Aid Worker Voices

Survey Results and Commentary

Thomas Arcaro, PhD

DEDICATION

To the countless women and men serving as aid workers around the world. May we all remain tireless in our efforts to forge a world of dignity for all humans.

CONTENTS

ACKNOWLEDGMENTS

Thanks to the 1010 nameless aid and development workers who took the time to complete the survey and especially those who provided rich narrative responses to the many open-ended questions. Also thanks to the dozens of aid workers with whom I Skyped, emailed or otherwise communicated with to get additional background information. Special thanks go to Annalisa Addis, Amelie Gagnon, Lucy O'Donoghue and Becca Price for reading, commenting on and contributing to early drafts of the manuscript.

I deeply appreciate all of the beta readers for taking time to provide feedback, among them Elizabeth Stanfield, Karen Mac Randal, Dee Zarnowski, Killian Barefoot, Stacey Oliver, Gabrielle Richard, Keely Alexander, Federica, and Joshua Sidwell.

At Elon University thanks go to the members of the Elon University Faculty Research and Development Committee for granting me a sabbatical so that I could devote concentrated time to pour through the data and write the blog posts which form the basis of this book.

My student assistant Laura Murphy kept me on track month after month and provided very useful feedback and valuable spreadsheet work.

Teresa LePors of Belk Library provided critical research assistance.

My editor Jennie Langley kept my spirits high and the manuscript in great order. Additional editing assistant expertly provided by Xernay Aniwar and Morgan Seijo-Vila'.

My most special thanks go to my partner from the very beginning of this project. He goes by the *nom de guerre* of "J".

Cover design and photograph by J.

FOREWORD

I first met Dr. Arcaro virtually after he read my second novel, *Missionary, Mercenary, Mystic, Misfit*. Something about that story grabbed him, and we made contact. Between his interest in studying people, and my own interest in telling my truth as a career humanitarian and being heard, we found the basis for that first conversation. Then another. Then weekly Skype chats, and soon after the idea for the project which led to this book was born. Among the first of its kind, a serious, formal survey of humanitarian workers worldwide.

This study—the survey entitled "Aid Worker Voices"—was as much about satisfying our combined curiosity, as about adding to the small but growing collective understanding of this mysterious, romanticized group of people: professional humanitarians.

I have spent most of my career as a humanitarian feeling misunderstood. As a younger person there were moments when I reveled in it. But as I grow older, I find that the consistent misconceptions, the popular culture portrayals based on inaccurate stereotypes – they begin to grate. But as I think about it, it is more than simply that some actress gets it wrong on the silver screen, or that some has-been celebrity starts a second-rate NGO. The more I think about it, the more I cannot escape the reality that these misunderstandings, or perhaps more accurately, the lack of understanding in the first place, matter.

Depending on which statistics you choose to accept, professional humanitarians comprise a global workforce, some 400,000 strong, in an industry worth upwards of $17 billion. These men and women, of all shades and colors, and from all parts of the world carry out the will of charitable donors, whether governments, corporations, foundations, or generous private citizens. They are tasked with going into some of the hardest places in the world to help those some of the most abused, disenfranchised, forgotten people there are. Despite diversity of background, humanitarian aid and development workers are now a global culture that transcends NGO and UN agency brands. But no one really knows them, as a group. No one really understands them.

The Aid Worker Voices project was specifically envisioned and undertaken to help fill that void. There were and are other complementary initiatives to study humanitarians, but that as may be, such efforts remain relatively few and far between, and so Aid Worker Voices stands as one of the first efforts of its kind.

This book, then, is the final output of the Aid Worker Voices project. Between January 2014 and March 2015 some 1010 anonymous humanitarians completed a 60-question census-style survey. You'll read about the survey itself, as well as the theoretical underpinnings of it in the Introduction and early chapters. The remainder of the book, then is discussion and analysis of what those humanitarians – you, if you're one of them – had to say.

Why did aid workers decide to become aid workers? (Chapter 5) How do those inside the industry see the future of humanitarian aid? (Chapter 18). What is the role of faith in the lives and motivations of humanitarians? Myself as a professional humanitarian who routinely has to supervise and manage aid workers in the field, knowing the answers to these questions helps me do my job better. I imagine that many in or with interest in the aid sector would also like to know.

As a long-time insider I found this book affirming one minute, and shocking the next. Aid worker thoughts on issues like corruption (Chapter 16) rang true, while some of the issues that come up in those sections which had to do with race and identity (Chapter 9) were surprising (in a good way) and enlightening. As a frequent manager of humanitarians, I will go into the field better able to work effectively with this engaging, spirited group. I cannot help thinking that many others will find this book similarly helpful, whether they're managing a stressed out and tired team, working on organizational strategy, or trying to make a movie about humanitarians!

–J

PREFACE

The world is changing rapidly, with each month providing a unique series of challenges and opportunities for humanity. Terrorism, war-related diasporas, climate change, weak and dysfunctional leadership, endemic corruption, and unchecked neoliberalism are hindering movement toward social justice, causing humanitarian needs to increase dramatically. Both natural events and misguided human actions continually create massive needs for both emergency services and long term development initiatives.

In our globalizing and ever-more-so-complicated world aid and development work – let's call it "aid work" from here on out – are becoming increasingly important, distressingly so, to meet the minimal needs of women, men and children caught up in natural and social forces that compromise their lives and dignity.

But what, exactly, is aid work? What does the typical aid worker look like? The short answer is that there is no typical aid worker. Aid workers can be the donors themselves, interested in implementing an HIV project, for example, in Vietnam to meet government-specific targets to eliminate the disease. They can be staffers working for international or local NGOs, receiving donor funding to implement an education project in Zimbabwe geared toward helping improve literacy rates. Aid workers can be medical doctors that rush to the scene in Guinea to help with the latest Ebola outbreak. There's no "one-size-fits-all" definition.

I would argue that at their heart, most aid workers are committed, passionate human beings interested in making a difference in the world. Many have always felt "the call" to get out and help others. Some may have fallen into the career by accident and found a growing passion for the communities and cultures they serve. Others may be aid workers borne out of tragedy who stand up to fight against persistent injustices. All deserve to be heard.

What I sensed in many of these 'aid worker voices' were the words of what I would describe as global citizens, with many (if not all) of the following traits:

- Ability to understand the long view, working toward the goal of making a better life for our children, their children and their children, on to many generations;
- A passion about working toward the goal of creating a more just world for everyone regardless of gender, ethnicity, tribe, clan or nation;
- Keen understanding of the urgency of needed engagement to stem the tide of poverty, malnutrition, illiteracy rates, etc.;
- Courage to stand up for their convictions, even if not the most popular route even if it means making personal sacrifices for the common good.

Why this book, why now?

We are moving toward a global consciousness that is facilitated by technologies that keep us connected in ways that would have been unthinkable just a half generation ago. A thinker ahead of his time, GH Mead, an American sociologist, anticipated as much nearly a century ago, writing of "international minds" developing in concert with the emergence of organized, functioning, international communities such as in the scientific, religious, economic and political worlds. Another sociologist Emile Durkheim talks of "collective consciousness" and, if we blend these ideas together we have what many have already argued, a global consciousness of sorts.

Could it be that, collectively, aid workers are the conscience of that pan-human consciousness? If indeed they are, we need to hear their voices just as much as they need to hear each other's. That indeed is the central purpose of this book.

What are the voices that appear in this book? Ultimately, these are aid workers who took the time to respond to a call to participate in a survey. This book can be imagined as an opportunity to listen in on an endless series of team-house, bar, or debriefing discussions. But perhaps more accurately, it could be seen as the private diaries –(or "Secret Aid Workers" who share their stories in *The Guardian*) - of many aid workers who have been in the trenches, seen and experienced things they have difficulty putting into words, and (hopefully) making a difference in the lives of the communities they're attempting to support. It's not always pretty, it's not always easy, but the accounts captured here are true reflections of aid workers, providing one-of-a-kind insight into this field, its contributors, and the daily opportunities and challenges they experience.

Aid and development work is being done in much greater magnitude and in more visible ways than ever before. International humanitarian assistance from the U.S. rising for a second year to $24.5 billion in 2014. The initial survey and subsequent book you're reading now are the preliminary steps toward discerning the voices of the folks brave enough to take the $431.6 billion, go into the field, work with local communities, and try to make a difference through a career devoted to aid work – a career they chose or just happened into. In our ever-changing, increasingly globalized world, these are important voices and experiences that deserve to be heard.

This book brings together hundreds of aid worker voices, covering dozens of topics and issues felt/experienced by aid workers and thus offers some clues as to how this the most globally-minded among us feel and think. A glimpse into how humanity —as represented to aid workers- responds to the humanitarian calling.

What's ahead?

Though this book is about aid worker voices, many chapters are filled with my attempts to explore the countless thoughts shared through my lens as a sociologist. The chapters on the impact of bureaucratization (chapter 3), the moral career of the aid worker (chapter 4), the ultimate efficacy of the humanitarian effort ("castles in the sand" chapter 21), are some examples.

Women make up a majority of respondents to our survey – 71% - and, as you'll see, show up in the data far more than men. The chapters below present aid workers' views on a variety of topics including corruption, MONGOs (MyOwnNGO), their level of idealism and what makes it change, reason why they got into – and stay in – the sector, thoughts on what it takes to get fired (or not) in the sector, and the future of humanitarian and development work. Chapters that touch on how gender impacts the aid worker's experience are longer and more personal. Chapters related to faith and the future of humanitarianism are also extended, based on the amount of feedback received on these important themes in aid work.

As a sociology professor and development work-oriented program director who has studied humanitarian aid and development work for many years, I took the license to add my thoughts in ample measure throughout the book. My analysis and comments are intended to sometimes amplify what I found in the data, but mostly to provide additional thoughts about how they might be understood. In all cases, my intent in poring over the narrative data was to find and then present with examples the themes which emerged. For largely practical reasons, only a relatively small percentage of the many thousands of comments respondents offered made it into the chapters, though there are countless others that easily could have been used to illustrate the same feelings, perspectives or points.

How to read this book

The intention of this book was to stay true to the title "Aid Worker Voices", but as a heads-up to readers I'll have to emphasize the subtitle "Survey results and commentary". The first third of the book is very much me reacting to the combination of my long-term study of aid and development work and the stimulation of reading survey results, especially all of the narrative comments. In these beginning chapters, I lay out some of my thoughts, conjectures and points of view related to aid and development work that – I hope – serve as a point of departure for more conversations about these topics. For those of you who want to skip straight to the aid worker voices parts of the book – that is, to find if what you wrote when you filled out the survey made the cut and was quoted – you can begin at chapter six, but – of course – I hope you don't.

For those of you who want to know more detail about the actual survey the entire survey instrument – complete with data – you can find that information on the blog (blogs.elon.edu/aidworkervoices).

If you are not an industry insider and are reading this book to get a general sense of what aid workers experience and think, great. Be warned, though, that many acronyms and "insider" terminology are used and you might need to Google a bit to catch up here and there. Consider that part of your research. Yes, "NGO" does stand for "non-governmental organization" but beyond that you're on your own.

One unique feature of writing the first draft of a book as a blog, is that I was able to invite readers to comment or provide to me any sort of feedback as drafts were posted on the blog. That is to say, what you will read in this book has already been read and vetted by many people. As well, my primary beta readers – all veteran aid workers themselves – read and commented on most posts before they went "live".

In the first pages of his book *That the World May Know* James Dawes asks, "What is the line that separates those who are merely moved from those who are moved to act?" The voices reported in the chapters below offer some answers to Dawes' query, and much more. I sincerely hope that I have succeeded in honoring the gift of the countless person-hours that went into completing the survey by so many who will remain nameless. My goal is that what you read below will provide a deeper understanding of what aid workers think and feel and, for my target audience *aid workers* that your thoughts, feelings and opinions are both affirmed and challenged.

Tom Arcaro
Elon, September 2016

INTRODUCTION

Smiles came across her face as she was reading

In the summer of 2016 I spent a couple weeks traveling in southern Africa with a few students and colleagues from our university. We were there doing our school's version of engaged learning which in our case ends up being a fairly thoughtful version of 'development-lite.' Having listened to the students and to my colleagues meeting and talking with community partners near Ndola – in this case organized by Habitat for Humanity-International, Zambia – I can say with conviction that our whole party clearly understands that development work is infinitely messy, complicated on many political, cultural, tuft and interpersonal levels, almost necessarily moves at a glacial pace and, at the end of the day, you can never be certain that intended changes have ended up a net positive, all factors considered.

As a layover break between my work in Zambia and Namibia I was in Livingstone. On our second night here I met a young female aid worker on R&R and, soon, the ritual surface chatting melted into a deep conversation about aid and development work and the frustrations thereof. Not long into that part of the conversation I invited her to look at what I was working on – this book. She spent a good deal of time reading through several chapters, spending the most time on Chapter 11 "How do you explain your job to non-sector people?".

Smiles came across her face as she was reading.

For any writer, or at least for me, the most fulfilling moment possible is when you know someone has read your work and felt something. In this case the "thing" felt was a deep sensation of being connected to other aid workers expressing the same sentiments she had felt at various times.

This is why I did this research and why I have put together this book: to have aid worker voices heard, shared and, for context, analyzed and commented upon.

Research ethics?

Reflecting on the "why" of this research I am reminded of a book I read as an anthropology grad student many years ago called *Through Navaho Eyes* by John Worth and Sol Adair.[1] Their research involved giving film equipment to various groups and asking them to "make a short movie," their premise being that films have language and are a window into the filmmaker's culture and *weltanschauung*.

Although their research was prior to the days when IRB approval was sought, before beginning with any new group Worth and Adair routinely met with the community leaders to explain the research and to get permission to proceed. When they went to a Navaho reservation, explained the process, and then asked the chief for permission he took a long moment to first ask, "Will it hurt the sheep?"

Worth and Adair, knowing the Navaho herded sheep, were only a bit surprised by the question and quickly answered in a respectful manner saying "no," the filming process most certainly would not hurt the sheep.

The chief took their answer and bowed his head in thought, finally raising his head with a second question, "Will it help the sheep?"

Again, though a bit more surprised this time thinking they had already answered the sheep question, Worth and Adair assured the chief that the sheep would not be impacted at all by the filming; it would not "help the sheep."

The chief took this answer, bowing his head again for what seemed to Worth and Adair a very long time, finally raising his head and asking, "Then why do it?"[2]

Indeed.

And, not inconsequentially, the same can be asked of all development work and sociological or anthropological research, for that matter.

I tell this sheep story to my sociology students before having them do research projects to introduce the topic of ethics. I also remind myself of this story every time I feel the need to "generate some data" about a topic.

So, why study aid and development workers? One short answer is that smiles came across her face as she was reading this blog. And those smiles were good.

What is *Aid Worker Voices*? Why this project? Below is messaging as it appeared on the blog (blogs.elon.edu/aidworkervoices) as we began our social media campaign intended to drive more people to the site and generate more survey responses.

- *Who's doing this?* This research project is being carried out by two researchers: Dr. Thomas Arcaro, Professor of Sociology at Elon University, and 20+ aid industry veteran, blogger, and writer, "J."
- *Why study humanitarian workers?* The global humanitarian industry represents a workforce of some 300,000-400,000 people, tasked with spending hundreds of billions of USD annually, for the purpose of making the world better. Yet these people are almost entirely un-studied. Understanding aid workers, of all origins, locations, and place in the industry is a necessary – critical, even – ingredient to making aid more effective.
- *What will be done with the results of this study? Will I be able to know what you find out?* Yes! The results of this study will be made available for anyone and everyone who cares to know what we learn about humanitarian workers. At this stage we're contemplating a number of options, depending on the quantity and quality of data we get back, possibly including presentations, book publications, and of course, further study. Watch this space – the Aid Worker Voices blog – for continuous updates, including in-process findings, as well as announcements of what comes next and where to find more formalized publications of findings.
- *If I take the survey, is my anonymity guaranteed?* Yes, absolutely. You are not asked for any specific personal identifying information at any point in the survey, nor are you asked to identify your employer by name. If you choose to self-identify in one of the spaces for open-ended answers, we will not publish that information.
- *Who can take this survey?* We're trying to gain the participation of anyone and everyone who is now, or who has in the past participated in any way in the global humanitarian industry. We want to hear from anyone who has ever worked for a NGO, INGO, or other charity, whether local or expat, regardless of your job or role.
- *The respondents you get are self-selected. Is this a "scientific" study?* We all know the drill: in the ideal world you identify a population and then secure a method by which you assure yourself of getting a stratified random sample of that population. What constitutes the population

of humanitarian aid workers is, at best, an open question, and we embrace that fact by recognizing that ours is an exploratory study intended to support the process of a more systematic research.

Some background

I'll start with some very deep and reflexive background. In 2000 I published a book that was used by colleagues here at my university in a required course by the same name, *Understanding the Global Experience*. When I was asked to teach one section of the pilot for this course in 1994 I used that moment to begin taking a deep interest in global affairs. I recall reading Benjamin Barber's *The Atlantic* article *Jihad vs. McWorld* and being immediately absorbed by the vague (or is that vacuous?) concept of global citizenship.[3] My interest in all things global only accelerated from there. As past President of the Association for Humanist Sociology my attention to social justice issues was already well developed.

In 2003 I founded a program at my university designed to offer a three year pathway for students who wanted to *do something* about global social issues as they deepened their disciplinary skillsets. Our program is now well into its second decade of creating and sustaining meaningful global partnerships. As director of this program I have made it part of my job to learn about humanitarian aid and development and have read, taught and written about this area for many years now. Of note is that the Core Humanitarian Standards are now a part of all course syllabi in the program.

As part of my reading I encountered *Missionary, Mercenary, Mystic Misfit* by this mysterious J person.[4] Through networking I found a mutual friend and he and I met on line, immediately connecting on the idea of finding out more about the lives and views of aid workers.

The survey

My collaborator (J) and I worked to construct the survey over many weeks, sending out versions to beta readers several times and making edits, adding and deleting questions, and finally ending up with a 60 item survey with 41 forced choice questions and 19 "elaborate on your thoughts" open-ended questions. The link for the survey was sent broadly via social media targeting aid workers worldwide. At the end of the survey was a link to the *Aid Worker Voices* blog so that people could see our reporting and comment on the results as they came in. J gave a detailed clarification of who should take the survey on the blog that casts a pretty wide net. His answer to the question "Who should take this survey?" was simple: anyone who has ever worked in the aid industry.[5] We stayed live for a little over a year and during that time we had 1010 responses, most coming in the first three months.

There were a total of 8,162 total responses to the 19 open ended questions, an average of 430 per question, including nearly 900 on the last two open-ended questions (Q58 and Q60), indicating that the interest levels of the respondents remained high and consistent throughout this long survey.

Our sample of aid workers

There is no master list of aid and development workers around the world nor for that matter any clear consensus as to (1) where aid ends and development begins (what is Dadaab, exactly?), (2) who could or should be included under the umbrella term "aid workers" (do volunteers count?) or even (3) how one would define the "aid industry" (does corporate social responsibility count, for example?)

To do a representative study of aid workers around the world we would need access to data bases of staff from everywhere in the aid industry, and effectively and efficiently get a culture and language specific version of the survey to a stratified random sample of these folks and hope that enough respond to make the results meaningful. If that were possible then we could make scientifically valid generalizations about the data.

Our survey was never intended to yield results that one could – with certainty – generalize to all aid workers. From the very beginning we were sober about the fact that our respondents were self-selected and, in the end, the survey was conducted only in English, narrowing that self-selection. What you read throughout this book are aid worker voices from women and men who graciously gave their time to complete the survey. In this book, I summarize and commented on the quantitative data and the themes that appear in the hundreds of responses to each open-ended follow-up question. I make every attempt to present a balanced representation of the responses as a whole, highlighting particularly well-articulated observations.

That the 1010 respondents tend to over-represent expat aid and development workers from "rich" countries (the Global North and in particular the US, Canada and Western Europe) seems quite certain from both the quantitative and qualitative data. The title for the blog is *Aid Worker Voices* because *"Mostly International Aid and Development Worker Voices from Primarily 'Global North and/or 'Rich' Countries"* was a bit too long.

What we have in this body of work is a positive step forward in exploring and giving voice to the thoughts, opinions and struggles of aid workers. Our results are scientific in the same sense as much social anthropology is and, in the end, adds to our knowledge about the aid industry. The hope is that the book-length treatment of the results will be useful to students, journalists and academics wishing to learn more about the aid industry and will provide interesting, entertaining and perhaps affirming reading for those already in the sector.

Our attempts at inclusiveness

Though we were able to generate over 1,000 responses to our survey it is clear that we have nothing close to a representative sample of all aid workers, however defined. Nor was that our goal. We simply hoped to move forward conversations about the lives of aid workers and to give voice to some of the concerns and perspectives of those willing to come forward, and I feel that that objective has been reached. In the vernacular of my academic area of sociology, our efforts represent an example of exploratory research intended to do exactly that, explore and share information about the lives and views of aid and development workers. More needs to be done, and a second version of our survey may happen at some point.

In the meantime, looking back at our efforts to get a wide range of voices I see some failed attempts and opportunities for future research efforts.

Why this lack of response? Two interrelated reasons are that (1) our social networking failed to get the word out effectively and (2) those that were reached felt unimpressed by our offer. But why? There are many reasons from various cultural perspectives, one of which is that the trust in the confidentiality of an internet survey may be low. Another is that the survey, if read at all, was seen as unworthy, off point, or otherwise not worth the investment in time.

We did find that those who did take the survey appreciated being asked to consider our questions. Here are a couple voices:

> "Very interesting survey and I appreciate the chance to share my views – it is surprising how little time (and few opportunities) one has to actually *think* about things in the busyness of the day-to-day. I wish your survey results could be shared in an open forum (not only virtual) where significant players can be present and honestly reflect for a moment."

> "These are great questions; very thought-provoking. It's rare to have an opportunity to share 'my truth' so I appreciate this initiative!"

So, given that many people thanked us for the survey and appreciated the chance to share, the question remains why didn't we get more responses overall?

Local aid workers

We were also concerned that we did not get many responses from local aid workers. Though our social media messaging about the survey was meant to reach all aid workers, the outcome was far more homogeneous and, well, white. Over half of the local aid workers that responded to our survey worked for humanitarian aid organizations and comprised a paltry 5% of our total sample. How this could have been more effectively addressed is open to question, but certainly one large gap in our goal of hearing and reporting the voices of aid workers is the very critical local aid worker segment. In some senses our book could be said to be "International aid worker voices," sadly so.

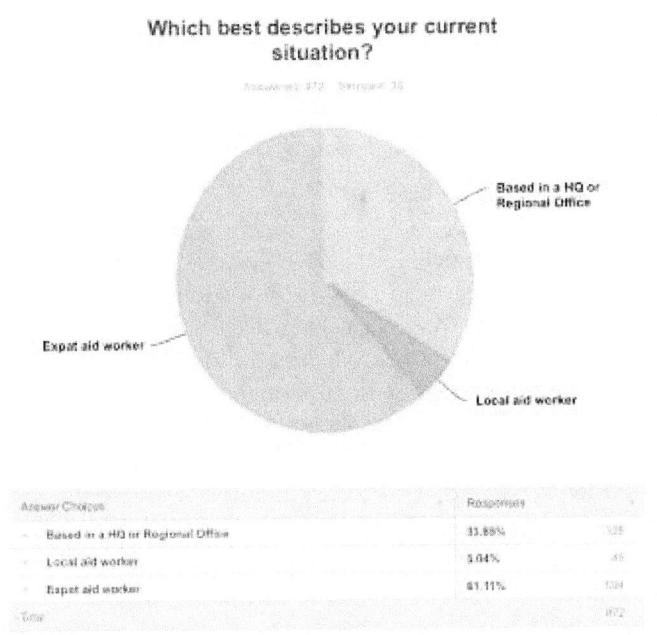

Which best describes your current situation?

Answer Choices	Responses	
Based in a HQ or Regional Office	11.88%	125
Local aid worker	5.04%	49
Expat aid worker	81.11%	1098
Total		1072

Concluding thoughts about being inclusive

That we had failed attempts at inclusiveness is obvious. But what can we learn from these failures? Here are a few thoughts:

- There could have been different versions of the survey pointed at various audiences and written in collaboration with (and in the local languages of) the local aid workers themselves and/or other academics and researchers.

- The Arabic version needed an Arabic person to lead the social media awareness efforts about the survey and that this version should have been written by an aid worker who is a native Arabic speaker.
- All versions of the survey could have been launched at the same time.
- A larger, more inclusive set of beta-testers could be identified.
- Our assumption that all aid workers want their voices heard needs questioning.
- Our means of making people aware of the survey need reassessment.

In the end, as they say "it is what it is" and the best that we can do is learn from the past so that we can make future efforts more robust and, yes, inclusive.

Comic relief as a critical element

Just as my colleague and silver back sector veteran J has found an eager audience for his aid worker fiction (HUMAN, and the series of books starring Mary-Anne), anthropologists have done the same for generations. I am reminded of the classic anthropological novel published under the name Eleanor Smith Bowen written by Laura Bohannan in the mid 1950's. Though this novel is mainly about the intersection of two cultures – something all aid workers know something about – in the last part of the book she illustrates beautifully words from Shakespeare's King Lear, namely "The worst returns to laughter..." and from there she gets her title. After a devastating epidemic comes through her fieldwork community (in Nigeria among the Tiv) she describes how they quickly return to being able to laugh at the situation, putting voice to the age-old truism that the difference between tragedy and comedy is the passage of time, and that healing from trauma is most quickly done by the social bonding (and re-bonding) that comes from laughing together.

And perhaps for some (most?) aid workers, social media and the Internet allow for just that, bonding with their peers through smirks, giggles and outrageous belly-laughs. A very human need, that.

In the following chapters what you will find can be seen as a focusing of this need to vent, share, support and laugh together. All this to bring smiles –born of shared understanding- to more faces.

NOTES

1. John Worth and Sol Adair, Through Navajo Eyes (Albuquerque: University of New Mexico Press, 1997).
2. Ibid, 2-4.
3. Benjamin Barber, "Jihad vs. McWorld." The Atlantic, March 1992. http://www.theatlantic.com/magazine/archive/1992/03/jihad-vs-mcworld/303882/
4. J. Missionary, Mercenary, Mystic, Misfit. (Evil Genius Publishing, 2013).
5. J. "Who Should Take This Survey?" Aid Worker Voices, March 9, 2014. http://blogs.elon.edu/aidworkervoices/?p=35

1 A THEORY-WONKISH EXCURSUS

"Not summer's bloom lies ahead of us, but rather a polar night of icy darkness and hardness, no matter which group may triumph externally now." - Max Weber

"...until we recognize how dependent we are on the oppression and marginalization of others for our own betterment and benefit (i.e. access to cheap disposable goods, foreign foods and fresh imports, temporary foreign workers to fill low-income job vacancies, etc...), humanitarian aid work is just another cog in this bullshit machinery."

The view from 35,000 feet

Encountering C. W. Mills' The Sociological Imagination early in my career provided me with a critical set of conceptual tools. Though the book offers much more, what I emphasize to my students is that the sociological imagination urges us to take the long view both geographically and historically, thus demanding a "the global is an interwoven social system the current state of which can only be properly viewed using a keen sense of world history" perspective. Mix Max Weber and his groundbreaking work on the inexorable stranglehold on humanity by capitalism and bureaucratic organization into that framework and that begins to explain the quotation above.

Understanding why the May 2016 World Humanitarian Summit was destined to "fail" begins here.

Contemporaries

That Karl Marx and Charles Darwin were contemporaries is well known, their intellectual and professional paths crossing in the UK, at least to the extent that Marx sent Darwin a copy of *Das Kapital* (that Darwin wrote back and thanked him for). I mention these two monumental figures because each is responsible for first articulating the two driving algorithms of our world, Darwin, evolution and Marx, of course, capitalism.

Just as Theodosius Dobzhansky argues that "nothing in biology makes sense except in the light of evolution," I would offer that nothing makes sense in the world of economics except in the light of capitalism.[1] To go further, I would point out that Marx' full-on version of economic determinism – that all aspects of modern culture are driven by the logic of capital (does the phrase "follow the money" come to mind?) – merits a serious look even more so in 2016 than when he first began to formulate it in the mid 1800's. A Guardian article by George Monbiot, "Neoliberalism – the ideology at the root of all our problems," does a great job of explaining the ideology of neoliberalism and provides deep insight into the massive economic and political forces that control our entire global social system.[2] This system includes within it, of course, the three parts of the humanitarian aid system, namely (1) aid organizations that get funding from (2) donors (be they individuals, governments, the UN, foundations or whatever) and (3) those who are the object of these efforts.

Side note: The irony that Henri Dunant experienced Solferino the same year *On the Origin of Species* was published – 1859 – is not lost on me. While Marx and Darwin were giving voice to the major forces determining our life on this planet, for his part Dunant was doing the same for our inner urges to respond to those in need through his book *A Memory of Solferino*.

A third person of note in this context, one of our contemporaries, provided us with a bridge between the biological and the social and must be mentioned. In the last pages of his 1976 book *The Selfish Gene* Richard Dawkins coins the term 'meme' and defined it as a "unit of cultural transmission."[3] Other thinkers, notably Daniel Dennett in the US and Susan Blackmore in the UK have done much to extend Dawkins' concept of the meme, Dennett pointing out that the process of evolution is substrate neutral and can/does include memes and Blackmore offering an extended discussion of the concept of 'memeplexes' by noting that just as human bodies are complexes of genes, social entities can be seen as complexes of memes (the Catholic Church being one of her main examples).[4]

Let's now consider Marx' observation that "The ruling ideas of each age have ever been the ideas of its ruling class."[5] Biological evolution is fundamentally Darwinian in nature (survival of the fittest and all that) whereas memetic evolution is partly Darwinian but also has an even bigger element of Lamarckianism (acquired characteristics can be passed on to others). Stated differently, the vectors of communication for genes are limited (sex, anyone?) and change takes place over many, many generations while the vectors for spreading memes are increasing – and increasingly rapidly – due in large part to technological change in how we communicate. The spreading of memes can be virtually instantaneous via, for example, YouTube and Twitter. Critical to note is that those most heavily influencing the flow of information, i.e., the spreading of memes, are those, typically, with money and power, i.e., "the ruling class."

Non-linear systems

Human life on this planet can only be fully understood as being part of multiple nonlinear systems. In her 2013 article "Nonlinear Systems Theory, Feminism, and Postprocessualism" Suzanne M. Spencer-Wood does an excellent job in probing and explaining this perspective, doing a very solid job in weaving in a discussion of the impact that human agency has on chaotic and nonlinear systems.[6]

Genetic and memetic evolution are impacted now by (and in turn impact) economic and cultural evolution. The bottom line is that engineering cultural change is extraordinarily complicated and that our efforts at "development" – despite our best intentions – can never yield predictable long term results and may in fact lead to negative impacts. Perhaps more distressingly, our short term specific (tsunami, for example) relief efforts are also injecting influences that inexorably will have unanticipated and unpredictable results both locally and in the global social system as a whole.

As one aid worker put it:

> "Compared to the money being invested, we're doing a pretty poor job of getting anywhere. A lot of misguided approaches or self-interested approaches or inappropriate interventions or I could go on and on. Why do we know that poverty is not simple or linear, yet still implement interventions as if it is? We need to get better. We need to be smarter, think more critically."

To understand the humanitarian aid sector you have to acknowledge that it is part of larger social and even biological systems. No part – even you, MSF – is disconnected from any other. Input into the system, however small or positively intentioned, at any one point can and does impact the rest of the system. A "fix" at one point can never be in isolation from the rest of the larger sociocultural system.

Said one aid worker,

> *"I think humanitarian aid work operates within a system that is built on inequality – we won't see large scale change happen in the lives of people, in terms of long term development, until we start to challenge the structures and systems that result in this inequity in the first place. And the heart of those institutions is within North America and Europe – until we recognize how dependent we are on the oppression and marginalization of others for our own betterment and benefit (i.e. access to cheap disposable goods, foreign foods and fresh imports, temporary foreign workers to fill low-income job vacancies, etc…), humanitarian aid work is just another cog in this bullshit machinery."*
> (emphasis added)

So, yes, the message that I heard from many aid workers about the future of the aid sector about the larger forces impacting the sector (e.g., neoliberal economic policies) are spot on.

NOTES

1. Theodosius Dobzhansky, "Nothing in Biology Makes Sense except in the Light of Evolution." The American Biology Teacher, 35 (1973): 125-129.
2. George Monbiot, "Neoliberalism – the ideology at the root of all of our problems." The Guardian, April 15 2016.
3. Richard Dawkins, The Selfish Gene (New York: Oxford University Press, 1976), 207.
4. Susan Blackmore, The Meme Machine (Oxford: Oxford University Press, 2000).
5. Karl Marx and Frederick Engels, The Communist Manifesto. (London: Verso, 1888/2012), 43.
6. Suzanne M. Spencer-Wood, "Nonlinear Systems Theory, Feminism, and Postprocessualism." Journal of Archaeology 2013 (2013): 540912.

2 WHAT IS THE "HUMANITARIAN AID SYSTEM?"

Context

This note is in part prompted by an op-ed piece in *The Guardian* by J in which he asks, "Is humanitarian aid really broken? Or should we all just calm down?".[1] J points out that, "The answer to 'What can we do to fix the aid system?' depends on what exactly you think is broken and what you think it was meant to do in the first place." Agreed.

But I would like to ask an even more basic question, namely "what is the humanitarian aid system?" This question became very germane to us as we imagined our survey of aid workers, the discussion of which is the purpose of this book. As a sociologist, the first thing I was taught in my research methods class was that before you sample and survey a population you have to, well, define exactly what that population is. In this case we are studying "aid workers" (hence the title of our book, *Aid Worker Voices*). But again, just who are these "humanitarian aid workers?"

Used as an adjective, as it is in this context, the simple dictionary definition of "humanitarian" is a person who "seeks to promote human welfare."[2] To be accurate, then, an inclusive definition of "humanitarian aid worker" would have to embrace a wide range of people approaching this goal of promoting human welfare from many directions and from a staggering array of organizational platforms.

That said, our data indicates that most respondents to our survey worked for what would be *traditionally* defined as humanitarian aid work, i.e., big budget, large global reach organizations.

Note

Here is what our sample population looked like, all self-identified and all presumably representing one time point along a career path. Less than 30% were what the public might stereotypically label "humanitarian aid workers," the rest doing some sort of development-related work. Our phrasing of the question left much room for interpretation by the respondent, but I think it is interesting that most (53%) put themselves in the "development" category.

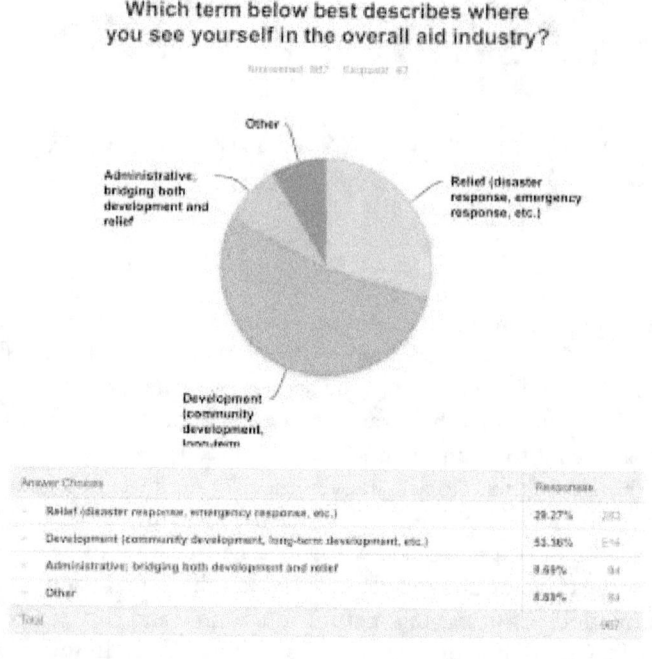

Which term below best describes where you see yourself in the overall aid industry?

Answer Choices	Responses	
Relief (disaster response, emergency response, etc.)	39.27%	283
Development (community development, long-term development, etc.)	53.36%	514
Administrative; bridging both development and relief	3.61%	34
Other	3.63%	34
Total		887

And now for this

Several points I want to make below, all interrelated and all critical to examine as we move forward in our efforts to understand and make more effective humanitarian actions of all kinds. These will come from my admittedly mostly US perspective, but nonetheless the points remain somewhat universal.

First, the humanitarian system includes innumerable points along a continuum from pure aid (e.g., emergency relief) to pure development. Ask those working for, say CARE in Ethiopia, to tell you exactly where aid ends and development begins and they will respond with a shrug. In the words of one aid worker, "...*it's always a challenge, especially in this context, in this environment, when does emergency begin, when is it development?*" And so it is with many individual aid workers as they progress from one point in their career to another, sometimes doing aid, sometimes development, most times a blur of both or neither.

A second point is one that seems obvious and was underscored in Caroline Abu-Sada's (editor) MSF commissioned book *In the Eyes of Others: How People in Crisis Perceive Humanitarian Aid* (2012).[3] From the "beneficiaries" perspective it really does not matter from where aid or assistance of any sort comes. Frequently, the outside entity offering immediate to long term "help" is only perceived in the most vague manner; organizational messaging and logos remain an undifferentiated blur. That is to say, the "humanitarian aid system" is a construct that can have very little relevance in the minds of those for whom the aid system's efforts are intended. Imagine you are working on a development project in a certain community, then a disaster affects those same people: "sorry, we only do development" does not seem a good way to lift them out of poverty. Luckily it is typically not the case, but you do have humanitarian actors that refuse to carry out development activities.

A third point, and one for which more detail is needed, is that actors within the humanitarian system include many entities and individuals outside of the traditional insider's definition of what aid or even development is.

Although I agree with the wordsmiths at The Active Learning Network for Accountability and Performance in Humanitarian Action (ALNAP), who describe the humanitarian system as, "an organic construct, like a constellation: a complex whole formed of interacting core and related actors."[4] I do feel that their model, elaborate as it may be, falls short of being usefully inclusive. Their premise is that aid work is a profession and their model thus emphasizes the 450,000 aid professionals worldwide.

To the extent that aid work is a profession – and I agree that it is and should be seen as a profession – there are umbrella entities like ALNAP that are taking proactive measures to both understand and make positive changes to the humanitarian aid system. Indeed, the establishment of the *Core Humanitarian Standard*,[5] a product of the Joint Standard Initiative, is a positive example of forward thinking efforts.

My point is that in reality the humanitarian aid system is far more inclusive than even the complicated ALNAP model infers, and this fact is ignored in discussions about "fixing the (broken) aid system."

Expanding on what they include, here are some additional – though far from exhaustive – thoughts where new categories are suggested and some that ALNAP does mention are elaborated upon. These appear in no particular order. My reason for this is explained below.

- Peace Corps volunteers and their European counterparts from other developed nations number in the thousands with impact in over 70 nations worldwide. They are doing – or at least are intending to do – humanitarian development work.

- MONGO's (My Own NGO) – of which there is an increasing number. Many are US based, but this creating your own non-profit organization to help "save the world" seems to be a generally Western phenomena that is only getting stronger. Note for example the rise of social entrepreneurship programs in US colleges and universities and elsewhere fueling the rise in number of small non-profits. Though MONGO's are largely a Western (and/or global north) phenomena there is a trend upward around the world of these entities, though some many have "ghost" partners from the north.

- Everyday individuals, part of the global diaspora, sending remittances while working and living in the US or in other parts of the developed world. These funds – totaling as much as US$550 billion in 2015 – are aid of the increasingly popular "cash transfer" nature and make a huge impact.

- All of the many Corporate Social Responsibility personnel working around the world. Corporate Social Responsibility (CSR) is becoming more of a factor in the sector in ways that can no longer be ignored or marginalized. The 10 principles of the United Nations Global Compact[6] to the cynical (read: realists) may sound like so much hot air, but increasingly the millennials and generation X students are making a change in CSR from within. In large part this is caused by a long term trend in higher education emphasizing community and global service in American higher education. Our own Periclean Scholars program at Elon University is an example where students who graduate from the program have global citizenship and humanitarian ethics embedded in their DNA and will take that into their professional lives. In the last 15 year or more US higher education has had an increasingly central focus on "civic engagement and social responsibly"; indeed there are many consortia specifically devoted to just that (Imagining America, Campus Compact, Project Pericles, to name a few). Of special note along these lines is the long history that CARE has working with scores of corporations.

- Academic/service learning students from American colleges and universities doing aid and/or development work (the "service learning" mentioned above) during both short and long term travel abroad experiences count in the tens of thousands annually.

- Church groups from the US (mainly) doing "mission" work and the many individuals doing 1-2 year outreach experiences (e.g.,

Mormons). European-based Catholic missionary work also continues apace. In many parts of the world massive sums of money go to "help the poor" from church, temple or mosque coffers and/or is simply done by individuals whose motivation is to satisfy religious expectations.

- Civic groups such as Rotary International have a footprint around the world that cannot be easily measured but certainly is part of the mix.

- Though this is obvious, the impact of those affected by disaster and/or long term needs who help their family, friends, neighbors is massive. The families in Jordan and Lebanon, for example, who have absorbed refugees from Iraq and Syria are not only doing humanitarian aid, but arguably are the largest provider. These are all cross-national examples (either working outside of their country of origin, or working with foreign populations), but clearly there are many who do feed the malnourished or teach the illiterate across US (or replace US with virtually any other nation) communities, and this highlights how broad the community is.

- People working for donor agencies, especially if headquarters-based. They often have technical expertise in humanitarian and/or development aid provision, and sometimes travel to the field for monitoring missions, but at the same time they are not your typical aid worker. They spend most of their time in western capitals with their families, they have somewhat regular working hours. Some of them are actually employed by another entity (e.g. ministry of Health or of Agriculture) and only temporarily seconded to the humanitarian/development arm.

- Consultants hired by external firms to provide for instance monitoring and evaluation of aid projects. Some of these firms focus solely on aid, but others work in several sectors. Are their employees aid workers? More broadly, how do we consider companies that are subcontracted to provide works/services for an NGO or UN agency in the framework of an aid project? Strictly speaking they are only doing business, not aid work. In practice however the type of activities they do (e.g. give out cash to beneficiaries, carry out a survey on beneficiaries' needs, etc.) are indistinguishable from the same things done by "real" aid workers.

- Civil protection/defense, fire brigades and other similar corps: they are usually among the first responders to emergencies. Sometimes they work together with humanitarians: for instance, the European Commission has a single structure that oversees both humanitarian aid and civil protection. Yet I would argue they are somewhat different, perhaps because their focus is "at home" rather than in third countries, but isn't it a bit neocolonialistic? Similarly, military personnel also sometimes distribute relief or implement development projects to "win hearts and minds" (and they often label their own initiatives as "humanitarian," as in the Balkans in the 1990s). But I would say they are not "true" humanitarian workers.

- Another example of work that is done to "promote human welfare" though not direct and hence not traditionally seen as aid work are the efforts of those international organizations (like UN agencies) working with myriad governments doing normative work (e.g., setting international standards or benchmarks) or developing capacity of national officials in, for example supporting the ministries of education or health in areas like planning or technical cooperation.

And the list goes on.

An organic construct

In short, the take-home from the above is as simple as this. "Fixing" the humanitarian aid system cannot be done. Period. Why? Because, inclusively defined, the humanitarian aid system is not closed, involves (literally) innumerable entities and actors along a complex and fluid continuum, and many of these entities and actors by their nature transcend governance and policy influences of any kind. Systems theory 101 tells us that although you can limit your definition of what is or is not included in your model – in this case "the humanitarian aid system" – the reality as it is perceived by the beneficiaries is more complicated and must be accounted for as you assess impact and imagine changes. And a butterfly flaps its wings. Take that, Joint Standards Initiative.

But there is hope. The "humanitarian aid system" in any one particular geographic/cultural context likely does have a relatively finite number of entities doing work. Efforts to maximize the communication, coordination, cooperation and principled functioning among these players in any given location is a step towards "fixing" the system. This will never be easy, simple, quick or, in the end, terribly effective. In the words of one aid worker, *"the aid/hum/dev sector cannot be considered as a whole, so we basically have to pick what we think is broken, define and circumscribe, and fix it."* Paul Currion adds additional layers of complexity to this discussion in his article "The Humanitarian Future."[7]

These local fixes will be by no means "one size fits all" in nature, and thus we're always back to square one as we move around the globe, location to location.

"Is the aid system broken?," J asks. Well, yes in some specific and narrow cases, as he accurately points out. The humanitarian aid system is a growing, amorphous and uncoordinated array of "do-gooders" being pulled by our natural human urge to respond to those in need, just as Henri Dunant did in 1859 in Solferino.

We are both blessed and cursed with this very powerful urge, but we can at least deal positively and productively with the our humanistic impulses by taking a broader approach to defining the 'humanitarian aid system' and earning satisfaction at successfully, on occasion, protecting some of our castles in the sand.

Post scripts

Though I say above that there is hope for 'fixing' the system I really am far short of closure on that point.

NOTES

1. J, "Is Humanitarian Aid Really Broken? Or Should We All Just Calm Down?" The Guardian, Jan 6, 2016.
2. Oxford Desk Dictionary and Thesaurus, 2nd ed., s. v. "humanitarian."
3. Caroline Abu-Sada, ed. In The Eyes of Others: How People in Crises Perceive Humanitarian Aid. (New York: MSF-USA, 2012).
4. The Active Learning Network for Accountability and Performance in Humanitarian Action (ALNAP). "What Is This System?" http://sohs.alnap.org/#what-is-this-system
5. The Core Humanitarian Standard. CHS Alliance, Group URD and the Sphere Project. https://corehumanitarianstandard.org/the-standard
6. The United Nations Global Compact. "The Ten Principles of the UN Global Compact." https://www.unglobalcompact.org/what-is-gc/mission/principles
7. Paul Currion, "The Humanitarian Future." Aeon, September 10, 2014. https://aeon.co/essays/humanitarianism-is-broken-but-it-can-be-fixed

3 OF BUREAUCRACIES AND AID ORGANIZATIONS

Framing the discussion

In his 2014 essay "The Humanitarian Future," Paul Currion points out that, "Of the Fortune 500 firms first listed in 1955, nearly 90 percent no longer exist in 2014, and this type of creative destruction is sorely lacking in the humanitarian sector."[1] This "lack of creative destruction" is my point of departure for further focusing on the question "can the humanitarian aid system be fixed?". Currion is spot on with his observation and below I discuss why this is such an important point from a sociological perspective.

There are many typologies of bureaucracies. For discussion purposes here is a simple version in which I include (1) *for profit* entities like Apple, Halliburton or Barkleys, (2) *governments or governing bodies* like the United Nations, the Parliament of Italy or FIFA, and (3) *not for profit* organizations such as Oxfam, the Catholic Church or the LSE.

One of those types is not like the other two relative to the pruning force of "creative destruction." The second two do not have nearly the same level of competition for survival as does the first. It is beyond the scope of this essay to discuss type 2, governing bodies, but much of what I point out below is as relevant to this type as it is the not-for-profit world of humanitarian aid organizations.

The business world functions according to Darwinian principles: big fish eat little fish, and only those corporations with the most myopic focus on maximization of profits tend to survive in the fiercely competitive global marketplace. Efficiency and focus of operation equals success, certainly, but in the long haul – say between 1955 and 2014 – the ability to adapt to all manner of cultural, technological and social changes is even more critical.

The not for profit organizations which are the core of the humanitarian aid system are largely outside this algorithm of capitalism, thus lacking a robust natural pruning process.

The "creative destruction" phrase that Currion uses above is perhaps misstated. "Creative" infers a mind and the algorithm of capitalism is merely a blind machine, allowing the survival of economically competitive businesses and selecting out the others. The forces of capitalism naturally prune weak/failing companies and failure is possible and actually imminent for those that don't adapt to changing social trends. Businesses are bureaucracies and therefore they are forced to be as efficient as possible to cope with the burdens of increased overhead, internal cooperation, and communication.

Weber 101: The problem with getting bigger

The intellectual grandparent of the analysis of bureaucracies is Max Weber. Below is some of what I have learned from studying his works.

A truism relative to bureaucracies is that all organizations have a tendency to get bigger as time passes. Two quickly stated reasons are (1) adding features is always less painful than subtracting and (2) the economy of scale comes into play. As bureaucracies get inexorably larger, many things begin to happen, most bad. Here's a partial list:

- Overhead – administrative and otherwise – increases
- Ability to alter course and mission – decreases
- Bureaucratic ritualism – increases
- Efficiency of internal and external communication channels – decreases
- Access to leaders – decreases
- Dependence upon experts at all levels – increases
- Ability of leaders to stay in touch with all aspects of functioning – decreases
- Tendency to gravitate toward exclusively quantifiable indicators of success – increases
- Overall efficiency in achieving mission – decreases

In the for-profit world these negative factors are muted and dealt with by the forces of competition, but much less so in the non-profit world in which the humanitarian aid systems inhabits.

It is a given that businesses that are on top, like those in the so-called Fortune 500, must stay lean, mean and on task to continue being successful. But how does a not-for-profit humanitarian aid organization deal with all of the entropic forces listed above?

One strategy is to avoid getting too big, and a second is minimizing noise by remaining focused on a specific mission. More discussion on these strategies below.

"Crisis caravans" are clusters of bureaucracies

Another critical dimension of this discussion is the hurdles faced when two or more bureaucracies must/need to interact with each other. In the business world market forces insure that over the long-haul inter-organization communication is done efficiently. In the not-for-profit world this is not the case and the forces ensuring smooth interagency communication and coordination are much less robust. To illustrate, here is a specific personal example.

I am director of Project Pericles at Elon University, Elon being one of 30 like-minded colleges and universities nationwide answering the charge to raise the level of civic engagement and social responsibility in our respective institutions. The directors of each institution meet once a year to share information and move forward collaborations and initiatives generated by the Project Pericles national office. The bigger picture is that there are a good number of other similarly missioned national consortia such as Campus Compact and Imagining America.

Here, yes, are gaggles of academic types who have common cause, are all passionate about their missions, and certainly are aware of the explosive and positive synergy that can come about when like-minded, well-resourced individuals come together. One might think that certainly within the Periclean institutions there would be constant, productive communication and that between the national Pericles office and the national offices of the other consortia there would be coordination and cooperation. Not the case.

Despite many and compelling reasons to make more and better inter-organizational communication, coordination and collaboration a high priority and despite the fact that, when asked, the various administrators and directors would say, yes, they would like it to be so, the grade card on this effort reads a C- at best.

One factor that plays a part in this "failure" is that we are all perpetually occupied with the day to day work on our campuses, always "putting out the fire nearest to us." The same is true for people in most jobs: looking at the big picture is a rare luxury, and spending time on activities which don't fall clearly in our job description (read: for which we get rewarded, i.e., "count") is hard to justify.

That is to say, if you think intra-organizational communication and overall functioning is a challenge, the situation only gets worse when you add efforts toward inter-organizational communication, cooperation and collaboration. It almost goes without saying that the more organizations in the consortia (or cluster of like-missioned entities), the lower the chances for productive, concerted action. This is not a problem specific to higher education, of course, but rather a general truism regarding interaction among and between large organizations in general.

And so it is with the "humanitarian aid system"; Polman was shooting fish in a barrel with *The Crisis Caravan*.[2] See chapter 16 for additional comment on the "crisis caravan."

Muting the inherent challenges of a growing bureaucracy

Though I have not done a thorough reading of the history of MSF (Médecins Sans Frontières, otherwise known as Doctors Without Borders), I'll suggest that the fissioning into now 24 semi-autonomous entities over the years was a natural reaction to the sense that they were getting too big to handle as one bureaucratic organization. MSF has, essentially, followed the franchise model from the business world with the Geneva main office remaining in charge of branding control and much of the administrative work while the many semi-autonomous affiliates remain smaller and leaner. They have also dealt with the challenges of inter-organizational coordination and cooperation by having stated and unstated policies of being as self-sufficient as possible. Cluster meetings, *peut-être*, but not much beyond that.

As a side note, another possible reason for having several affiliates in different countries is making the most of fiscal regulations (i.e., some governments offer tax relief on charity donations as long as the charity is registered in country) and/or local grants (again, some grants are restricted to charities registered in a specific country). It's not necessarily the case for MSF but it is for other organizations. For instance, the European Commission Humanitarian Aid & Civil Protection Office (ECHO), which is one of the biggest humanitarian aid donors, only funds charities that are registered in one of the EU member states.

Though there are other examples of organizational fissioning, here are just two more. OXFAM is now a confederation of 17 organizations around the world. The International Federation of Red Cross and Red Crescent Societies (IFRC) was founded in 1919 and today it coordinates activities between the 188 National Red Cross and Red Crescent Societies. Smart strategic moves, these.

The brute force of positive human will

It is a testament to the dedication of workers within the humanitarian aid sector that coordination and communication among the various humanitarian aid entities happens at the high level that it does. In May 2016 the World Humanitarian Summit (WHS) was held in Istanbul. The WHS happened in spite of the overwhelming challenges to intra-organizational coordination. It happened because of the brute force of positive human will and collective desire within the humanitarian aid sector to respond in dignity enhancing ways to the needs of those who have been crushed by wars, famine and marginalization of all types. More and more humanitarian aid organizations are adhering to trans-organizational agreements on standards (e.g., the Core Humanitarian Standards). Sector-wide cluster meetings are becoming increasingly organized and coordinated. The humanitarian aid system moves forward despite a multitude of challenges, such as:

- the above mentioned inherent and inevitable bureaucratic functioning hurdles
- a work force that tends to have dysfunctionly high turnover
- a mission that is increasingly compromised by the actions of various militaries
- changing technology allowing for real-time social media scrutiny and kibitzing
- all manner of MONGO-types muddying the waters
- a decreasing respect for the sanctity of the humanitarian space (read: good people die in the line of duty).

Is the aid system broken?

That there will be constant chatter about how the "aid system is broken" is a given. Recent *The Guardian* op-eds by J and Currion are great examples.[3,4] People experience frustrations when they see inefficiency, stupidity, waste and lack of coordination, especially when lives are on the line.

But is the humanitarian aid system broken? No. Are there aspects of the system that could be improved? Definitely. My guess is that Weber would be astounded at the frequently creative but always relentlessly stubborn actions of many devoted individuals who have mightily resisted and overcome the many challenges faced by these large, complicated bureaucracies.

No, the humanitarian aid system is not "broken." Just the opposite, it embodies a heroic response to the greatest human challenge of them all, that of harnessing our innate human urge to make the world a little bit more free of unnecessary suffering and indignities.

I agree with J. We should all just calm down. But at the same time we can never ease up in our efforts.

NOTES

1. Paul Currion, "The Humanitarian Future."
2. Linda Polman, *The Crisis Caravan*. (New York: Henry Holt and Company, 2010).
3. J, "Is Humanitarian Aid Really Broken?"
4. Paul Currion, "The Aid System is Broken – How Can We Fix It?" *The Guardian*, January 14, 2016.

4 THE MORAL CAREER OF A HUMANITARIAN AID WORKER

Sit back. This one may take a while.

The goal of this chapter is to meaningfully apply the concepts of "moral career" and "looking-glass self" to better understand the lives of aid workers as they move through their professional lives. In this chapter I want to emphasize the overall journey of a career as opposed to a snapshot of single moment. This will make it possible to consider the evolution of self identity that occurs over the course of an aid worker's career.

Moral career and self identity

I borrow the phrase "moral career" from sociologist Erving Goffman. His classic book *Asylums*, was published in 1961 as a "collection of essays on the social situation of mental patients and other inmates". Goffman defines moral career as "...any social strand of any person's course through life...the regular sequence of changes that career entails in the person's self and in his imagery for judging himself and others." He continues by explaining that,

> *"The moral career of a person of a given social category involves a standard sequence of changes on his way of conceiving of selves, including importantly, his own....Each moral career, and behind this, each self, occurs within the confines of an institutional system...and can be seen as something that resides in the arrangements prevailing in a social system for its members."*

Finally he concludes that, *"This special kind of institutional arrangement does not so much support the self as constitute it."*[1]

Here Goffman brilliantly foreshadows the groundbreaking works of first Stanley Milgram (author of *Obedience to Authority*) and then, later by Phillip G. Zimbardo (famous for the Stanford prison experiment and *The Lucifer Effect*). Both researchers stress the "institutional arrangement" and its impact on behavior and, hence, sense of self as one reflects on their behavior. And, oh, their free will as well.

Is it possible that in most instances instead of thinking and then deciding to act, we act and then explain our actions to ourselves and then to others? Questions of this nature are challenging, to be sure, but important to consider.

There are two main points to keep in mind as we move forward. First, the idea that we all go through stages in various parts of our lives is now fairly standard social science fare, perhaps made most famous by Elizabeth Kübler-Ross' book *On Death and Dying*.[2] Her detailing of the five stages of coming to grips with death remains a useful tool for many. This chapter will serve to extend the idea of stages to include the lives of aid workers. The second point is harder to grasp because it is counterintuitive, namely that our sense of self is in many ways outside of our control.

Social psychologist Charles H. Cooley is generally credited with the term "looking-glass self."[3] One's sense of self is, to a certain extent, a product of how we imaging others to see us – both physically and our behaviors, how we imagine others evaluate what they see.

We all know intuitively how beneficiaries will see us when driving up in a white land cruiser or, alternately, on public transport.

To merge another of Goffman's ideas with Cooley for a moment, we all manage our identity by manipulating how we are seen by others. What both Cooley and Goffman are saying is, simply, that our identity is in flux and depends upon social context to a good extent. For aid workers, the "social context" one finds themselves in can be a challenge and is something that is thrust upon more frequently that chosen.

That said, we can put everyone on a continuum with two end points. On one extreme there are people whose sense of self are totally driven by how they see others seeing them. We'll call these chameleon-like people "other directed." On the other extreme are those who are totally unwavering in their self concept and are driven, as it were, by an internal gyroscope. We'll call these people "inner directed." The two ends of the continuum are, of course ideal types and only exist as points of reference.

Key to note is that where one is on the above continuum is in flux most of the time and depends on many factors, perhaps most importantly (1) the age and maturity of the person and (2) the social context in which the person finds himself/herself. Very young people are always reading social cues from others and, in general, are very other directed: if an authority figure tells a young person they are stupid they tend to believe it.

All of us, in various social situations, look for cues to see how we are fitting into our social surroundings with appropriate cultural sensitivity.

The remainder of this chapter will focus on using Goffman's term to better understand the lives of aid workers and to suggest that they too have a moral career.

A fitting, fictional example

Perhaps the most prominent example of fiction writing about the lives of aid workers is the series of books by J. Here Mary-Anne and Jon Langstrom speak to us from *Missionary, Mercenary, Mystic, Misfit*:[4]

> *"Somewhere I read—can't remember where, exactly. Anyway, it was a description of aid workers as missionaries, mercenaries, mystics, and misfits. And the longer I stick around, the more I see it." Jon looked around for the waiter, and then motioned for two more bottles of St. George. Mary-Anne could already tell that she'd probably miss curfew. Again.*

> *"The problem is that when people use that phrase, they're usually describing where we've come from. They mean it's what we were before we accidentally found our way into humanitarian work. But I think they're wrong. I think it's about what we become. It's a description of states of being toward which humanitarians gravitate."*

> *Mary-Anne was suddenly on the edge of her chair, hanging on every word.*

> *Jon Langstrom's tone was matter-of-fact. "We all start out with these altruistic intentions. We're going to save the world, or at least a little corner of it. We're going to do everything properly, we're on the 'right' side of all the issues all the time. We're self-styled warriors for truth and light. That's the 'missionaries' part."*

> *Two more bottles of St. George appeared and Jon held one out to her. Mary-Anne took it although somewhere in the back of her head she knew she'd probably regret doing so. But for now she was in the mood to drink a bit more and listen to Jon Langstrom bequeath his wisdom. She took a sip and said, "Go on.""*

> *Jon took a sip himself and nodded.*

> *"So, we're all on the side of right and light, warriors for the poor, and all of that. Then we get into it a little way and we see that it works by calculus, not math. We see what goes into the sausage. We see that for all of our dialogic,*

participatory, multi-stakeholder, community-led, bottom-up, embrace-and-empower-everything-local ideals and maybe even practice, that the decisions that truly matter are made elsewhere and on the basis of other things entirely. We come to understand that we have to play hardball. If we stick around long enough, we usually get to the place where we're willing to fight for a program or strategy we think is the best one, even when it means throwing a colleague under the bus. There are times and places in this industry where, for all of our professed love of all humanity, a win-win is just not possible. We choose this poor community rather than that one because the donor wants this one, not because the needs are greater. We sacrifice little bits of who we are and what we believe in the service of some alleged bigger picture. Then the little bits get bigger. We become extreme. We're willing to execute more tactical bad in the name of an increasingly elusive and vague strategic 'greater good.' For some, it becomes an 'ends justify means' thing. But one way or the other, we become mercenary."

He exhaled sharply. It was almost totally dark in the courtyard at Billy-Bob's now. Without waiting for a response from Mary-Anne, Jon continued.

"That altruism, or what we took as altruism that drove us to this line of work isn't a bad thing. We want the world to be better. We can envision a more just or a less unjust world. Some of us become hyper cause-oriented. We delve into the theory or maybe the technical nuts and bolts of practice in a particular sector. And in that sense some of us become mystics."

"But as in everything else, there are trade-offs. There is always the danger of spending so long immersed in the language and culture of humanitarian aid that anything outside feels incomprehensible. We spend so long focused on a particular way of thinking about issues, like reproductive health or third world hunger, that we lose our ability to engage with those who see the issues differently. Or, and this is the even greater danger, we lose the ability to really engage with those who simply haven't thought about them at all: the ordinary people in our families and social circles."

"It's a paradox, but we can spend so long out here that we begin to treat home like we treat 'the field.' Which is to say that we become perpetual temporary interlopers who embrace our 'not from here' status as an excuse to see everything clinically and still always have a way out. Our visa is about to expire and we have to go home or to the next mission. Or we have another mission and have to leave home..."

Jon stopped mid-sentence and paused, as if weighing his words.

"We become misfits."

J does several things with this dialogue. First, he acknowledges that the alliterative phrase "missionary, mercenary, mystic and misfit" is an oft used trope, but he immediately distances himself from the traditional two-dimensional use of these words as mere labels for static categories. An example of this is the otherwise insightful article published in 2006 by UK researcher R. L. Stirrat entitled *"Mercenaries, Missionaries, and Misfits: Representations of Development Personnel,"* J's character, Jon Langstrom, is quick to note that these four stages – missionary, mercenary, mystic and misfit – are "states of being" and points along a journey; he anticipates the utility of the moral career concept.[5]

But what exactly is this utility? Let me be clear in pointing out that neither J nor I are selling any version of the truth, but rather doing what comes naturally to those who seek to understand, namely describe and categorize and then offer, tentative as it may be, analysis and explanation. In the words of Miguel de Unamuno,

> *"My intent has been, is, and will continue to be, that those who read my works shall think and meditate upon fundamental problems, and has never been to hand them completed thoughts. I have always sought to agitate and, even better, to stimulate, rather than to instruct. Neither do I sell bread, nor is it bread, but yeast or ferment."*[6]

That is to say, any conceptual framework that one imposes on social reality can be usefully judged by the kinds of questions it generates. Since this book intends to report on data gathered rather than spin out deep analysis, I will not go into answers to some questions below, but perhaps simply suggest them as useful points of departure.

So, what questions do emerge as we think about the "moral career of the aid worker?"

- Can further describing these stages be of therapeutic value to an individual aid worker as she attempts to examine her career?
- Are human resource personnel responsive to and aware of these stages?
- When mental illness becomes an issue, how does this impact these stages?
- Are these stages different/progress through these stages different for relief/aid versus development workers?
- How do life-partners help or hinder awareness of stages?
- How does this play into the concept of compartmentalization (e.g., deployment smoker)?

- To what extent are these four stages exhaustive? Are there stages that are missed, jumped over or just ignored? If so, what are they?
- What kinds of events or experiences move a person from stage to the next?
- How long does one stay in each stage? Is it possible to get permanently "stalled" in one of the early stages?
- Can you regress through the stages and/or can there be a cycling through?
- How do you communicate with someone in another stage? How is social networking helping or hindering progress through stages?
- After misfit....what is there? Does one ever fit back into their "home" world?
- Finally, how do you know who you really are? As Berger pointed out, we are all reinterpreting our past. How do we know out present self is fully formed? How can you know your motivations are true to who you are? When are you *you* and when are you just playing the role into which the social situation places you?

Yes, the above list does drill down to the existential core. Too deep for some, but valid nonetheless since considering these questions might serve as a useful backdrop for more deeply understanding the data. Asking these weighty questions allows us to better understand the reality of the aid workers experience and it allows us to better represent aid worker voices.

For example, chapter 9, "Race, Identity, and Branding," includes numerous touching and thoughtful statements from aid workers as they reflected on their identity and, in retrospect, on their journey though some stages. Other chapters include similar points of departure for our understanding. Take a look at chapter 7, "The Impact of Gender on the Lives of Aid Workers," regarding the impact of gender on identity.

I'll end here with a nod back to Goffman. He argues that only by understanding both one's structural context *and* the internal dialogue that takes place can we fully understand not only our own identities but as well the identities of those around us. I agree.

NOTES

1. Erving Goffman, *Asylums* (Harmondsworth, England: Penguin Books, 1961).
2. Kubler-Ross, Elizabeth. *On Death and Dying* (New York: Simon & Schuster, 1969).
3. Charles Horton Cooley, *Human Nature and the Social Order.* (New York: Scribner, 1902).
4. J. *Missionary, Mercenary, Mystic, Misfit.* (Evil Genius Publishing, 2013).
5. Roderick L. Stirrat, "Mercenaries, Missionaries and Misfits: Representations of Development Personnel," *Critique of Anthropology* 28 (2008): 406-425
6. Miguel de Unamuno, *Perplexities and Paradoxes.* (New York: Greenwood Press, 1968), 8.

5 WHY DID YOU BECOME AN AID WORKER?

"To make the conditions present for a life of human dignity for all."
— 36-40 yo female expat aid worker, white

"It comes down to this: there is serious injustice in the world, and that makes me really fucking angry."
— 18-25yo female expat aid worker, non-white

"I think it's a mixture of accident, the lure of adventure, and (self)righteous indignation over how messed up the world is combined with an (arrogant) sense that maybe I could make things suck slightly less."
— 31-35yo female expat aid worker, white

An overview

Our personal lives seldom unfold in a linear, logical, preplanned fashion. We rarely know exactly what external forces will push or pull us in various directions. Even the assumption that we are sole masters of our fate, unfettered by cultural currents and eddies, can be called into question. Perhaps anthropologist Miles Richardson said it best in his essay "Culture and the struggle to be human": "Rather than thinking and then proceeding to act; we act and then proceed to explain."[1]

Here's one respondent, a 26-30 yo white female expat worker, that states this nicely:

"It's too simplistic. Yes, I wanted adventure... yes, I wanted to do something productive with winning the birth lottery... yes, it's kind of an accident..."

This next statement comes from a 41-45 yo white female aid worker in the sector for more than ten years who had indicated she became an aid worker "by accident":

> *"I would hope that I am no longer in it by accident, but to be honest, I am not entirely sure."*

Yup. That said, what did our survey respondents have to say about their life-path decisions?

The quantitative data

That said, our Q22, *Which statement below *best* describes your primary reason for becoming an aid worker?*, put the respondent in a position of trying to explain the past.

Somewhat predictably, at 34%, the most frequently selected closed ended response was "None of the above even comes close to articulating my reason for becoming an aid worker."

Males and females responded very similarly to this question, though males were almost twice as likely to choose *"I needed adventure in my life and being an aid worker seemed like a good idea."* Females were slightly more likely to indicate the altruistic response, *"I was following my dream to provide aid to those less fortunate than myself."* and also to say, in effect, "it's complicated." These specific differences were apparent as I read through the many narrative responses.

	Ended up as an aid worker by accident or "unintentionally"	I felt called by God or a higher power.	I was following my dream to provide aid to those less fortunate than myself.	I needed an adventure in my life and being an aid worker seemed like a good idea.	I could not find any other employment.	I followed a friend or significant other into the field of aid work.	None of the above even comes close to articulating my reason for becoming an aid worker.	Total
Q4: Female	16.22% 81	5.17% 29	33.51% 188	8.56% 48	3.18%	0.71% 4	35.33% 201	63.39% 563
Q4: Male	16.53% 40	6.20% 15	23.14% 71	16.53% 40	0.83% 2	1.65% 4	28.93% 70	36.14% 242
Total Respondents	121	44	259	88	3	8	271	805

Which statement below "best" describes your primary reason for becoming an aid worker?

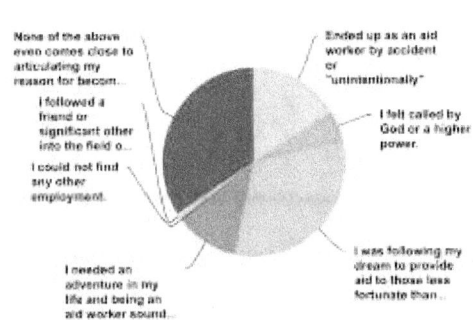

Answer Choices	Responses	
Ended up as an aid worker by accident or "unintentionally"	18.78%	
I felt called by God or a higher power.	5.57%	
I was following my dream to provide aid to those less fortunate than myself.	31.72%	
I needed an adventure in my life and being an aid worker sounded like a good idea.	11.02%	
I could not find any other employment.	8.48%	
I followed a friend or significant other into the field of aid work.	3.97%	
None of the above even comes close to articulating my reason for becoming an aid worker.	34.14%	
Total		

Some narrative responses

The open ended invitation to elaborate on Q22 generated a very robust 596 narrative responses (out of a total of 1010 that started the survey), 410 from females and 187 from males. Q24 asked a two-part follow-up *"What are your primary reasons for remaining an aid worker? Are your reasons for staying in this field different from the ones that brought you to it in the first place?"* and 615 people responded (426 females, 189 males).

First we'll take a look at some of the reasons people gave for becoming an aid worker.

This first example is both interesting and representative of many other respondent's thoughts. This 36+yo female aid worker working for a "big box" organization indicated that she came into the field because *"I felt called by God or a higher power."*

She goes on to say,

> *"I bought into the Liberal narrative fed to me by my left-leaning university professors and supported by a guilty and near-sighted North America: "The*

Third World" was an innocent place "out there" where innocent good people suffered, because of the Big Bad West – due to All Catastrophic Colonialism – both historical and neo. I could not call myself a Good Person, a Good Christian, or on the Right Side of History if I didn't Make The Sacrifice and Go Out There and Do Something (sorry for obnoxious capitalization)."

Why does she remain in this sector (Q24)?

"Salary and Benefits. Though no longer idealistic and no longer buying the narrative in Q23, I don't see the aid industry as being any worse (or better) than anything else out there. It's still more interesting than working at A-1 Insurance Company and more sophisticated than being a high school teacher...you do still get to travel and see and learn things most other careers do not afford you. Finally, expat colleagues are really great even when annoying. You can't really go back. Besides, not sure what else I would do at this point. Yes, reasons are very different. But I've learned to accept a different narrative so it makes it ok."

This transition from idealism in the early going to pragmatism in the later career seems a common pattern. Here is a white 26-30yo male expat aid worker's description:

"Slowly changing indeed. Even if my organization is the biggest and most present actor in the medical emergency field, we still spend 65% of our annual budget in stable projects where the emergency is long gone and we don't know how to get out. Which ultimately leads to a normal office job for me. It's still ok, mainly because the challenges and level of responsibilities are much higher than what a guy my age would be able to get at home. If I remain an aid worker in the next years, it will be because this organization offers a lot of opportunities to get more important responsibilities. The altruist feelings I had at the beginning are still there, but much less present."

(White privilege) guilt seems a quite common force pushing people toward this sector. Here are a couple typical responses.

"Ever since I was a child I felt like I didn't deserve my privilege of being an upper middle class white American, and I've known since then that I wanted to dedicate my life to making the world a better place for everyone to live, but actually living in Rwanda and doing the expat aid worker thing sorta happened by accident. I thought for a long time that I'd be helping people in the United States." 18-25 yo female expat aid worker

"I felt like the postcode you are born in, or on a larger scale, the country you are born in, should not dictate your opportunities for the rest of your life. It is a politically motivated decision to be an aid worker, I do not think the Western world deserves the right to the best standard of life." 26-30 yo white male expat aid worker

So many of the responses were heartfelt and thoughtful, few more than this one from a 26-30 yo white female expat aid worker.

"I believe in solidarity and mutual aid; whenever possible, elevate and act on the priorities and needs of people advocating for themselves, for example in justice-oriented social movements. I do aid work for my job because it's a way to offer help and resources at the moment when people most need it, with (I believe) less harmful impacts than 'development' that's done without the active centering of social movements. The rest of my (nonworking) life is devoted to organizing and solidarity activism. Aid work is my compromise: I get paid, I get to help, I get to learn first-hand what is going on and how, and I get to feed my cowboy streak without buying too deeply into a development project that dictates long-term distribution of resources according to funder pleasure. I realize this sounds naive at first typing, but I do really think that the long-term balance falls (generally, with many exceptions) on the side of humanitarian aid as a necessary, useful tool, whereas development projects led by foreign NGOs tends to undermine local organizing over the long-term. Philosophically, I'd rather be an advocate or researcher with Food First working to support the work of La Via Campesino. And I have been – I've participated in plenty of protests and campaigns against smallholder farmer-damaging free trade agreements and for local community gardens in US cities. But I also want to be a direct participant, embracing the moral dilemmas and engaging with (instead of studying) the complexity. Aid work seems like a good way to do so."

There is much more to add at this point, but I'll close with the assertion people gravitate toward life paths that makes them feel good and responds to their basic urge to have justice.

"I believe that we have an obligation to correct structural injustices in the world and enable each and every person to realize their full potential, irrespective of where they live or what privilege/underprivilege they access." 18-25 yo white female HQ worker

45

NOTES

1.   Miles Richardson, "Culture and the Struggle to be Human." *Anthropology and Humanism Quarterly* 1 (1976): 2-4.

6 FAITH AND AID WORK(ERS)

"Besides [being a] calling it was also a sense of adventure."
– 41-45 yo white female HQ worker

"None of the answers above describes why I because an aid worker, but I did choose the 'closest' response. It was never a life-long dream to provide aid to those less fortunate than myself. I'm not sure if I really have a strong, concrete answer. Compassion? Righteous anger? Indignant injustice? Fighting against "The Man"? God's calling?"
– 36-40 yo non-white, unspecified gender HQ worker

"I think it is a bit disrespectful to ask about the level of idealism of aid workers. Aren't people working on a 9-5pm job idealists too thinking they will have a better life and get promoted? I think aid workers have an aspiration, something guide them and do not lack a sense of realism."
– 26-30 yo white female expat aid worker

Inferences from the data

We did not directly ask questions about faith (or lack thereof), but both our quantitative and qualitative data do shed some light on the topic of faith and aid work. A significant subset – nearly 1 in 5 – in our sample (17%) identified as working for faith based organizations. The World Bank lists nearly 500 such faith based organizations around the world ranging dramatically in size, reach and mission.

As I looked through all of the quantitative data I found few differences between those working in faith based versus non-faith based organizations. The numbers were fairly comparable when looking at demographic data such as gender, race, and education level. The faith-based workers did tend to be, on the whole, slightly younger than those working in non-faith-based organizations. There was one dramatic exception.

Q22 asked, *"Which statement below *best* describes your primary reason for becoming an aid worker?"* Below are the results comparing those who reported working in faith-based versus non-faith-based organizations. Of note is that while almost a third (29%) of those in faith-based organizations indicated that the primary reason they became an aid worker is because *"I felt called by God or higher power."* By contrast only slightly more than 1% of those based in non-faith-based organizations indicated the same. Wow.

	Ended up as an aid worker by accident or "unintentionally"	I felt called by God or a higher power	I was following my dream to provide aid to those less fortunate than myself.	I needed an adventure in my life and being an aid worker sounded like a good idea.	I could not find any other employment.	I followed a friend or significant other into the field of aid work.	None of the above even comes close to articulating my reason for becoming an aid worker.	Total
Q17: Faith based.	15.87% 20	28.37% 36	29.37% 37	4.76% 6	0.79% 1	0.79% 1	18.84% 25	15.37% 126
Q17: Non-faith based.	16.26% 113	1.44% 10	32.13% 223	12.10% 84	0.43% 3	1.01% 7	36.74% 255	84.76% 695
Total (Respondents)	133	46	260	90	4	8	280	820

Q23 asked, "Please elaborate on the response you gave to the question above on why you became an aid worker," and nearly 60% of the respondents chose to take us up on that offer. Many gave specific mention that there was a strong social justice component to their motivation, but that is grist for a separate chapter. Below are some comments from the faith-based respondents.

26 of the 94 respondents – 28% – from faith-based organization specifically referred to God/the Bible/being "called" in their narrative answer.

Here are a few:

> *"As a Christian, I feel God gave me a passion to work with those in need especially those in East Africa."*
>
> 26-30 yo white male expat aid worker

> *"I think God had a large part in my becoming a humanitarian aid worker. But I could have stated home and helped people. My skills and passion were more focused on issues of global poverty and injustice. So put them together and I followed my dream of becoming a humanitarian aid worker."*
>
> 31-35 yo male expat aid worker

"In my opinion, there is very little difference in my feeling called by God and my following my dream to provide aid to those less fortunate than myself. I believe I have dreams and passion and skills that God uses for the good of others; at the same time, I believe Christians are called to do justice for those less fortunate in some way or other. In my case, it is working in development."

26-30 yo white female expat aid worker

There was this comment from an aid worker in a faith based organization that stood out:

"I have always engaged in work with a social conscience. I 'fell' into this work in the 1980s as a destitute backpacker in West Africa. Incidentally, I am an atheist."

56-60 yo white, unspecified gender expat aid worker

This is the word cloud from the 94 responses made by faith based organization workers.

Choice Service Justice Process Wanted to Help
Given Career Human Fortunate Support
Called Serve Development Learning
Living Place Skills Humanitarian Aid
Country Entirely Social Led Started Resources
Christian

Big differences not there

One place where perhaps one could have anticipated a difference in responses is Q28 *"Regarding your sense of idealism, which statement below best describes your experience?"* and Q29 which asked for a narrative response asking about changes in the respondent's level of idealism. The numbers differ little between those working in faith based versus non-faith based organizations, and that a slightly higher percentage of faith-based workers reported lower levels of idealism compared to their view before becoming an aid worker.

In Q59 we asked the respondents to give their views about the overall direction of humanitarian aid work and the numbers indicate that the faith based workers had a consistently (though slight) more optimistic view of the impact being made.

Concluding thought

To what extent does faith play a part in aid work among our respondents? For a small percentage it seems to play a crucial role, but for most aid workers it does not appear to be a major factor. My view is that we are wired to seek fairness and justice. Like most physical attributes, this wiring is not binary but rather distributed within a population likely in something resembling a normal curve. Were there tools of analysis sophisticated enough, we would find that aid workers generally come from one end of that curve, the end that accents the human need to ease pain and, ultimately, to do unto others as we would have them do unto us. Some are – yes – called to do humanitarian aid work, but the calling is being done by forces from within, not from "above."

Yeah, I just said that.

A (second) note on faith and aid workers

Overview

Just as I blogged about on our survey data relevant to faith and aid workers EvilGenius was putting out two mini-polls on that topic. As with our longer survey, many respondents were generous with their time and offered extensive and thoughtful comments.

EvilGenius asked first for the respondent's views on the net impact of religion as a force for good or bad in the world. Though this question is clearly very complex, there is precedent for asking it. The Tony Blair vs. Christopher Hitchens debate that took place in Toronto, Canada back in 2010 examined the same question, specifically, "Be it resolved, religion is a force for good in the world."

The second mini-poll is a bit more specific and probes into the question "does being faith-based impact the efficacy of aid organizations?"

I'll present some data on both of these questions and then conclude with some observations of my own. Please note that the response rate to both of these mini-polls was low and we are very interested in more viewpoints. If you are reading this and have not yet take the polls please do so now. Each is here and here and below.

Is religion force for good in the world?

The specific question was *"Based on what you've seen and what you know from your experience related to aid or development work, is religion on balance a force for good, or a force for bad in the world?"* The vast majority of those who responded to this question also indicated that "I have an inside knowledge the aid, development, or charity sector/industry. I work or have worked for a charity or NGO, an institutional donor like DFID or the Gates Foundation, a beltway bandit like DAI, or I have been a consultant to one of these kinds of entities."

The results, though clearly tentative, are dramatic. An anemic 13% of those responding felt that on balance religion was a force for good in the world. The rest were either not sure at 35% or, actually a majority at 52%, felt just the opposite.

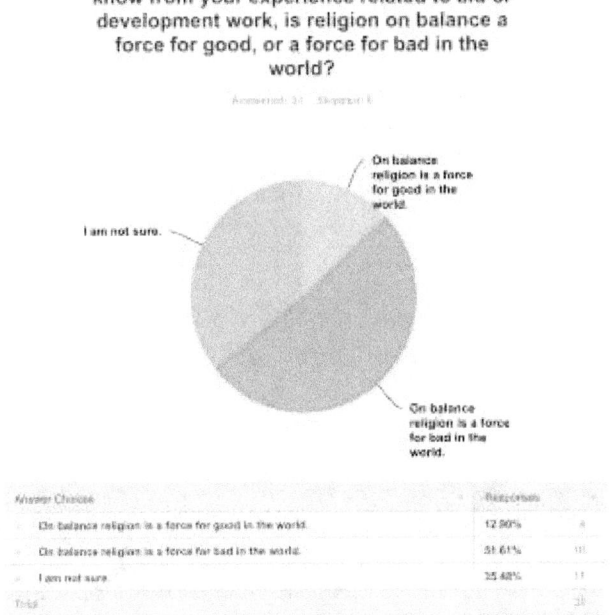

Based on what you've seen and what you know from your experience related to aid or development work, is religion on balance a force for good, or a force for bad in the world?

Answer Choices	Responses	
On balance religion is a force for good in the world.	12.90%	4
On balance religion is a force for bad in the world.	51.61%	16
I am not sure.	35.48%	11
Total		31

Below are responses representing all three choices. I have highlighted what I think are particularly salient points.

First, 'on balance a force for bad.' I have included two since this was the majority view, with the second representing a view evoking Marx:

"To begin, I think that it is difficult to say on balance whether it is a force for good or bad, as many of the effects of religion are not necessarily quantifiable or equivalent, but considering the harm that is caused by religion, which cannot be negated by its good impacts, I'm comfortable saying that it is a force for the worse in the world. Between the manipulation of religious beliefs to oppress, marginalize, and dehumanize people, often by religious authorities, and the conservative and reactionary character of many religious institutions, religion causes great harm around the world, especially when it comes to social justice.

Being from the US, I'm very aware of how religious conservatism is a major driver of polarization and oppression in my country. That being said, I think there are many benefits of faith, and I know many people who are driven to good due to their faith or spirituality. From what I have experienced of the world, I think faith is seldom if ever an actual cause of things like oppression and conflict, but due to its fundamental and existential place in many people's lives, it is susceptible to manipulation by people with power, especially those who have some form of religious authority. Faith and spirituality drive people to seek justice and make the world a better place, but religion can be used to exclude certain people from those deserving of sharing the betterment of the world.

Finally, being an atheist, I find that many people still think having faith of some form is a prerequisite for being a moral person, and in many situations, not least at home in the US, I am not comfortable revealing my lack of faith. This I think gets at one of the greatest problems with religion, that it tends to prevent people from accepting without judgement others who are different from themselves, which is absolutely critical in the modern world if we are to successfully live together and achieve the aims of social justice and development that we strive for."

"Divisive regressive tool for social control."

Next, 'on balance a force for good:'

"The majority of people in the world are religious. The majority of people in the world live their lives peacefully (and are only unfortunately caught up in conflict if they are in a conflict area). Their faith brings them personal strength, and meaning as well as strengthening and organising communities. At the local level (which is ultimately the level aid should be concerned with), religion is a mostly a force for good."

And finally, 'I am not sure:'

"I see the strength and support it can give people, and a platform from which people perform generous acts, but I also see how it excludes, marginalizes, or

encourages people (from many faiths) into more extreme posturing on issues of social justice and compassion."

"I see the importance of faith + humility and understanding. No faiths can be proven and the religion I believe in is no more evidence based than another faith. I therefore cannot say or think that my faith is the correct one but it is just something that speaks to me in my heart and is very personal. I wish religious institutions would promote understanding and knowledge of different faiths. I wish they would not preach their way as being the only correct path. I wish they would also encourage enquiry and address the limitations of their histories and sources. Sierra Leone provides the perfect example of different faiths living harmoniously, 'Jesus loves Allah', 'Allah loves Jesus' written on cars."

To the respondent who wondered, *"Can we get away from these dichotomies?* I will point out that though the question is certainly very complex, as is evidenced by others responses, pushing people to take a position on the question does generate useful dialogue.

Faith based aid organizations "bad?"

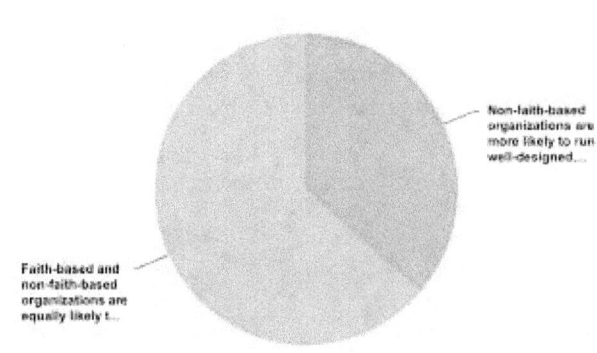

Which of the following statements best reflects your view on the issue of whether faith-based orientation has an effect on an organization's effectiveness:

Answer Choices	Responses	
Faith-based organizations are more likely to run well-designed, effective, efficient programmes than non-faith-based organizations.	0.00%	0
Non-faith-based organizations are more likely to run well-designed, effective, efficient programmes than faith-based organizations.	36.36%	4
Faith-based and non-faith-based organizations are equally likely to run well-designed, effective, efficient programmes. The determinants of well-designed, effective, and efficient have nothing to do with whether or not the organization is faith-based.	63.64%	7
Total		11

The next mini-poll generated some thoughtful responses as well. The key question was, *"Irrespective of anything else, does the fact that an organization is faith-based or not faith-based have an effect on the quality, and ultimately the impact of its programmes and interventions in the field?"* The results to this, 55% "No" and 45% "Yes," and what went behind these responses is hinted at in the follow-up question. Here are the quantitative results indicating a majority of this small sample felt, of course, that it all depends, but minority opinion was biased toward non-faith-based organizations.

Here are a couple representative narrative responses that articulate some of the nuances.

> *"Truly, my answer is "depends." I have seen both stellar examples of how FBNGOs leverage faith to the advantage of the population they serve and terrible examples how faith is used to excuse bad projects. Ultimately, the failures are due to bad management, which exists regardless of faith."*

> *"Depends on the context that the organisation is working in. If a faith based organisation is working in communities of the same faith then they can be more effective than others as they can engage deeper with people's worldview and behaviour. However if working outside this context or in communities hat are not religious then their impact would not be different to non faith based organisations."*

Religion is a major social force all over the world and has clearly shaped most of our past and clearly much of our present (see: ISIS). Understanding this force is critical for this who concern themselves with effective aid.

Let's continue the conversation.

Oh ye of little faith

Faith based NGOs

Faith-based aid organizations are now and have always been a major factor in the sector. Collectively these organizations continue and refine a trend – most especially among the Christian religions – that has gone on for centuries and, historically, is indeed an integral dimension of colonization. These organizations range from the "big box" globally influential mega-NGOs to the classic "MONGO" or My Own NGO based in a specific church. The larger organizations tend to avoid overt proselytization while the smaller ones less so, some being almost aggressively pushing their faith messages.

Which best describes the humanitarian aid work organization with which you are (or were) most recently affiliated?

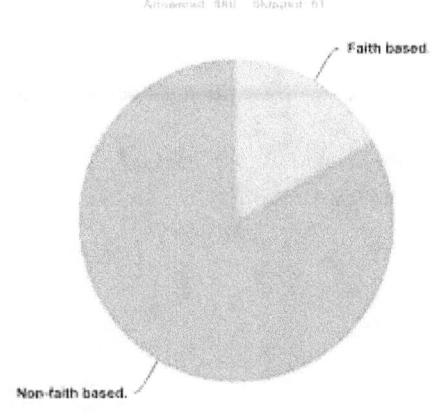

Answered: 480 Skipped: 51

Answer Choices	Responses	
Faith based.	16.77%	161
Non-faith based.	83.23%	799
Total		960

Q17 asked simply, "Which best describes the humanitarian aid work organization with which you are (or were) most recently affiliated?" Of our respondents, 17% indicated they were affiliated with faith based organization.

Given the nature of what some aid workers experience in the field, especially in those locations that have undergone what an anthropologist might call "cultural disintegration" i.e., conflict zones, what do aid workers have to say? How do they address the sometimes massive gap between the lofty messages of religion and the realities they witness?

Venting from an aid worker

Here is what a veteran aid worker deployed in a post-conflict environment ranted to me over Skype:

> *"So, there's this place where my employer built houses, a mosque, latrines, etc. for a small community of IDPs. Classic relief infrastructure. Was a worthwhile*

project. At each corner, there is an elevated guard booth for UN soldiers to stand guard at night to protect them. It's been great-ish for the past 9 months.

Last week, the UN peace-keeping mission in-country decided it was time to stop posting guards. So the booths have been empty at night.

The very next evening, the local community came and stole the metal doors off the latrines. So now no one can poop in privacy.

What kind of asshole steals the bathroom door from IDPs?

Anyway, we concluded the visit and walked out. 50 meters away sat the chief of the local police and the local religious leader. They were all anxious to pump my hand. 'Thank you, [my employer]… let's pray for peace.'

Or, you could just stop stealing from IDPs."

Taking time to share one more time this aid worker went on.

Sorry, but I gotta vent. Here's another….

"Apparently, taking a machete and murdering people against whom one had a grudge of some kind, or to whom one owed money, and then tossing the corpse down a well was so widespread (and continues, to some extent) that it has negatively moved the needle on clean water access nation-wide.

Call me ethnocentric. But this does not seem complicated.

STEP. AWAY. FROM. THE. GODDAMN. MACHETES.

But everyone's all, 'pray for peace.'

I swear, if I hear 'pray for peace' once more, I may actually lose it."

Pray for peace?

Both of the anecdotes above illustrate the deep and perhaps pervasive hypocrisy that exists in much of the world regarding faith and religion. Go to church on Sunday, cut up or steal from people the rest of the week. Appearing religious for show only perhaps, or, cynically, to apply a smokescreen covering essentially immoral actions.

In my conversation with this aid worker I responded to his comment *"Call me ethnocentric"* by offering, "NOT ethnocentric. Warped values are warped values universally."

The view that says culture forms us completely, the Standard Social Science Model (SSSM) as described by Leda Cosmides & John Tooby in their essay "Evolutionary psychology: a primer,"[1] is wrong. We are not born, as Steven Pinker points out in *The Blank Slate* with a formless blob of a brain but rather with myriad and complex modules that with timely stimulation comprise our "human nature" individually and collectively.[2] We are a moral animal from the inside out; morals come from our primate and pre-primate past, enhanced by further evolution and our expanding frontal cortex. There is right and wrong, at base.

That said, we are a species prone to contradictions because we have seemingly competing modules in our brains. Anthropologist Miles Richardson poetically summarized it long ago. Listen to his words:

> *"Blind, senseless, uncaring nature produced us. She cast us out of the primate troop, by cursing us with the ability to imagine God and thereby making us one of the most successful species, and certainly the most lonely. Being human is not to be a passive reader of blueprints, it is not to be a puppet on a string of norms, but it is to be man the hero, fighting to make sense of what nature has accomplished with us, the creation of a paradox: a species who can dream of eternal life but who must die, a species who preaches peace but who is more effective at waging war, a species who can imagine perfect beauty but whose shit stinks like all the rest."[3]*

The importance of this insight for aid workers is clear: it is NOT ethnocentric to view machete killings and rape as a tool of war or dominance as cultural practices to be accepted. You do NOT have to adopt a convoluted "cultural relativity" I-must-see-things-from-their-perspective point of view regarding all cultural practices you see. The third position – the one between ethnocentrism and blind acceptance of the cultural relativity – is the one embraced by the Universal Declaration of Human Rights adopted in 1948.[4] This third position says there are exactly that, universal and transcendent human rights the violation of which is wrong.

As I mentioned above, I do believe that morality is woven into our being as humans and that we do know the difference between right and wrong. The problem is that, as we have been told many times by anthropologists and writers, oftentimes "things fall apart" and cultures can all too commonly foster dysfunctional and, yes, immoral behavior.

A central part of the cannon in the sociology of religion is Emile Durkheim's *The Elementary Forms of Religious Life* in which he points out that religions evolved as a mechanism serving to externalize and to give voice to our moralities and in so doing function as a controlling and cohesive force in society.[5] That aid workers frequently hear the refrain "let's pray for peace" among those with which they work in the field (and at home) is to be expected…as is the feeling that this refrain can be excruciatingly hollow and hypocritical.

Grappling with the frequently massive gaps between the "is" and the "ought" is an occupational hazard among aid workers. The sector as a whole can be seen as our global community's effort to bridge that gap and confront head on the contradictions inherent in our species.

I think it will be a long time until "how things are and how we say things are, are one." And so it goes.

NOTES

1. Leda Cosmides and John Tooby, "Evolutionary Psychology: A Primer." Center for Evolutionary Psychology, University of California Santa Barbara, 1997.
2. Steven Pinker, *The Blank Slate*. (New York: Penguin Books, 2002).
3. Miles Richardson, "Blind, senseless, uncaring nature produced us."
4. The United Nations. *Universal Declaration of Human Rights*. G.A. Res. 217A (III), U.N. Doc. A/810 at 71. 1948.
5. Emile Durkheim, *The Elementary Forms of Religious Life*, Trans. Carol Cosman (Oxford: Oxford University Press, 2001).

7 THE IMPACT OF GENDER ON THE LIVES OF AID WORKERS

"Being a guy is like playing the easy setting. Less harassment, more respect."
 – 18-25yo white male expat aid worker

"Being female and working in many male dominated cultures I have to be extra mindful about how my actions are perceived, especially in management positions. Also, safety."
 – 26-30yo white female expat aid worker

Women comprise a majority of those in the aid and development industry and ours respondents – mostly female – had a lot to say. This chapter has three "acts" with the first act based on the survey results and acts two and three based on more in-depth responses from two female aid workers, Lucy and Becca, each with different and valuable contributions to make.

Act 1 One person's view from 50,000 feet

Just like most other animal species, among humans one's gender is a factor in daily life is a truism, a cultural universal. Gender differentiation has always existed among human cultures all over the planet and for our entire existence, starting in those caves hundreds of thousands of years ago in what is now South Africa. Humans, a species blessed – or cursed – with the ability to engage in complex thought and having the ability to possess and, more importantly, pass on cultural learning from one generation to the next, have made gender differentiation a major and lasting and social factor.

Though with only rare exceptions all of us have either a penis or a vagina – and the attendant secondary sexual characteristics that go along with said equipment – unlike other mammalian species, humans have socially constructed gender. Further, we have taken our sexuality – who we feel an urge to have sex with – and conflated it with gender identity. We are a complicated species and, unfortunately, have tended in most cultures to find a way to morph somewhat benign and perhaps functionally useful gender *differentiation* into a not-so-benign and, for 50% of the population markedly not advantageous, gender *stratification*. My personal theory is that gender stratification is fairly new and that up until about 15,000 years ago we lived actually most of our existence in a non-sexist manner. Social differentiation transforms into social stratification in cultural settings where a surplus of food, etc. is being regularly generated (i.e., concurrent with the rise of the domestication of plant and animal species) and this transformation, methinks, gives rise to gender stratification, i.e., sexism.

Yes, sexism. An ideology of domination and subordination based on the assumption of the biological and/or cultural inferiority of those with vaginas and the use of this assumption to legitimate and rationalize (commonly grounded in our modern Abrahamic religions) the inferior or unequal treatment of these vagina possessors.

Are we doomed forever to a world based in gender stratification, dominated by varying degrees of sexism? Perhaps not, but I think it will take several more generations before we live in a world where we simply enjoy our differences instead of exploiting them.

Same same, but different; now, from 35,000 feet[1]

Aid work is, well, work. It is a job in a sector. Of the 400,000-500,000 people around the world which might fall into this category depending on how you define "aid," there exists a healthy mix of both males and females. In many organizations there are more females than males, and of those that took the time to complete our survey, 70% were female. Representative of the sector? Likely not, but a good indication of strong female presence in the sector.

Given that we live in a gendered and, yes, sexist world, one can conclude that there are few if any occupations where to one degree or another one's gender is not a factor. Well, duh.

On to data from our survey.

With which gender do you identify?

Answered: 977 Skipped: 23

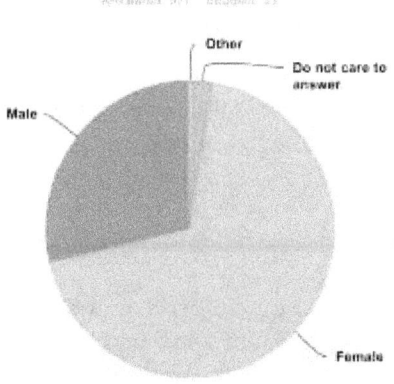

Answer Choices	Responses	
Other	0.20%	2
Do not care to answer.	2.56%	25
Female	68.68%	671
Male	28.56%	279
Total		977

Two questions

Which of these four factors is the most important in influencing how we
see ourselves: (1) race/ethnicity/cultural status, (2) social class/relative
wealth and power, (3) gender or (4) age? Which of those four factors is the
most important in influencing how others perceive and react to us?

Certainly every one of these factors is critically important for all of
us no matter where we are in the world or what our occupation might be.
Indeed, that is a basic truism in the social sciences. Though Max Weber was
referring more narrowly to wealth and power when he first used the term,[1]
his concept of "life chances" can be usefully applied more broadly to all
four of these factors. Each can and frequently does play into how we go
through our lives and our work days, that is, what "life chances" we enjoy –
or don't enjoy – depending upon where we are vis-a-vis these four major
social variables. Which factor is the most important for an individual can
change quickly, even moment by moment as we transition from one social
setting to the next, for example getting off a plane to a deployment faced
with immediate and dramatic cultural shifts. In short, all four factors are
critical, and various combinations can lead alternately to open or closed
doors.

63

This comment from a young, white, male expat aid worker sums this point up nicely:

> *"In Muslim countries, being a male makes a lot of things easier, even though in West Africa you are generally perceived as white before being perceived as a man or a woman. The only disadvantages in being a Male in some unstable countries are that it makes you more of a target for 'extremist/hostile' groups in some contexts."*

Vaginas and penises

That one's perceived gender can influence how a person is responded to is the focus below, and by presenting some representative narrative responses from our survey I hope to shed light on the deeper contextual nuances of perceived gender identity among aid workers.

As a related note, how you feel about yourself at any one moment is influenced by how you believe others are seeing you and how they are evaluating – judging – what they see. Perhaps that is part of the allure of being an aid worker: "How wonderful you are to help other people!" Though the "looking-glass self" can have that positive side, the way you are perceived by others can sometimes be negative (*"When two thousand years old you are, see how many times a week you are accused of being 'too male, too pale, stale.'"* stated one male respondent to our survey).

To go one step further, looking through the lens of sociologist Erving Goffman's concept of "impression management"[2] when we are at home and/or in our cubicle environment we are able to use myriad props, cues and affectations to enhance – or mute – any or all of our gender, ethnic/race, age or class statuses. We are in control of how we are seen by others and can manipulate – albeit most times doing so unconsciously- the looking-glass effect, somewhat. By stark contrast, while in the field there are times when we have very little control over how we are perceived. One important interpersonal skill any aid worker must have is the ability to imagine what people in an array of contexts see when they look at them and then act in accordance with that knowledge. To the point: a young, black, female American aid worker gets off the plane in [fill in the blank]. What do the beneficiaries see first, i.e., which of these four demographic variables is most salient? Yes, it varies. Yes, it is culture/situation specific. But in the end, the person getting off the plane is not the one in control of how she is being perceived, how she is identified and reacted to. The choice of whether or not you wear your aid organization branded t-shirt is trivial. You will – despite your intentions otherwise – be seen as a Westerner first.

Some results

Below are our results to the question related to gender being a factor for aid or development workers. On one level I am a bit surprised that nearly a third – 30% – of the respondents indicated their gender was not a factor at all in their work. When broken down by male compared to female, the percentages differ in what I would consider a predictable manner with females lower at 28% compared to 36% for males. I can understand that a male might not be habituated to thinking in terms of gender, but for a fourth of the females to report gender not a factor sounds, well, a bit odd, especially as I look more closely at the other numbers and read through some of the comments that were offered in the open-ended follow-up question (Q41). That said, perhaps these numbers nod at the points I made above.

What we do see very clearly in the data below is that by a very wide margin gender is a more negative factor for females than for males, with 39% of the females indicating that their gender was a negative factor compared to only 7% of the males indicating the same.

Q 40: To what extent has your gender been a factor in your humanitarian aid work experience?

	Not a factor at all	Overall has been a very positive factor	Overall has been a moderately positive factor	Overall has been a moderately negative factor	Overall has been a very negative factor	Total
Q4: Female	27.56% 148	8.57% 46	23.46% 126	38.55% 207	2.05% 11	69.42% 538
Q4: Male	35.71% 85	21.85% 52	34.87% 83	5.88% 14	1.68% 4	30.71% 238
Total Respondents	233	98	209	221	15	775

Combined responses:

Answer Choices		Responses	
Not a factor at all.		30.28%	241
Overall has been a very positive factor		12.69%	101
Overall has been a moderately positive factor		26.63%	212
Overall has been a moderately negative factor		28.27%	225
Overall has been a very negative factor		2.14%	17
Total			796

In the words of women – and men – in the field

Among the 443 (thank you all!) that provided a response in the follow-up open ended question (Q41) several themes and patterns emerge. Gender impacts both relationships with colleagues in the aid worker industry and those with the non-aid workers (both aid/support beneficiaries and non-beneficiary community members) in both negative and positive ways. Below are examples.

> *"It's been creeping up on me ... I never thought it is an issue but over the years I did notice that it is. Either with project clients and sometimes with colleagues."* –31-35yo white female expat aid worker

> *"I would say the positive aspects outweigh the negative. As a woman, I have been able to work with women and children in communities more closely than if I was a man. I also feel blessed to have close female friends in this field and we try to support and nurture each other as much as possible. I have not witnessed men bonding in this way. However, I have experienced sexism and harassment quite a bit in the course of my work. In some countries the harassment was significant and carried with it the threat of violence. On a couple of occasions I have not received jobs due to my gender. I have also experienced female bullying."* –36-40yo white female expat aid worker

These next ones gets pretty specific regarding power dynamics and expresses anger that I suspect may generate some head nods among the women reading this chapter.

> *"Because white women like me can still be viewed negatively, dismissed, ignored, by other white men - yes, really. So, a white woman in a senior position in Africa? Tough. African men ignore me routinely, especially if I am in the company of a male colleague, I may as well not be there sometimes. Only when they realise they need me to get to the money, do they talk to me. By then it is too late. Enough assholes in aid work, I am not supporting those who do not acknowledge a white woman."* – 41-45 yo white female expat aid worker

> *"More risk associated with being alone/out Sometimes I get the sense that people don't take what I'm saying as seriously, and I noticed they'll look to or defer to the man in the group, even if I'm the one in the position to answer/position of authority."* – 26-30yo white female expat aid worker

The next few examples highlight the nuance of gender impact and, importantly, voice clearly the point that in gender stratified cultures getting free access to – and generating a sense of trust with – women is much easier for female aid workers.

"My answer will change based on the day. It is definitely a large factor but in some instances it is positive and in others it is negative. I deal regularly with sexist rules and comments made by other expat staff members who I am sure do not even realize what they are saying or doing (e.g. no you cannot ride a bike, no you cannot drive a car. you are too emotional you must not be able to cope with stress. no you cannot attend this meeting with us, etc. etc.) When dealing with locals I have found that being a woman is often a positive as people seem to open up and trust women more than men and are more likely to feel they must take care of a woman, therefore offering me more access to people's homes to be able to talk to them." – 31-35yo white female expat aid worker

"Being a woman can be exceedingly difficult, especially in conflict zones where I'm working with mostly men. All of the decisions are based on a 2-dimensional perspective. It takes a lot of explaining to bring about a holistic approach and/or incorporate the lives of women in planning. Sometimes, as an expat woman, I'm considered androgynous and given the same access as a male. But that can also be isolating, depending on the context since I end up in the male category and have to fight to speak to a woman or plan things that factor in women's lives. Sometimes, I'm a critical bridge between the women/vulnerable and decision makers, a "voice" for women when they're kept out of the process. That can also be a burden if decision makers are expecting you to be the voice for millions of women." – 36-40yo white female expat aid worker

"In my organization, "rank and file" staff at HQ level are dominated by young women, whereas senior managers and leadership continue to be dominated by men. This is changing, but still observable. In the HQ setting, being a driven female was positive because my motivation was rewarded with opportunities. In the field, the overwhelming majority of "rank and file" staff (local nationals) are men, as well as heads of local organizations and government, and often fairly traditional. This made being a senior leader challenging at times, as I had to work harder to earn respect from my male counterparts." – 31-35yo non-white female expat aid worker

Thoughts on safety, sexism and the advantages of being a female

Many respondents referred to the fact that being a woman carried – or was perceived to carry – more risk:

"This was a challenging question. While I don't feel I have ever been discriminated against for being female in my job, there are certain implications. In my organization, the majority of staff at HQ are actually female - so I am

at a slight disadvantage were I to try and work at HQ. In the field it is different - there are some perceptions by male coworkers that some deployment areas are 'too dangerous' for women so this can limit your movement."
— 31-35yo white female HQ worker

"It's been difficult in two ways: 1. There is certainly an "old boys network" in my work context. My bosses are more likely to listen to other male workers' opinions, especially on academic or theoretical topics. 2. Being a woman in a Central American context is frustrating on a daily level (catcalls, threats to security) which I think decreases my productivity."
— 26-30yo white female expat aid worker

"I have experienced sexual harassment from "locals" and staff alike too many times to count. I have at times felt like a liability to male staff when confronted with armed groups who use the threat of rape and kidnap of females as pressure to get what they want. I also believe my gender has enabled me to connect with children despite language barriers and open conversations that may not have happened otherwise." — 31-35yo white female HQ worker

"The only issue that my gender has caused is that it was a factor in deciding whether or not to go to work in Afghanistan. That's the only time it has influenced any decision I've made."
— 18-25yo white female expat aid worker

"In a lot of countries being a woman means working ten times harder than men just to be taken seriously (even by your own colleagues). And I have been in situations when me being a woman put me in more physical danger."
— 31-35yo white female expat aid worker

This pithy response provides a great summary of the above:

"Sometimes positive (interviewing female participants) and other times more dangerous."

Which is the most salient demographic variable? In many cultures (most?) age is traditionally a major factor regarding to whom respect and attention is given. The first comment below captures just that, and the second one, from a male, illustrates that even physical stature can have an impact.

"I think as a woman, there are still issues in respecting me in some cases, likely. I think my age (I'm still young compared to most local colleagues) has probably been a bigger factor than my gender though."

– 26-30yo white female local aid worker

"Being a (tall) male has helped to gain respect, especially among beneficiary communities and local partners."
– 31-35yo white male HQ worker

Being able to access female beneficiaries is critical and is an advantage for females.

"Being a woman can sometimes help in communication and negotiation"
– 26-30yo white female expat aid worker

"When I am able to work directly with poor or marginalized women in visual storytelling processes, my gender creates a more open and safe environment for them. As such, I always ask for a female translator, if needed, when working with women." – 41-45yo white female expat aid worker

"It has been relatively easy to speak with authority figures in other countries as a male, however I know how much is lost because I have not been able to speak to some females in some countries."
– 26-30yo white male expat aid worker

Here is the view of the same situation from a few male expat aid workers stressing the access issue:

"Being male, and given the strong pro-male bias in all developing countries, it makes the decision making aspect and coordination aspects of the work easier; however, due to my focus on maternal health, it is a problem in getting full access to women in all cultural contexts and when you do have to do a needs assessment or medical interview, you may not get all the information you need, you need to rely on translations that are often not so good."
– 41-45yo white male expat aid worker

"In most of the world, being male has come with added respect, increased security access, and the ability to bully when necessary. Unfortunately, I don't have access to the female voice." – 31-35yo white male aid worker

This final thought comes from Annalisa, a female aid worker who wonderfully sums up most of the above.

"Regarding Q40, a partial explanation of why so many respondents said that gender was "not a factor at all" might be due to how the question was

formulated (i.e. too generic and/or lacking a "mixed impact" answer). Let me elaborate a bit. It is clear that gender might play a role in several aspects of the life of an aid worker: for instance in their recruitment, in their interactions with their bosses, in their interactions with local colleagues, in establishing relationship with beneficiaries, in the way they spend their free time, and so on. For some of these things, being a woman might be detrimental (e.g. personal security), but for others it can be an advantage (e.g. easier access to female beneficiaries). Some people (like me) may feel that, on average, the impact of their gender is neither negative nor positive, and thus they may have chosen "no impact". But literally speaking, "no impact at all" is very different from "there are both positive aspects and negative ones, but I can't choose which one is stronger as they somehow even each other out". I bet that you would have gotten different percentages had you asked to evaluate how gender has affected a series of separate things (for instance: recruitment, professional relationships within the office, professional relationship with local authorities, life outside of the office)."

Some take-home thoughts

Being a female aid worker is, in sum, not the same as being a male aid worker in many, many ways. The quantitative results from our main question highlighted the fact that one's gender is more of a negative factor for women. The qualitative data produced the insight that though there are negatives and positives of being a female when working with colleagues as well as with beneficiaries and locals, the negatives working with colleagues were much more commonly cited than the negatives when working with beneficiaries or locals. Indeed, what I am reading is that in terms of doing her job, being a female was frequently a distinct disadvantage.

One take-home point from all of the above is that aid and development organizations recruiting and hoping to retain qualified females need to be constantly aware of the impact of gender and ceaselessly work to minimize the negatives in whatever ways they can. They should begin by hearing the voices of the women already in their ranks and using their insights and growth to support those who come behind them, both males and females. A second and critical point is that the gender mix of the team in any aid situation needs scrutiny and work needs to be done to ensure maximum effective use of gender differences. Finally, this comment from a male expat aid worker nails much of the above pretty well.

"I find that most people in this sector are women. They have a monopoly on a lot of jobs around gender and child welfare. So for a man, it is good as we are under-represented in a lot of areas. Having said that, it seems to me that there are too many men at the top end of the sector, and this should perhaps change,

although I think the humanitarian sector must be better than average regarding equality."

With regard to the different demographics variables (gender, age, ethnicity, nationality) and how all of them, not just gender interact is critical. There is a growing literature about "intersectionality" focusing on how an individual's many biological and social identity characteristics interact on multiple levels, and for me this phenomena is even more complicated when imagining how aid worker identity is understood both from a first person perspective and in the eyes of the beneficiaries.

In the words of Annalisa (cited above),

> *"In the context of aid work, all these things get reshuffled, so being a woman might actually be an advantage (or a non-issue) in certain situations, but you may still get problems (or special treatment) due to your skin colour, or your age. At the end of the day, you are ALL these things at once – what changes are the implications attached to each of them, and which ones prevail. This resonates with those respondents who felt sort of genderless, but very much racialised, in the context of aid work. Crucially, intersectionality illuminates why the simple fact of "being a woman" is not sufficient to make any sort of generalisation (you need to differentiate among women of different ethnicities, from different backgrounds, of different age groups, etc.). Local authorities may listen to NGO country directors regardless of their gender, because they can provide or withold critical resources: in this case power is more relevant than gender, but there may be millions of examples where other considerations prevail."*

Perhaps the sociologist Erving Goffman was on to something when he said "This special kind of institutional arrangement [that we find ourself in] does not so much support the self as constitute it."[3] Indeed, in many respects we are as others see us, like it or not.

Special thanks go to Annalisa who contributed to this section.

Act 2 Aid Workers as Parents

How does that work?

A small but significant subset within our survey population – 21% – were aid workers who have one or more children. Being an aid worker can be a complex, demanding and all-consuming occupation. The fact that many aid workers are also parents – a complex, demanding and all-consuming job – brings up many questions. Here are just a few.

- In a sector characterized by international travel and frequent deployments how can an aid worker be a parent?
- How does the parenting role differ between males and females, and what are the problems unique to each and those that are common to both?
- More generally, how do aid workers deal with their part in the family ecosystem of which they are enmeshed either by choice or necessity?
- What are the leave policies of the big box aid organizations and smaller NGO's and how can the maternity/paternity leave policies of these organizations become more progressive?

All big questions, these.

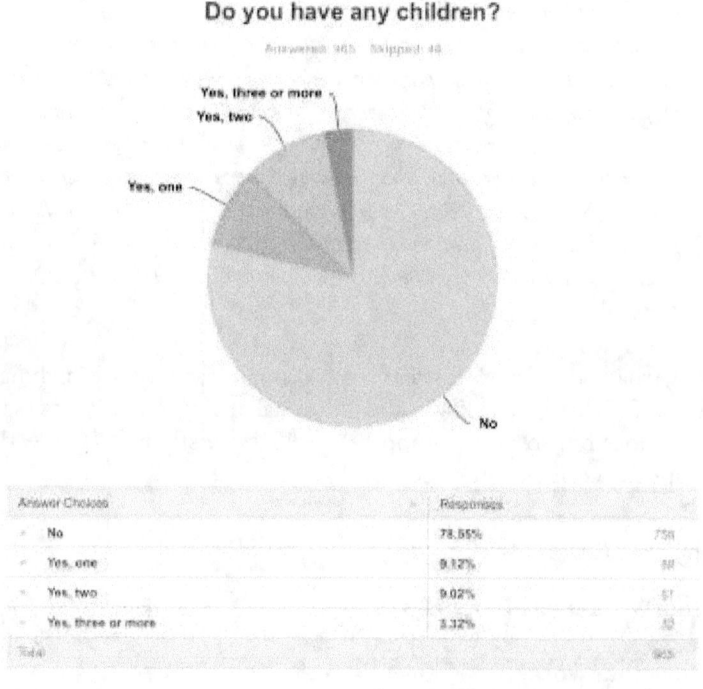

Do you have any children?

Answered: 965   Skipped: 44

Answer Choices	Responses	
No	78.55%	758
Yes, one	9.12%	88
Yes, two	9.02%	87
Yes, three or more	3.32%	32
Total		965

To get deeper insight into how to address these questions (and more) I was fortunate to talk with the founder of a new but rapidly growing group called "AidMamas." Some members meet in person, in Google hangouts, on Facebook and most recently members have begun blogging. Topics of conversation tend to focus on the struggles of juggling the role of parent with that of aid worker. Though most members are women, men are welcomed to the group and help serve to expand the conversation to family life in general.

The founder, Lucy, is a young mother, now more on the edges development work. She has embraced the challenge of bringing together – at least virtually – other men and women like herself and facilitating 'frank and full conversation about being a parent and working in the international aid and development sector.

What follows are anecdotes and observations from our conversations.

Maternity/paternity leave policies

This is not the proper place to call out any specific 'big box' aid or development organization, but I think that a safe generalization to make is maternity and paternity leave policies are overall very weak throughout the sector. One young female aid worker put a harsh point on the situation.

"You have a choice: come back to work after 3-6 weeks of unpaid leave practically still bleeding post childbirth, find someone to watch your poor infant who is still physically attached to you, or lose your job."

The irony of this statement is even more rich when you know that this particular development worker is the primary bread winner in her family – in development terms a female headed household – going back in the field.

Lucy points out that,

"If you examine the parental leave policies of many organisations, paternity leave (if it exists at all) still lags woefully far behind maternity leave (if it exists at all). Maternity leave that is long enough to both enable women to maintain job security and adequately provide that early nutrition source that the sector so strongly supports for beneficiaries without demanding acrobatic feats of logistical planning and awkward office encounters, is rare. Support transitioning back to work is patchy at best across the sector."

In a more perfect world where the best interests of both children and the family were made top priority, the option of both maternity and/or paternity leave would be standard and provisions for at least 6 months of breast feeding not only provided but aggressively encouraged. What is keeping the sector – and the West in general and the US more specifically –

from this model is the steamroller which is capitalism. The pervasive logic is "no work, no pay," simple as that. But perhaps this logic is flawed.

When women make the choice not to come back to work immediately – or in many cases not at all – because of childcare issues, their practical experience and institutional memory is lost; the human capital and expertise that is wasted by losing these women is considerable. Think of it this way: much like setting fire to a warehouse full of blankets or food losing these women is a waste of valuable human resources. The questions about the overall values in the sector and who determines those values is in play here in a very important way. The management of human resources within the sector is critical; this is not "just a women's issue" but rather impacts the efficacy of the entire sector.

Can you be a parent and an aid worker? Yes, but this role juggling feat could be made whole lot easier with more progressive sector-wide policies.

Is cred gendered?

In terms of self-concept, many aid workers endure what might be called the "imposter syndrome." Are those who work in aid more 'legit' than those doing development work? Does working in a conflict zone give you a more respected seat at the table? To the point of this chapter, can an aid worker who is also an active parent – a breastfeeding mom, for example – ever compare with a single male (or female) who can jump to the front of the line for any deployment? Given that, yes, women bear children and in the best case scenario can have the support and freedom to choose to breast feed their children for an extended period the answer is yes, cred is gendered.

Yeah, so what?

Diminishing the contribution of the majority of aid workers who choose to be breeders and family members is not only counterproductive but also a textbook example of sexism. The question is how to address the situation. In Lucy's words, "Ultimately it's a culture change, not just a policy change."

This is not a woman's issue but an issue of family relationships. Most aid workers have mothers, fathers and siblings and all to a certain degree are part of a family "ecosystem" that, when they are away, is compromised and must adapt. Yes, maternity leaves should be standard, but more broadly the fact that all aid workers have family lives must also be taken into account not just within HR policies but more broadly as a cultural issue.

A cultural universal

That this most fundamental form of role conflict has existed for parents for all of modern history all over the world is a basic anthropological fact. Beyond parenting duties, women have always worked – though frequently in a seamless fashion – in and around the home, close to the children. Fetching water and fire wood, tending gardens, running small entrepreneurial enterprises; these examples are played out everywhere in the world. The iteration of role conflict that groups like AidMamas is addressing is where the mother works "outside the home" in a formally paid position.

Can the global culture change to being less paternalistic and more family-friendly? Not in the short run, to be sure. The efforts of the many internet-based groups bringing together like minded and situated individuals is a move in the right direction. Not to put too fine a neo-Marxist point on it but the fostering a class consciousness must proceed revolutionary changes in culture, and so the efforts of groups like AidMamas is a small, though critical, step in the right direction.

One small warning for these groups is to avoid the creation of a self-serving echo chamber of ideas and dialogue. Affirmation and sharing are good but is best tempered by sobriety that comes from always seeking to relate all micro-issues to the broader humanistic goal of maximizing all human potential.

Summing up the above Lucy puts it thusly:

> *"Take a closer look under the 'hood' of the sector and examine in your own organisation, how well do we support those female-headed households – both among those we're working to assist, and among the staff? If we don't know how to support the female-headed households among our staff, how well are we really supporting the female-headed households in local communities? We need to get it right from the inside out."*

Many thanks again to Lucy of AidMamas for sharing her insights.

The fact that our survey was not completed by the many women and men who left the sector because of the issues discussed above is ironic, and I wonder what those voices would have said.

Act 3: You do you

Our survey respondents were overwhelmingly female – 71% – and they had a lot to say on all topics. Below Becca, a 36 year old expat aid worker, currently living in the US but – no new story here – a frequent traveler to Southeast Asia and west Africa. Her career story reflects many themes that appeared in our data:

- She entered the sector very early post-university, not quite knowing what was ahead.
- Though she has seen some of the worst conditions – think Ebola response in Guinea – she maintains a deep commitment to what she does.
- Her deployment record is lengthy, varied, and seemingly never-ending.
- She is challenged by the countless times non-sector people have questioned her job, motives, life choices and even the meaning of her life's work.

Before we get to her thoughts, a personal aside. I too have trouble with communicating what I do and why I do it up to and including putting together this book. When I have nothing to gain – in terms of extrinsic rewards – why devote so much time and effort? How will this help to pay the bills? The push back is sometimes subtle, but it is there, making the time when I can burrow down into this work all the more valuable to me.

But, now on to Becca. Below she shares her story as it relates to personal relationships, both current and prospective. A single, 30+-year-old woman, she is embroiled in an internal clash between her moral, humanistic calling to be of service to others and her very human urge to engage in long-term mate bonding. We know from research on the topic of happiness that both making meaningful impact upon our world and close family relationships are essential factors. Her dilemma is that, though she has good relations with her family or orientation she lacks even the beginning of a family of procreation.

What's a girl to do? Here are Becca's thoughts:

Becca, aid worker

"Are you married?" "Do you have kids?" "Are you in a relationship?" "Have you met anyone?"

These questions can bring any woman over a certain age to their knees, but when you're an aid worker, they often lead to additional questions and comments which can be downright debilitating.

"Well, would you like to be married?" "How do you expect to meet someone if you're always traveling?" "You work such long hours; it must be difficult to meet someone." "Honey – I really want a grandchild – don't you think it's time to settle down?"

And with every "no", the final comment is usually something along the lines of "Well, at least you get to travel such exotic locations – I'd give anything to see what you've seen". The grass-is-always-greener syndrome.

Becca's pooch, Belle.

If "Aid Workers Anonymous" was a thing, I'd start each meeting with – "Hi, my name is Becca, and I'm 36 years old, female, unmarried, and don't have children", in an effort to address the elephant in the room straightaway and not give others the chance to ask the dreaded litany of questions.

Because in the United States, a woman over thirty that is career-oriented, unmarried, and without kids is almost sacrilegious. Our media touts stories either applauding or lamenting the ability for women to "have it all" … but what does that mean when you're an aid worker? Does having it all <u>have</u> to include kids and a husband

77

and the white picket fence and a dog named Spud and giving up the international travel and life experiences you're having in the field?

Of course not – in fact, that stereotype doesn't have to exist for women in any profession, though – as I'm starting to sound like I'm standing on a soapbox – I'll stick with what I know and describe my experience as an aid worker and how it's impacted my relationships – past, present, and future goals.

I literally fell into the aid worker role. I'd been working in Charleston, South Carolina for a year, hating my job working in the very upper-crust, blue-blood preservation world (turns out I'm neither upper-crust nor blue-blood), and responded to an advertisement to get back into the project management world through an organization largely funded by the U.S. Agency for International Development (USAID). I stopped in Chapel Hill, NC for the interview on my way home for Thanksgiving, was awarded the job on the spot, and the rest is history.

That was more than 10 years ago, and I've had a million opportunities since then. I've traveled extensively throughout sub-Saharan Africa supporting a malaria prevention program; I lived in Hanoi, Vietnam for 14 months supporting an HIV prevention program focusing on key at-risk populations (men who have sex with men, drug users, and sex workers; as my mentor would say – "sex and drugs and rock 'n roll"); I've been to Bangkok and Jakarta more times than I can count; and was lucky enough to spend a full month touring the Caribbean on an HIV/Human Resources for Health (HRH) project. I'm currently based in Wilmington, North Carolina, am managing 2 staff, four international projects (2 each in Guinea and Thailand), and am pretty content in my job. Every day isn't rainbows and unicorns and the travel can be wearing, BUT … overall, I'm content.

One specific question I've often been asked and _have_ given some thought to is "What about a job in a different field that doesn't require so much travel? You've learned so much – surely your project management skills are transferable?" And they're right – I'm a Project Manager. Whether or not I'm managing an HIV project in Vietnam or managing an IT project for IBM, it's basically the same series of steps to get from Point A to Point B/deliverable.

Flying into Guinea

But the thing about aid work that they don't tell you ... you can't un-see what you've seen, good or bad. I can't un-see or un-experience the amazing days I spent at the beach on the South China Sea in Vietnam any more than I can un-see or un-experience working in an HIV orphanage in Uganda. And the truth is, I don't want to - all of those experiences have made me who I am, and I think my life is enriched for them. Sure, they're difficult to explain to folks that haven't seen/done things along a similar vein, but ... they're part of my story – and I think it's a story worth telling.

While my career is in a pretty good place, I'd say my relationship life is ... meh. I have great friends and a supportive family, but ... I'm the only one in my group of friends that is unmarried and without kids. I'm currently single (and ready to mingle, fellas!), but tend to work a godawful number of hours in a week, travel frequently, and spend any free time I carve out sleeping, or binge watching Netflix, or traveling domestically to see friends and family, or hanging out with my dog. I've recently realized that I live for my job, as opposed to the other – "normal" – way around.

Most of the time, I'm perfectly content – I recently bought a house, have some disposable income to play with, and get to travel the world. But sometimes – like during a recent anniversary party celebrating two of the best friends a girl could ask for; or after spending 3 weeks with best friends made in Hanoi and my godson – it gets a bit lonely. And then I look at my life and think – "Shit. I'm 36 years old. Yes, I get to travel the world, and yes, I love what I do, but … is this all there is?"

Going into the field is always a treat as a single woman as well. I find that, globally, folks have NO PROBLEM asking how old you are, if you're married, if you'd like to be married, if you have kids, if you'd like to have kids, and commenting generally on anything from your hair color to your weight to your clothes in relation to why you're single and don't yet have kids.

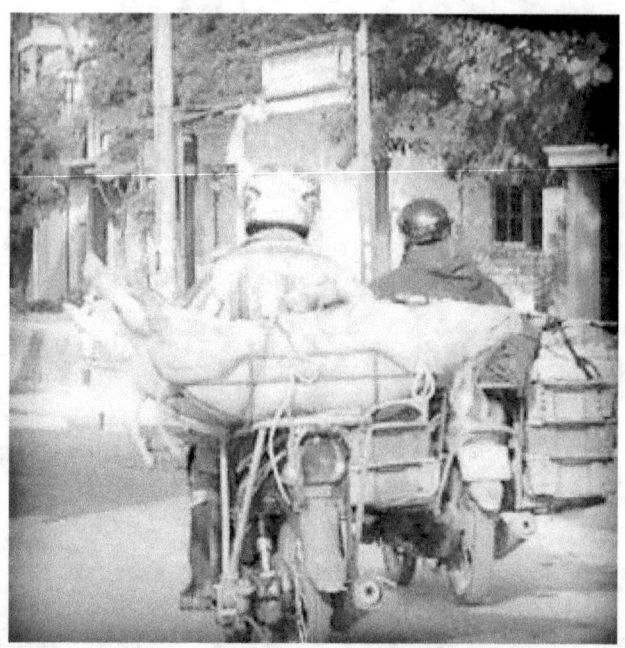

Translation – people can (unknowingly) be rude. And those rude comments can be hell.

I didn't make a conscious choice to "give up" one dream (the husband, babies, white picket fence, and all that) when I became an aid worker. I also FIRMLY believe that that the two don't have to be mutually exclusive … you can ABSOLUTELY be an aid worker, follow your dream, travel the world, and still have a family.

In thinking about other women I work with in the aid world, there's quite a mix out there. There's people like me – single, over thirty, no kids; others that are married, but chose not to have children; and still others that have a nuclear family with the white picket fence, husband, kids – the whole shebang. Often, those women don't travel as often as they used to, and tend to have progressively less responsibility, but there are always outliers – one example is a single mother colleague living with her 3-year-old daughter in Zimbabwe and doing swimmingly! There's SUCH a breadth of experiences among women in aid work … so why do I, personally, feel as though I'm not filling the "right" mold?

I do think that the United States is a bit harsher in terms of timelines and reminders of a woman's biological clock. I never felt old or any pressure to procreate when I was living in Hanoi … women around me – single AND married – were in their 40's and just either having or adopting their first child. My best friend from Hanoi used to constantly tell me, "Becca, you're 34 years old … why in the world do you think it's over for you" when I would lament the fact that I wanted a husband and wanted kids (I can get a bit whiny, truth be told).

When I moved to Hanoi, I was convinced that I was going to meet my Prince Charming – a like-minded, expat individual living in Vietnam, interested in seeing the world and experiencing, in situ, REAL culture. While I did meet amazing people and made friendships that will last a lifetime, the available men pool was … disappointing. Those that were single (and straight) were more interested in experiencing the local flavor of Vietnam than meeting a like-minded, American, 36-year-old aid worker. They were always good for a laugh, but … there's just something about Asian women that I absolutely couldn't compete with!

Along that vein, it felt like my family and friends who thought my Hanoi stint was just a blip … "surely, she'll return to the real world and settle down and start that family she's always talking about".

Coming home from Hanoi was eye opening, and not just related to the husband/ baby pressure … I'd been away 14 months and my entire world had changed. I'd experienced and seen things that my family and friends never would. I'd been put through the ringer by my company and the donor, and lived to tell the tale. I made friendships that I was convinced (and have been proven right) would become some of the most important in my world.

But I was expected to fit right back into the "Becca" mold I'd previously inhabited. I should forget about Hanoi, go right back to work, and FIND A HUSBAND SO I CAN FINALLY HAVE THE BABIES I'VE ALWAYS WANTED.

Oof – just thinking back to that time is exhausting.

Sitting here writing this, I've just come off of a 2-month period where I've been to Guinea for 2 weeks, Bangkok for 3, and spent 2 weeks with friends that traveled from the UK for their first-ever visit to America. I've put a moratorium on work travel for the foreseeable future, and think it's time to start focusing on me and meeting those relationship goals I do have … I would like to meet someone, and I would like to have children one day … and half the battle of even TRYING to meet someone is having the time to do so – to go on dates and decide if you're a match. When you're traveling all the time, it's really hard to make that a priority. So I've drawn a line in the sand with my job, and am ready to turn the focus back to me.

Will it work? Who knows. But ya gotta try, right???

I don't know if I've got any great wisdom to share or true conclusions to be drawn, but I think it's important for aid worker women to know a few things:

- *There is NOTHING wrong with you because you've chosen a life in aid work as opposed to a more "traditional" job (but even as I write that, I think "what does that even mean?").*
- *Being an aid worker does <u>not</u> preclude you from having a husband and babies (if you so desire).*
- *NOT having a husband and babies is TOTALLY cool too!*
- *Being "of a certain age" should not provoke knowing head nods and slight grimaces when you tell people how old you are and that you're single. Those people are assholes.*
- *Aid work is about passion … if you love what you do and are fortunate enough to have the husband and babies too – more power to you. If the other half of the equation hasn't come along just yet … relax … you're still doing amazing work for the world and should feel proud of that!*

In other words…

You do you … and tell any naysayers to go fuck themselves.

The malady of infiniteness

I suspect that many aid workers can relate to Becca's story and will nod that "the struggle is real." This tension between the moral and mating callings within the heart is timeless and certainly not restricted to females, and, as Becca points out, there are no easy solutions. The sociologist Emile Durkheim told us long ago that we are destined to wrestle with the "malady of infiniteness", with social possibilities being many and life paths being limited. One female expat aid worker put it this way.

"I wonder if the fact that we've seen so much compared to the "normal" American working in a different field, meaning that we've seen so many more options and choices, makes us less likely to pick and choose something and stick to one place/person. I've read the idea that the more choices we have, the less likely we are to actually decide. Maybe women that travel more are more likely to bounce around in their relationships and location because we've seen more choices and don't want to make a decision."

Being human means to be constantly battling contradictions and dealing with multiple options; we are a species who can frequently imagine and desire more than our finite lives can provide.

And so it is with most everyone, including SWF aid workers.

NOTES

1. Max Weber, *Economy and Society*, ed. Guenther Roth and Claus Wittich (Berkeley: University of California Press, 1978).
2. Goffman, Erving. *The Presentation of Self in Everyday Life*. (New York: Doubleday, 1959).
3. Goffman, *Asylums*, 154.

8 AID WORK AND THE LGBTQ EXPERIENCE

Filling a gap

Our original survey did not target the opinions of those who identify as LBGTQ+. Toward the goal of making it possible for *Aid Worker Voices* to include this significant subpopulation, I did some additional interviews and, on the suggestion of several people, worked with my colleague J to construct a "mini-poll" exploring the question "How does your LGBTQ+ identity affect your aid industry workplace experience?"

We began the online survey with these words:

> *The aid industry goes to great lengths to persuade itself and others that it is a champion for justice and equality in the world. The UN system, NGOs of all sizes and kinds, and individual humanitarians invest time, energy, sometimes even money to make the point that they are forever on the right sides of all the issues. If there is one apparent element of aid/dev/NGO/UN worker identity, it would be this notion that we are all open-minded and inclusive.*
>
> *Since we're all so open-minded, it would make sense, then, that our organizations are havens of peace and light, that our workplaces are sanctuaries from an intolerant and sometimes downright cruel outside world. Right?*
>
> *There are many issues over which relationships and workplace tolerance can unfortunately break down (including in the aid industry): Nationality, ethnicity, religion...*
>
> *In this mini-poll we'd like to take a look at how sexual preference and gender identity can play out in the context of the aid industry workplace.*

Specifically we'd like to discuss perceptions and experiences from our LGBTQ+ colleagues.

Note: Yes, we do understand that sexual orientation and gender identities and expressions are complex and personal issues that can vary in time. When we asked people what terms and acronyms they felt were most appropriate, we literally got a different response from every single person. For the purposes of this survey, we're going with LGBTQ+ to refer to individuals who identify as lesbian, gay, bisexual, queer or otherwise non-heterosexual, as well as trans.

Note: This survey is not limited to LGBTQ+ people. If you do not identify as LGBTQ+ yourself, we would like you to answer each question as you believe it applies to LGBTQ+ people in the aid industry or in your place of work.

Survey says...

The response to the survey has been good and the vast majority (96%) of those who gave their opinions are industry insiders and/or have an intimate knowledge of the sector, and 86% indicated that they identify as LGBTQ+. So, cred level appears high among those responding, which makes the voices shared worth a close listen.

The mini-poll contained ten questions, all but a few allowing for open-ended comments. As with our original survey (the data from which are reported and commented on in *Aid Worker Voices*), I was overwhelmed by the thoughtfulness with which some people responded.

So here are the results.

In response to the question "In your opinion how accepting of those who identify as LGBT+ is the aid and development industry?" predictably only 2% thought there were no problems which many – 39% – indicating that the industry had serious problems. The fact that (1) the industry is very large and diverse and thus it is difficult to generalize and (2) there is a significant difference between the organization home base and "in the field" was highlighted in some comments. These comments articulate well both points.

"There are obviously vast disparities between different organisations and different offices within the same organisation.

However, as an industry there is very limited recognition of LGBTI staff and/or how their security, health and well-being might be affected by their identity and orientation. So, although many individuals who work in this industry are accepting, the industry as a system is not."

> *"While the AID industry in certain ways can be quite progressive in certain ways, it also continues to perpetate a lot of the same problems that underscore homophobia within our global discourse. It silences LGBTI staff versus raising their profiles or supporting the issues. They fail to understand the complexities of why Gender and sexual diversity issues, just like gender, underscores all development issues beyond just staff."*

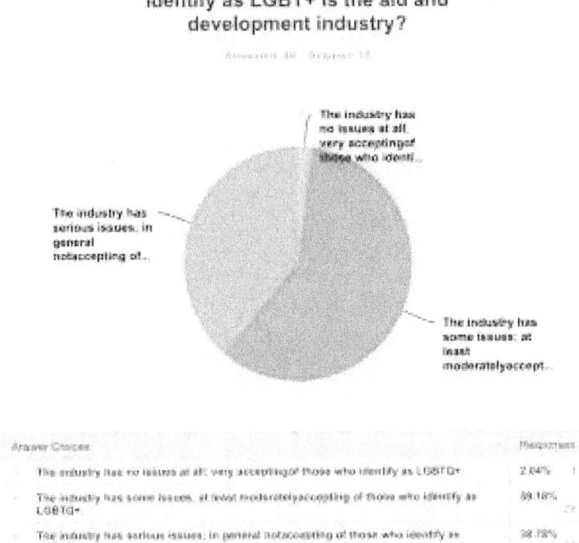

In your opinionhow accepting of those who identify as LGBT+ is the aid and development industry?

Answer Choices		Responses
The industry has no issues at all; very acceptingof those who identify as LGBTQ+		2.04%
The industry has some issues, at least moderatelyaccepting of those who identify as LGBTQ+		59.18%
The industry has serious issues; in general notaccepting of those who identify as LGBTQ+		38.78%
Total		

> *"There is not enough programming for beneficiaries who identify as lgbtq nor is there enough support for national and expat (although a bit more) who identify as lgbtq."*
>
> *"There is a "culture" of general social justice, "the left", and being inclusive but both institutionally and culturally humanitarian aid is much less accepting than it thinks it is. There is minimal support and knowledge of how to support and deal with LGBT issues that can arise in the field and generally LGBT people are just told to keep quiet and not cause trouble for their organization."*

So my read of the above is that though the sector may appear progressive it lacks complete followthrough on the idea that being inclusive means just that, and that if efforts toward this end fail to account for those who identify as LGBTQ+ there is still much work to be done. On this note, here is what one respondent said regarding a lack of action.

> *"Zero appetite for including LGBTQ+ in protection programming – at least explicitly – so little wonder that among staff the issue is largely ignored."*

But can the sector as a whole really pivot in a more progressive direction when there are many faith based organizations for which this type of inclusiveness flies in the face of religious doctrine? Said one respondent,

> *"I work for a Christian aid agency, some colleagues are homophobic and the organisation has an official stance against equal marriage."*

How many degrees of "out" are there?

Are LGBTQ+ aid workers "out"?

Were we to live in a world of binaries, that might be a simple question. We do not.

Here is what the respondents indicated, and as you can see there are many degrees of disclosure. In my field of sociology we make the distinction between "emotional telling" and "instrumental telling", that is, between opening up to those with whom you interact because you care about them and vice versa and in telling others only for practical, necessary purposes (for example telling your dentist that you are HIV+). In aid and development work both kinds of telling happen and this varies considerably from situation to situation. While deployed in some areas of the world the decision to "tell" or not can be critical. Listen to these next voices.

> *"I could possibly be forced out of my job in the Middle East at my (very large and respected NGO) because of my sexuality. They, in general, do not like the issues associated with having out gay men. There have been instances where gay male nationals who were too effeminate have been forced out of the organization."*

"I work for the UN and it has pro-LGBT policies and the environment is tolerant in HQ locations based on my experience. However, I have worked in E. Africa and many staff were highly homophobic – international staff – mainly from all over Africa. In my current field posting, many staff come from conservative countries or religious backgrounds that are homophobic, so despite working for the UN the atmosphere is entirely different from HQ and I have seen the bullying of LGBTQ+ and open homophobic comments."

Our data were clear on this topic with the vast majority – 77% – saying that "I feel more threatened, marginalized, or just offended from host governments, communities, and beneficiaries, etc. than in the workplace." And even when your immediate workmates in the field are open-minded, there are still major safety and career concerns.

"I feel that I have open-minded colleagues in the field. I am openly gay to them but as they don't have many other LGBTQ+ friends or colleagues, I worry that they may inadvertently put me in a difficult or dangerous situation. The management of my workplace have little appreciation of this challenge that I face. I wouldn't be sure that they would stand by me if a homophobia incident caused a breakdown with a partner that threatened a project. They'd probably just move me to another project, and this wouldn't necessarily be good for my career."

"I do not feel it would be safe for my career or wellbeing to be open in the UN compound and environment in which I work. Only the younger, western or westernised, professional level and higher educated colleagues seem to be non-homophobic and open. However, the majority of colleagues are not of this type and homophobic remarks are rampant amongst security, pilots, administrative staff etc. It sounds snobbish but it's true. In my section I don't feel threatened at all despite that some colleagues are a bit homophobic in general, despite being human rights workers. For national staff, homophobia is normal, nobody could ever be out to national staff here or anyone in the host community."

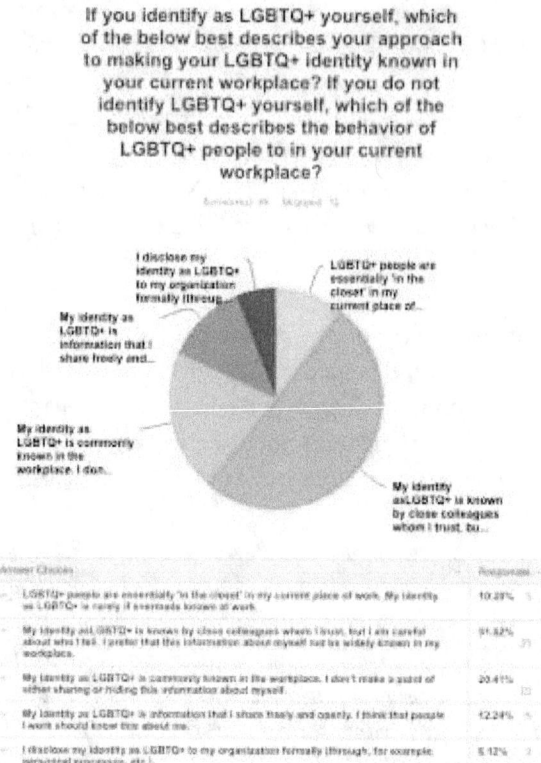

If you identify as LGBTQ+ yourself, which of the below best describes your approach to making your LGBTQ+ identity known in your current workplace? If you do not identify LGBTQ+ yourself, which of the below best describes the behavior of LGBTQ+ people to in your current workplace?

Answer Choices		Responses
LGBTQ+ people are essentially "in the closet" in my current place of work. My identity as LGBTQ+ is rarely if ever made known at work.		10.20% 5
My identity as LGBTQ+ is known by close colleagues whom I trust, but I am careful about who I tell. I prefer that this information about myself not be widely known in my workplace.		51.02% 25
My identity as LGBTQ+ is commonly known in the workplace. I don't make a point of either sharing or hiding this information about myself.		20.41% 10
My identity as LGBTQ+ is information that I share freely and openly. I think that people I work should know this about me.		12.24% 6
I disclose my identity as LGBTQ+ to my organization formally (through, for example, personnel processes, etc.).		6.12% 3

Do managers make deployment decisions based on LGBTQ+ status? here is what one respondent said,

"While difficult to substantiate, I believe that I have not been considered for a series of overseas assignments for which i was highly qualified, due to my status. I was once inadvertently included in an email trail from senior HR managers confirming that I would not get a post because of my status. This was extremely demoralizing to me from a career standpoint."

Moving forward toward policy solutions?

In the final two questions of the survey we asked what could be done to move the needle in a more positive direction to make the work experience for those identifying as LGBTQ+ better. The responses were thoughtful and, in some cases, provocative. This respondent suggests what might be considered an unreasonable pathway forward given the fundamental humanitarian mandate to provide assistance as neutrally as possible. But, then, when and how do we make progress?

> *"Insist with the receiving countries that all staff be accepted without reference to race, gender or sexual orientation. Easier said than done, but someone needs to set an example. I believe that if the state discriminates against its LGBTQ minority, it should be sanctioned by the HRC and denied development/aid assistance."*

Many respondents suggested something along the lines of "change HQ policies to have them explicitly include language – and put teeth to that language – protecting staff identifying as LGBTQ+." One went on to include the point that beneficiaries need also to be considered.

> *"I believe more funding and programmes should be available for this very vulnerable group. In displacement or refugee settings, LGBTQ+ communities are often twice or thrice times the victims or prejudice, assault and socio-economic vulnerability."*

This next respondent who sums up much of the above while making a specific suggestion.

> *"The UN bureaucracy needs to get over its squeamishness about the "third sex". It needs to take a much more principled stance with member states that persecute their gay citizens through punitive laws and state-sanctioned violence. Perhaps it's time for a 'UN-Gay' organization to emerge that will lobby for the rights and interests of 10% of humanity? But good luck getting funding! On a personal level, I genuinely feel that my career prospects have been stymied by my coming out at work and that senior managers in my organization do not feel empowered to support my advancement. I also feel that HR will only 'reward' those who remain closeted and single. Of course, prevailing attitudes in the UN reflect the membership of 193 states, the majority of which are socially conservative. But aren't we allowing the membership to dictate policies that only add to the prevailing climate of prejudice against LGBTQ people? The UN needs to lead by example and adopt truly inclusive policies that really do assist its gay employees."*

I'll end this section with the touching and very personal words from one soul willing to share. Certainly many aid workers sacrifice, but perhaps LGBTQ+ bear an additional layer of psychological pain.

> *"Intimacy is the biggest hurdle. Imagine going for months without any expression of a deep part of your personhood. It is isolating and safe spaces are definitely needed."*

More details from a happily married gay woman

One veteran development worker took the time to address the questions in the survey with a bit more detail.

> *"The degree to which the aid and development industry is accepting of LGBTQ+ people is a tricky question, and the answer has an individual and an institutional level.*
>
> *Let me explain part of the complexity. Although the organisation I am familiar with includes in their staff rules that everybody should embrace diversity, not discriminate, and respect each other's differences. At least officially there is a safe space created for everybody to be who they are, so technically, the industry – or at least my organisation – is quite open and welcoming to every kind of person really.*
>
> *But the reality is that these same organisations have offices in many countries where there is State-sponsored homophobia – so de facto, LGBTQ+ people (or at least myself) are excluding themselves from employment opportunities by fear of being harassed, threatened, or even jailed (this happened to someone in Senegal, because they were gay). If one wants to progress in their career, try something new, get other experiences, it might be difficult to rotate if you identify as LGBTQ+.*
>
> *Last year I contemplated a post in Nairobi. Knowing that Kenya criminalises homosexuality and that social climate might be hostile regarding this issue, I had to ask myself if I wanted to put my wife in such environment, and most importantly our child. So we considered living apart (i.e. in different countries), moving in Nairobi with a gay male couple (to pass as two straight couples), living in a high-security bubble, only interact with like-minded expats – we seriously considered even the craziest options.*
>
> *I have no trouble in serving in countries that have laws that I am against, but will I put my family at risk for sheer career progression? I am not able to take that step. I am lucky enough to be based in a European capital,*

and I get to work in countries where I could never dream of living in with my family.

What I have become to realise is that when I was a more junior professional, I tended to avoid social situations from colleagues, especially colleagues that I could not have 'checked' if they were open or not on social issues. Not so much because I would fear their reaction, but mainly I guess because I would not want to deal with the awkwardness of having to explain. Once, I introduced my wife as 'my wife' to a colleague and right there, in front of us, she literally replied "what do you mean?" That was awkward.

Now, older? Wiser? That I am positioned in a more senior position? In another country? I feel that I do not owe anything to anyone and that I do not have to deal with their reaction, basically.

In my office, everybody knows I am gay: peers, supervisors, interns, etc. It's a relatively small office where we are all very social, so from the start it was a no brainer for me to be transparent about my personal life—and I felt very free about it. At my HQ, also, as soon as discussions become personal, I am absolutely open about being gay. I take it for granted that if someone asks about my intimate life, they are able to deal with any reality that it might entail. If not, too bad for them.

By contrast the reality is that when I work with my clients, outside of my organization, I am absolutely mute on my spousal situation. The great thing in having a child, is that I can redirect any discussion (or just focus on) things about children. That's my joker. And I don't need to lie.

What I try to do is to position myself as an ally to anyone who is not 'conforming'. There was a colleague in one of our small country offices that I thought was gay – others were teasing him about not being married, and I could feel that he was not so comfortable with the teasing so I supported him not to be wishing to marry (quoting my grandma: "don't get married!") and made a case about living one's own life etc. Then a few months later, colleagues were still teasing him about not being married, and then he said he had found someone but that this person 'did not fully meet his family expectations' or that it was something like 'socially impossible'… and I was like "I knew it!"… but what happened next is that he basically declared he was in love with me. And then I was like 'this is sooooooo wrong, if he only knew'!

I don't really feel threatened or marginalized, in the field than when back at HQ but I do feel in the closet with my clients, and totally free with my peers, colleagues, supervisors, etc. In fact, one thing I find very comforting is the fact that my office peers with whom I am open (out of the closet) are very sensible and sensitive to potential threaths to me when we travel together —

when discussions fall into very heteronormative issues or when I am asked about my "husband", colleagues do not hesitate to tag with me in adding more nuance, or even to help me protect my cover. I find this unspoken alliance very sweet!

What could the industry do to change for the better the work experience for those who are LGTBQ+? Perhaps there is a distinction to make between single, couple, family LGBT situations. Single people can deal with their lives themselves, perhaps. For couples, there might be a need for the employers to facilitate or help with employment of the partner… but for families, I really do not know what would be a workable solution. The only concrete thing I could see the industry doing is to lobby on government to abolish discriminatory legislation, so at least people can feel safe, or at least not threatened by law.

Being gay absolutely limits your posting/employment opportunities when you have a family. If I were single, I would probably be ok to take a few years of potentially dry spell, or try something new:)

But when you are not alone, the professional benefits have to be weighted by the living conditions on your family, and that is not easy. I am happy because I get to travel frequently to work with my clients, while being posted in an open city, but I do see the limitations on my career."

Others in the closet?

As a final note I'll mention that as part of this research process I interviewed a number of aid and development workers who live in a parallel closet, namely those who are atheists. In particular, many non-believers who happen to work for faith based organizations feel compelled to play the game of "passing" with their colleagues and superiors, remaining "closeted" atheists, as it were. That there are laws against nonbelievers in some countries and that the lives of "out" atheists are in danger – as is the case in Bangladesh – cannot be ignored, especially given the fact that there are likely more atheists in the aid sector than there are LGBTQ+. A final take home point here is that we need all to work toward a world where there is tolerance for all and that a "you be you" attitude is more globally accepted by individuals, organizations and governments.

I am not holding my breath on that happening anytime soon, though.

9 RACE, IDENTITY AND BRANDING

Some introductory thoughts

Racism and sexism are, sadly, cultural universals. The recent evidence of human warfare going back at least 10,000 years reported by Tia Ghose for livescience.com points to how long we have found reasons to kill in large numbers.[1] Evolutionary psychologists present data-backed arguments that we are ethnocentric by nature and some degree of racism is inevitable. Just as gender differentiation easily can devolve into gender stratification (read: structural sexism), racial/ethnic differentiation perhaps as easily degenerates into racial/ethnic stratification (read: structural racism). Though we cannot change human nature we can change human institutions, and though socially created institutions can and do increasingly mute and redirect this negative part of our nature (e.g., the Universal Declaration of Human Rights[2]), we will have to be forever vigilant in our control of our darker angels. Expanding on that idea is beyond my present task, but those are my views as a sociologist.

Both racism and sexism exist in the sector, but which is worse within the sector? Here's how a small sample responded to that question.

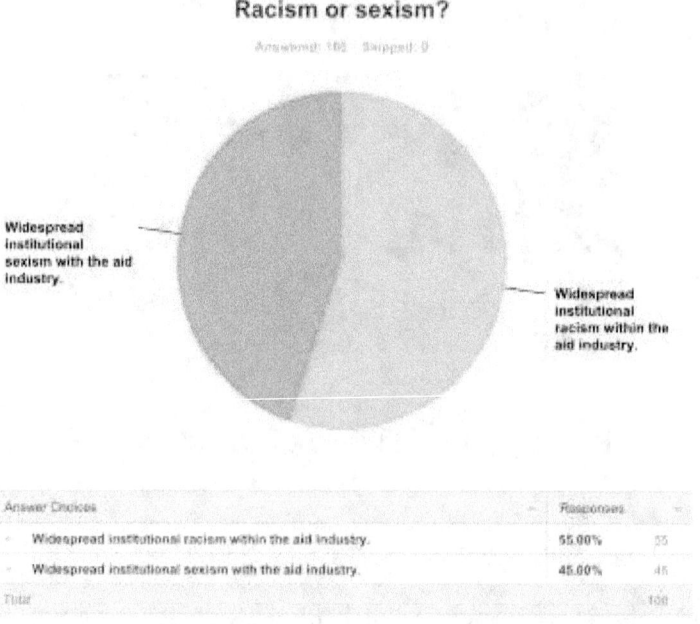

Racism or sexism?

Answered: 100 Skipped: 0

Answer Choices	Responses	
Widespread institutional racism within the aid industry.	55.00%	55
Widespread institutional sexism with the aid industry.	45.00%	45
Total		100

So, by a good 10% margin, those sampled see widespread institutional racism as a bigger problem with the aid industry than institutional sexism. Given that, let's explore some aid worker voices on the issue of race.

In chapter 7 I address the impact of gender in the aid industry. This chapter addresses race, racism and the intersection of race and identity. That racism and sexism exist within the humanitarian aid system is not in question, nor, to point out the obvious, is that fact of one's perceived gender and race impact the construction and maintenance of one's self identity. Though this discussion raises the issue of intersectionality of race/ethnicity and gender, that also is for another chapter.

Our survey responses

Below I go into detail presenting, analyzing and commenting on our data relative to the topic of race. The voices presented below are in most cases on point, insightful and bitingly critical.

As an appropriate place to start, here is one comment written in response to Q7: "*Why does it have to be white as point of reference?*" Indeed.

Why, in discourse related to development work, is white the point of reference? This is an on point, critical question, the answer to which the likes of Jared Diamond and other cultural historians have grappled with in great detail. Ironically, the thinkers of which I am aware are all Westerners because I am from the Global North, speak and read, embarrassingly, only English and hence this is all I know. My point of departure for all thought and analysis is, well, necessarily Western/ethnocentric and, since I have a penis and identify as male, perhaps even phallocentric. And so it goes, my cards – embedded biases – are on the table.

Branding is for all of us

Branding is important. Indeed, organizations spend a great deal of time, effort and money to "get their name out there" and to have their logo be recognized as something desirable or positive. The vast majority of all social entities – be they for-profits, political parties, social clubs or, indeed, non-for-profit humanitarian aid organizations – worry about public relations and will make efforts to "spin" what is known about them using social media, press releases, advertising and a myriad of other techniques.

You and I do this as well constantly albeit not always consciously. Sociologist Erving Goffman's work on impression management remains part of the canon, and his 1959 book *The Presentation of Self in Everyday Life* could be useful reading for aid workers at any stage of their career.

Brand = identity to some extent regarding both units of analysis, the organization and the individual.

One of the key insights that I gained from reading Abu-Sada's (ed.) *In the Eyes of Others* is that though an NGO – in this case MSF – may go to great lengths to brand themselves, people on the receiving end of aid tend to see the aid workers collectively as a monolithic Western entity. Just as organizations can only be partially effective at managing their identity, the same is true for individuals. All of us, though we may try to "brand" ourselves as our own unique person ("I am truly wonderful! – in a complex and nuanced kind of way, of course") find that sometimes we are not seen as who *we* think we are but more so a generic category like "female," "white," "young person," "Western." And, yes, that does describe our modal survey respondent.

Here is what our sample population looked like.

Which below best describes you?

Answered: 962   Skipped: 48

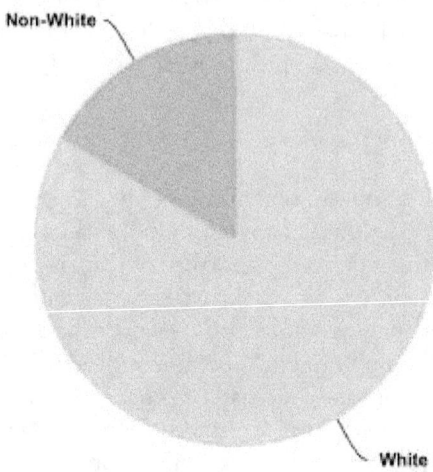

Non-White

White

The race question on our survey

Most surveys ask at least some demographic questions, and the phrasing of these tend to get complicated and for good reason. When writing the "race" question for our survey we wanted to get at the tremendous depth and complexity of this part of one's self concept and in the end decided a more or less direct approach. Q6 asked "Which below best describes you?" giving only "white" and "non-white" as the only possible choices. That was the bait. The follow-up Q7 then asked "Please use the space below to (1) react to the inappropriateness of the choices in the question above and (2) describe how you identify yourself based on common cultural-linguistic, ethnic, racial, tribal, national or other categories."

Most everyone who started the survey, 991 people, answered the "race" question (Q6) and 542 (56%) giving at least some narrative comment in Q7. The bait worked, and in numerous instances the respondents were insightful, articulate, poignant and often hilariously funny. As is the case when nuance is used, some did not appreciate and/or understand our intent.

Of note – but somewhat predictable – is that a higher percentage of "non-white" respondents chose to write a follow-up Q7 response, nearly two thirds, 66%, doing so as compared to just over half, 53% of those identifying as "white." Not only did more "non-whites" respond, their average word count was about 19% higher as well. They had a bit more to say.

Many themes in the written responses

This first example hits well on two main themes generated in the responses to Q7, and is well worth a close read, methinks:

> *"(1) I think the choices in the question reflect the notion that aid workers can be classified in just two categories: white (either North American or European, expats with higher salaries and more leadership positions than locals) and non-white (the locals from whichever developing country the organization is established, working alongside the white leaders, doing most of the grunt work on a lower salary. Much like the Lone Ranger's Tonto, if that's not too rude of an analogy). Is this notion inappropriate/politically incorrect? Perhaps. Is it false? I don't think so. They're simply caused by the resulting power dynamics in a context where whites are generally better prepared to handle the global networking required for the growth and expansion of an organization, and the non-whites/locals, who are better prepared to conduct all the field work without wreaking culture-shock havoc on the beneficiaries.*
>
> *(2) As for myself... I always say I have a nationality crisis. I was born to a Costa Rican mother and an Jordanian father. I have dual Costa Rican/Canadian citizenship, and spent most of my childhood and adolescence between countries in a culture-neutral household (because of the cultural differences between my parents, my home life never mirrored the culture of the outside world, wherever we may have been living at the time), so I grew up as more of a cultural observer rather than replicating any of it. Physically, I'm ambiguous, people can never place where I'm from. I think and express myself more naturally in English, but I write all my "romantic, thought-out masterpieces" (I'm one of those frustrated writer people) in Spanish, I also speak French and I read and write Farsi (although the vocabulary has long been locked up in my brain, having fallen out of use when I was three years old). The only place where I don't feel completely external to the culture around me is in an office full of converging personalities from all over the world where the dominating atmosphere is "tolerance", not some unspoken attitude pattern that everyone seems to know except for me. And this is not because it sounds so "Oh, I'm a citizen of the world, y'know?", but because everyone is just as awkward and culturally-misplaced as I am. But, for practical purposes, I am Costa Rican in Costa Rica, and Canadian everywhere else (less visa issues)."*
> – 18-25yo non-white female HQ worker

The first theme has to do with white being the point of reference. The gap between how things are and how we would like things to be is wide in this context. In the field, at HQ and perhaps especially in our personal lives we want for skin color to be no factor at all, but it is. Can we ever close that gap? We all create or happily find color-blind bubbles in certain contained contexts and for some limited periods of time, but most of the time, especially in the field, this is not the case. To pull a line from the above, *"Is this notion inappropriate/politically incorrect? Perhaps. Is it false? I don't think so."*

The second theme has to do with identity and how people define themselves. That we live in a globalizing world is obvious. There is a small but rapidly growing number of people worldwide for whom national/racial/ethnic identity is very complex. Cosmopolitanism is on the rise, and the 400,000 or so humanitarian aid workers worldwide are a rapidly growing part of this trend. All the more reason to hear their voices and tell their stories.

More themes

We have the pithy:

> *"Outraged at above question, passed on outrage to the office, before seeing this question [Q7]. Identify as White, British."*
> — 18-25yo white female, expat aid worker

Some appeared to dislike the question and judged: *"(1) This is racism and sexualism. (2) World inhabitant."* and others just the opposite: *"I love this question but (predictably) fit into the categories above."*
— 26-30yo white female, HQ worker & 31-35yo white female expat worker, respectively.

Funny/Sarcastic

These examples made me smile, though all for different reasons. The last one hits what was a common point made above, i.e., whether we like it or not, color matters.

> *1. inappropriate response to inappropriate question. 2. I identify myself and others based on a complex correlation of the amount of stamps, number of passports held and whether or not a person uses a mac.*
> — 31-35yo non-white male, expat aid worker.

> *I had to check with my colleagues about what my answer should be. I have a white skin, but the definition of white in survey usually is Caucasian white, which I am not. I am Lebanese first then an Arab.*
> — 26-30yo non-white female, local aid worker

1) I get it, most expats are white, f*ck us for caring 2) Yooper
— 36-40yo white male HQ worker

I'm not sure "white" appropriately captures the whiteness of a white Canadian woman working in development. You should have used "pasty".
— 26-30yo white female HQ worker

HA! I was wondering why that was so horribly stated. Points for humor. I am American, white, English-speaking, blue-collar rust belt SES, yet ultimately over-privileged in the grand scheme.
— 31-35yo white female HQ worker

White but not Anglo-Saxon. No post-colonial guilt trip.
— 31-35yo white male, expat aid worker

1) Sadly reflects the world view in many cases. 2) Why can't we all just have two boxes: human and non-human?
— 26-30yo white female, expat aid worker

I'm really white. White, middle class American. Blonde, even.
— 41-45yo white female, expat aid worker

Not surprised -- when we're "in the field" we are often self-identified as being either white or non-white. It's icky, it feels wrong, and yet, there it is. Skin color tells half your story for you before you've even opened your mouth.
— 31-35yo white female, HQ worker

Some perhaps missed the point

1) only albinos would consider themselves 'white' in my opinion. 2) I am me. I accept me. Just the same as I accept all those not me. Colour is irrelevant.
— 26-30yo white female, expat aid worker

The world thank god is not so black and white.
— 46-50yo white male, HQ worker

Appropriate or not, skin color simply does not provide any meaningful data. Despite its limitations, a regional identity would be more significant here. In my case, my identification as a European suffices for this survey.
— 18-25yo white female, expat aid worker

This description works for me as I am white bread, but if I had to identify as non-white as my only option I would not be very happy! It is like colonizer or colonized. Possibly we could look at a description of pigmentally challenged vs not pigmantly challenged? But seriously I have never understood the value in these types of questions...

— 31-35yo white female, HQ worker

Thought provoking

There were many responses that underlined the main point I am making in this chapter. Here is one that hits that perfectly: *"Those choices were very inappropriate. Yet, I am still white. It is not so much that to me, this is my most distinguishable feature, but living in Africa, it somehow seems to be so to others."* Where you are in the world — your social context — has a big influence on how you are seen. The following examples restate that point in various ways and illustrate the sad fact, again, that skin color matters.

I've noticed that in the African country where I work, everyone who is not ethically African (black) is "white." So I'm not sure how this question plays out with say ethnic Indian Africans?

— 26-30yo white female, expat aid worker

I think that there's absolutely a place for this question, provided that we're given the opportunity to react. Perhaps the question is halfway there, and you should be asking how we identify versus how we're perceived. This probably comes from my time prior to entering the aid sector, when I worked with Indigenous Australian communities, and was familiar with extensive debates regarding whether you were "black enough" — I worked with a number of Indigenous Australians who appeared outwardly 'white' but identified strongly with their Indigenous heritage. So while these people were absolutely Indigenous, they were often treated as 'white outsiders' who had no place making policy decisions or managing community programs. It's a complicated issue, but it's often perceived as (pardon the horrendous pun) black and white. So maybe the question comes from this perspective and is appropriate in that sense. I would be really interested in hearing the discussion that took place around this question some day! As for me, I'm a white Australian of German and Namibian heritage. I was raised speaking English and some German. Aside from the cultural-linguistic/ethnic/etc business, I also identify as a queer woman.

— 26-30yo white female, HQ worker

It sets up a dichotomy and forces one to choose between two categories that don't best describe an individual. There are many more adjectives that I would use to

describe me. It sets up a world view which I have to deal with on a daily basis but would like to see us move beyond.
— 41-45yo white female, HQ worker

It would be best if it didn't matter, but it usually does, and it's most often the distinction above that does matter. you can't list every race, every selection will be inappropriate to someone... I'm European.
— 31-35yo white male, HQ worker

It's pretty blunt. It's certainly imbalanced and biased to see a global minority written down as a majority, and other majority generalised as a "other" group. Many expat aid workers are white, and are defined as such by each other and local populations (whether ethnically white or not), so the options reflect conversations you hear but it's stark to see written down.
— 26-30yo white female, expat aid worker

This last one makes the point so clearly.

In terms of how whiteness tends to inform differential treatment of and reactions to aid workers by both their organisations and the populations they serve, this split may be depressingly appropriate.
— 26-30yo white male, expat aid worker

"White" and "non-white" differences SEP

There was a slightly higher percentage (66%) of "non-white" respondents that chose to respond to Q7 than "white" (53%), indicating that this was a slightly more important question for those that self-identified as "non-white." What I have found in these "non-white" responses are the same patterns as in the "white" responses, mostly that identity is both incredibly nuanced and at the same time quite binary. This one sums it up well:

"I am Filipino-American. Colleagues in the Philippines treat me as a local/ national with a foreign passport. I have similar experience in other countries within South East Asia. In West and East Africa, I am often perceived as Chinese. In the Middle East, my ethnicity is often associated with hired domestic help. I am extremely proud of my ethnic background and cultural heritage but there have been times in the field when I wanted to look like the typical expat aid worker - 6 feet tall, blond and very white. The color of one's skin shouldn't matter especially in this line of work, but who are we kidding?"

– 26-30yo non-white female, HQ worker

Here are the "word clouds" from both. Quite obvious which is which.

Showing 26 most important words and phrases

African Aid Workers Asian
Asian-American Care Categories
Chinese-American Depends Developing Country
English Family Filipino Hispanic Indian Indonesian Means
Mexican Mixed Mountains Not Necessarily Origin
Pakistani Question Racist Sri Lankan White

Showing 28 most important words and phrases

Anglo Anglo-Saxon Categories Caucasian
Consider English Speaking Ethnic
European German Identify Italian
Jewish Latin Middle Class Native English Speaker Non-white
Not Inappropriate Question Relevant Rural Scottish
Skin Color Two Choices WASP White Australian
White British Workers World View

Aid worker voices regarding identity

Many respondents used this open-ended question to riff and reflect on their identity, and I was a bit surprised at the range of identifiers that were used beyond the obvious country/region of birth, etc.

"*Atheist*" was not uncommon as was "*queer*". Many used the opportunity to express a sense of global citizenship ("*Global citizen of Georgian origin.*") and/or anti-or a-nationalism. One respondent simply wrote "*nomad.*" Those who were comfortable as seeing themselves as fitting neatly into a category (e.g., *German* or '*Murican*) were one large group, but a roughly equal number went into some detail about how what they saw themselves as was quite complicated (as seen in many examples above).

Conclusions?

What, if anything, can be concluded from the responses to Q6 and Q7? First, aid workers in general have a sense of humor but more importantly most have an in-depth and critical sense of identity – both who they are and who they are seen as. Most recognize the reality of white bias both within and outside of the aid industry and many struggle with the "race" question on many levels. Those with more stamps in their passports will recognize the fact that "white" or "non-white" matters a great deal in some parts of the world (much of Africa) and less so in others. I will hazard that seasoned aid workers manage their identity as much as they are able in order to maximize their effectiveness (and/or personal safety) in various situations and locations, accenting or downplaying gender, race, Social-Economic Status or SES, or other status markers so as to get by successfully in various contexts. But despite our very best efforts and intentions we are as we are seen by others much of the time. Here is an example that sums up the complexity of identity and ends with a direct statement about how clients view her (emphasis added).

> *"I am European but I left my home country to go to university and have not lived there ever since, so I don't think I can be defined by my nationality. Language, none talks my language so that does not work either. As silly as it sounds I am global, my colleagues speak the same language I do and they understand the issues I talk about. I think my identity is very much linked to my work, or not work rather to a community of people who have to move around a lot too working on similar thematic areas I do. Yes I am white, but it is not an important part in my own identity but it does play into how clients I work with perceive me."*

This response from a female aid worker adds an additional twist to our understanding.

> *"I just choose white as the locals here perceive me as a white woman in a political sense. That's what I have been felt here, and that bothers me a lot."*

What is true on the personal level is also the case for organizations. All of the logo flags, branded t-shirts and other forms messaging cannot fully counter to naturally monolithic impression that many beneficiaries have of the generic 'do-gooder" organizations that they encounter. In chapter 15 I wrote about the views aid workers expressed about

MONGOs, most of them negative. I'll assert that one factor is the fact that the actions of one small MONGO can despoil the image of the entire array of humanitarian aid organizations. One bad apple spoiling the bushel is, well, a universal phenomenon.

What are the take home messages from all of the above for individual aid workers and aid organization staff who are tasked with monitoring the branding? For the aid worker, you should take the message that your struggles with identity are shared by many of your colleagues, certainly, but as well the obvious message that you need to see how you are seen by others both in the field and elsewhere and act accordingly.

Postscript

A question: What does it matter how you see yourself or even how others see you – that is, what is happening in the minds of people – as long as the job gets done? Perhaps the more important question is to what extent does your sense of self and how others see you in the field impact what you do and what gets done?

NOTES

1. Ghose, Tia. "10,000-Year-Old Battered Bones May Be Oldest Evidence of Human Warfare." *LiveScience*, Jan 20, 2016.
2. *The Universal Declaration of Human Rights*, 1948.

10 WHAT DO YOU LIKE – OR NOT LIKE – ABOUT BEING AN AID WORKER?

> *"I don't like that people see what aid workers do as "charity" work. I am not a socialite here for the feel good factor. People don't actually acknowledge that this field is a "real" career."*
> – 31-35yo white female expat aid worker

> *"Sometimes you wonder what the hell you're doing, and why. Sometimes I think that aid is categorically harmful and we should all pack up and go home. Other days I don't feel like this."*
> – 26-30yo white female expat aid worker

> *"Hate the feeling of inequality, being patronising, being seen as the rich white girl, etc. But like the feeling of being somewhere that matters. And meeting people - the basic human interaction with people across the world - love that."*
> – 31-35yo white female

> *"Urban cholera outbreak - I am secretly excited. I know it's wrong but it's what I do and I'm good at it. Aid workers are macabre like that."*
> – 31-35yo white female, expat aid worker

Cathartic moment

In the middle of the survey were two questions included to provide data for us and a cathartic moment for those offering their input. Q30 asked *"In general, how much do you like what you do as a humanitarian aid worker?"* and Q31 invited the respondents to *"Use the space below to elaborate on what do or do not like about being a humanitarian aid worker. An illustrative anecdote will be useful, perhaps."* That over half (433) of those who responded to the closed ended question (816) took the time to follow up with elaboration and example is evidence of a need for the cathartic function of these specific questions and perhaps the survey as a whole.

One female aid worker summed up her feelings this way.

> *"This has been a very interesting and thought-provoking process for me. I realise that I have become more cynical in some ways and at the same time more hopeful. Even with middle-age bearing down on me like a drunken uncle at a wedding, I'm still with Elvis – "what's so funny about peace love and understanding?" and still idealistic enough to believe that it is not only possible to change the world but that the point is never to give up trying."*

Another noted, *"This is a great survey. The questions really dig into the issues and doubts at least I as an expat aid worker face."*

This one sums up the feelings of many caught in the immediacy of the now, I think.

> *"Very interesting survey and I appreciate the chance to share my views – it is surprising how little time (and few opportunities) one has to actually *think* about things in the busyness of the day-to-day. I wish your survey results could be shared in an open forum (not only virtual) where significant players can be present and honestly reflect for a moment."*

The results on these two questions are rich with thoughtful perspectives regarding the aid sector in general but more dramatically with a insights about how aid workers feel about their jobs and their lives doing this kind of work.

First the quantitative data

Reading all 433 narrative responses after seeing the numbers was a bit of a disconnect as you'll see below. The numbers suggest that, on the whole, our respondents like what they do, with 57% indicating "to a great extent" and another 44% at least a moderate extent. If my math is correct, that means an overwhelming majority – 97% – of those responding to our survey like what they do. That said, "liking" and "being snarky/critical/cynical about" are not mutually exclusive.

In general, how much do you like what you
do as a humanitarian aid worker?

Answered: 519   Skipped: 134

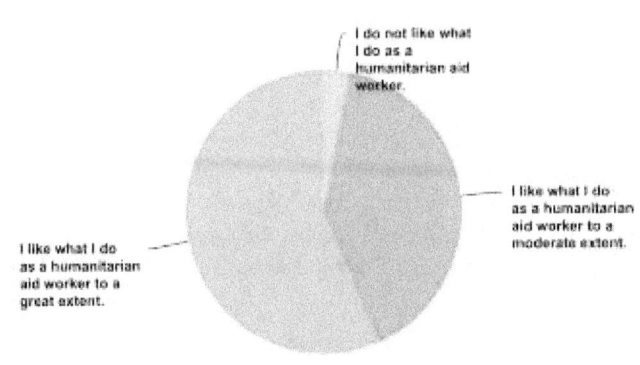

Answer Choices	Responses	
I do not like what I do as a humanitarian aid worker.	3.06%	25
I like what I do as a humanitarian aid worker to a moderate extent.	40.44%	330
I like what I do as a humanitarian aid worker to a great extent.	56.50%	461
Total		816

What do aid workers like about being in the sector?

Given the quantitative data results above, I expected to read volumes of glowing anecdotes about being an aid worker. There were many, indeed, though many of the voices included both positive and negative and sometimes these were the same things, as in this comment.

> *"The change and variety is something I like and don't like at the same time. It keeps things interesting and sometimes exciting but having to adapt frequently gets tiring. I like meeting new and different people. I like seeing new places. I get to talk about things I like. I don't like being away from immediate family and friends."*
>
> – 26-30yo white male expat aid worker

This next one critiqued the word "like" in our question and captures the sentiment of many with her words about how the job makes her feel.

> *"People ask whether I "enjoy" or "like" what I do. I always find that a very hard question to answer. Enjoy? No, not really. It can drive me crazy at times,*

111

but it's what makes me feel most alive. There's a depth of experience not often found in a "normal" job in the UK. The things I don't like would be similar in any role, e.g. dealing with difficult colleagues."
— 26-30yo white female expat aid worker

I love the phrase "niche parts of the human experience" in this next one.

"What I like most about being a HAW is that I find the work I am able to be a part of extremely meaningful and compelling. I have the privilege to bear witness to and affect change to some niche parts of the human experience. I find one of the most difficult parts of the job to be coping with the stress and the feeling of disassociation." — 26-30yo white female expat aid worker

This next respondent makes an interesting distinction between being and doing.

"It's not that I like being an aid worker. I like to do things that utilize the skill sets and strengths I have -- being adaptable, empathetic, culturally sensitive, organized, and analytical. I like to engage issues that I feel passionate about. I like work that reflects my own values. Aid work allows me to do all of that." — 26-30yo non-white female expat aid worker

I found that many did not like what the sector did in terms of their personal life yet felt good about the contributions they were making. Here is a perfect example:

"I like knowing that I make a difference in people's lives and that I've prevented suffering. I like being amongst like-minded people. I like that I don't have to get a mortgage and do the same mind numbing work in an office in the same place every day. I don't like that I can't keep cats as pets and that relationships are always complicated by work and distance."
— 26-30yo white female expat aid worker

These next two highlight the satisfaction that comes from the simple act of connecting with other people.

"At the end of the day, I love analyzing large social problems and trying to identify ways to solve them, in community with other people. I appreciate the human connection that is involved in my job, and the relationships across boundaries that can be developed."
— 26-30yo white female HQ worker

"It is the small moments for me that I like. Getting national staff recognised or promoted in an organisation. Giving a tarpaulin to an old lady who has lost her roof. Taking a football to a group of children and playing with them. That moment when someone comes to you and says 'Thank you for coming. Nobody else has.' Accepting a mango from someone who is so poor they don't even have a shirt, because they insist they get to show their appreciation somehow. Watching a group of young men build a bridge with materials your project provided, and having them laugh at you when you join in and can't even move a full wheelbarrow. Any positive interaction with national staff and beneficiaries. And randomly bumping into a colleague at an airport bar and discussing the most recent locations of common friends and then detailing your latest gastrointestinal mishaps and tropical diseases."

– 41-45yo white female expat aid worker

This one touched me as I read it, and I still am at a loss as to how to respond.

"It depends on the day and/or hour. Example: In the morning I am trekking through the mountains to visit a classroom and train our M&E officers. In the evenings, I am sitting alone in a mud-walled compound eating the same beans I have eaten for the last 3 weeks and silently sobbing myself to sleep."

– 26-30yo white female expat aid worker

As with other sections on the survey, this question brought out a thoughtfulness that is striking. This one represents many that mention liking "making a difference," travel adventures and the challenges they face in their jobs, how their work is misunderstood, "good" aid versus "bad" aid, and finally, the frustration of dealing with donors.

"I like the feeling of making some sort of difference in people's lives. I like that I am constantly exposed to new adventures and new challenges. I like that I've gotten the opportunity to live and travel in all sorts of places most Americans have never heard of. This was a career change for me about 6 years ago, getting away from the corporate world, and I think it was the best thing I could have done for myself. I don't like the fact that everyone assumes I'm an English teacher when they hear I work abroad. I don't like that some organizations seem to be doing more harm than good and even though I don't work for them, I'm still lumped together with their aid workers. I don't like the way some aid is forced to be based on donor interests and not necessarily what's best for the community."

– 31-35yo white female expat aid worker

Many talk about the joy of specific accomplishments and small "victories." Here's a detailed comment that illustrates just that.

> *"I like meeting with the direct recipients of our work (we work on repairing obstetric fistulas, a very specific facet of maternal health). I like getting a better understanding of the environments in which they live and learning a bit about their lives, rather than reading all the worst-case scenarios we're inundated with in the media. These are real people with real smiles, real problems, real senses of humor. I especially like candid conversations with the surgeons we work with and with the "local" aid workers we partner with. Nothing ever goes quite as planned, and it's usually the conversations over a beer or in a quiet, un-planned moment that give you the best information."*
> — 31-35yo white female HQ worker

What don't aid workers like about being in the sector?

Many talked about frustrations dealing with bureaucracies and especially with donors. Here are some representative examples, the three showing an awareness of a fundamental truism regarding bureaucracies, namely that there is an inverse relationship between size and flexibility.

> *"I absolutely DETEST the fact that we are called upon to feed the machine of HQ (media and comms) and that our size has now brought us to the point of creaky inefficiency instead of speedy lifesaving responses."*
> — 26-30yo white female expat aid worker

> *"I do not like the bureaucracy and lack of innovation and creativity that seems to be hard to implement at many of the larger organizations that fund most of aid (e.g. UN agencies, USAID, etc.). I also do not like how, try as we might, the people we aim to help still seem to be lost and forgotten in the conversation. For example, if a community health worker or short-term volunteer is paid $5 a day to help us, is that really improving the person's livelihood, or are we just using them to achieve our project's goals?"*
> — 26-30yo white female local aid worker

> *"Sometimes it [aid work] is incredibly rewarding, but it can also be incredibly frustrating, particularly when one is stymied by bureaucratic inertia/ineptitude that prevents being able to respond effectively."*
> — 46-50yo white female

> *"Frustrating amounts of bureaucracy, poor communication, etc. lead to a decrease in the quality of services provided to targeted populations. This is frustrating."* — 18-25yo white female expat aid worker

These next two are especially critical of and frustrated by donors.

> *"I am frustrated by donors who push an agenda -- a checklist -- with no recognition of the limitations faced by the beneficiaries."*
> — 66-70yo white female expat aid worker

> *"I dislike dealing with funders who try to control projects with extremely narrow parameters and don't understand how the projects often have to adapt to accommodate shifts in contexts; but I especially dislike funders who say crap like 'I want to come see the poor knocked up teenage mothers'. First, keep your damn money, Second: No; they are not animals in a zoo; and Third: Seriously? I am so over this post-2015 malarkey: it is such a waste of resources and energy; especially when every development agenda that has been formulated since the 1970s is *still* unfinished..."*
> — 26-30yo non-white female expat aid worker

> *"My work on the ground with people who need and appreciate any support they can get is very rewarding. At the same time I hate the amount of bureaucracy I have to deal with and the competition between different aid organizations. Sometimes it is also sad, that projects are failing for different reasons.'*
> — 51-55yo white female HQ worker

There are many who refer to a frustration for knowing their efforts could be more effective but that there is in invariably a gap between the "is" and the "ought", the ways things are and the way things could/should be in a perfect world. This woman is one of many who show a keen understanding of the bigger picture but are challenged by the reality that we live in a world dominated by political forces and maddeningly inflexible bureaucracies.

> *"I work with great, intelligent and committed people but development work is bureaucratic and frustratingly political while pretending it is apolitical. It is complex and messy but politicians want it to be quick and 'results-oriented' in unrealistic timelines. It often tinkers with things rather than asking difficult questions about wealth and poverty; have and have nots or asking if we need to fundamentally rethink how we have imagined our world."*
> — 36-40yo white female HQ worker

This veteran male aid worker sums up perfectly what many voiced in different words.

"The gap between the narrative the aid industry tells about itself, and the reality." – 36-40yo non-white male HQ worker

And now for the snark

Below are some representative comments, the first few adding to the reputation of aid workers being, well, snarky.

"No brainer. The politics in it. Shocking. Laughable levels of discrimination. The blindness to privilege, power and responsibility. Do I like my day-to-day work? Hell no! I am in HQ. Far removed from most things remotely interesting and bang in the middle of the BS that characterizes intl. dev. Plus everything I do is beyond my control. I fight battles that I have already lost in a war that is never-ending." – 31-35yo non-white female, HQ worker

The comment above underscored what I have found as a theme throughout all of the data, namely that there is a frustration with control over the outcome of one's efforts and the sense that as an individual the aid worker is "only" part of a bureaucracy within a sector dominated by even larger, intertwined bureaucracies which are in turn impacted by political, economic and historical forces beyond anyone's control. These next two comments are same sentiment, different wordings.

"The mind-numbing, soul-numbing, stifling layers of bureaucracy. The pretense of it all. The hypocrisy and peddling lies. Everyone pretending to care when everyone is really around the table to please their paymaster (direct boss or donor) at the end of the day. The matrices and RBM word smithing. Needing to fill out multiple and contradictory bureaucratic reports to address every donor demand ever made over the years. Being a cog and not really being able to have a personal say. Losing yourself and independence to the collective. Perfunctory tasks and meetings. Turf wars. At least in private sector there is a handsome pay-off, but in our work it's all the more pathetic bc it's not worth it – it's just petty egos. Also the pretense behind the New Snarky Aid Narrative that portrays the white western aid worker as a clown vs. the wise local. That's bullshit too. Locals/nationals are not off the hook in any way - they don't get carte blanche and auto-cred. They come with their own class and racial baggage internally too. No one is innocent here. No one gets a free pass."
– 36-40yo white female HQ worker

The last couple sentences above are particularly on point, methinks.

"Not like: being shout at by hierarchical superiors. being a threat to their incompetence. lacking tools to work. feeling a cog in the machine, or a lemon to

be pressed till exhaustion before being thrown to the rubbish bin. The arrogance that makes the sector think they can save the world, and without professional competence. The lack of privacy, being always 'a child'. Living with colleagues. Abuses that would get someone fired in the private sector here can get land them a better position. I like: discovering new realities, learning about humans and their ways of living, coping, leaning from others."
— 36-40yo white female expat aid worker

"I do not like telling people what to do with their lives, even if only by implication. Moreover, I don't like the sanctimony and hypocrisy inherent in an industry that's ostensibly about 'service to the poor' (and other such self-congratulatory rhetoric) but in fact serves primarily to support comfortable lifestyles for people from rich countries who want to feel like they're doing something more meaningful than their investment banker classmates."
— 36-40yo white male HQ worker

And final words from the dark side?

"I like the cultural context, specifically related to nutrition and feeding practices. But sometimes everything just seems like a well intentioned clusterfuck." — 31-35yo white female expat aid worker

"It's a job, at the end of the day. I'm in it for me - we all are. I just hope others benefit from my selfishness, to a higher extent than if I was in another job."
— 26-30yo white female expat aid worker

"Aid work still has a dark side - winning over donors and competing over space. Every new disaster is like the moon-gotta get that flag up 1st. Can't we just get along while getting work done?!?"
— 26-30yo white female expat aid worker

Conclusions? Of the 433 written responses to this question several stuck out in terms of the breadth, depth and thoughtfulness. This first one, I think, does the best at summarizing the complexities regarding how aid workers feel about their jobs and lives. Her "likes" are rich and complex.

"I like the complexity and power of the issues I face in my work. I know its potential to have a real impact on people's lives and I strive to see that realised in my work. I also find it stimulating in various ways that resonate for me - issues at the heart of humanity, aspects of spirituality (although I'm not religious), intellectually stimulating, understanding different cultures, religions, histories, etc. I have met some truly remarkable people. All of this has indelibly changed who I am."

– 36-40yo white female expat aid worker

Her "dislikes" strike deeply, and I was touched and saddened as I read...

> *"I don't like the politics of the work - dealing with people who care more about their careers and reputations than doing good work. I wouldn't call it frustration with bureaucracy, it's frustration with pettiness, apathy and cowardice. At the worse end of the scale, I have met and worked with some of the worst people I've ever known. They have been corrupt, spying for government, sexually exploiting staff and community members. But typically it's just working with people who refuse to take risks to improve responses because they are more concerned with their own career goals. As most of my work requires coordination and consensus-building, these people can make it impossible to do good quality work. And they're not a small minority, unfortunately."* – 36-40yo white female expat aid worker

This next one tips more toward the "dislike" in making some good points reflecting the general frustrations of many.

> *"I like to interact with local staff, and try to position myself as a friendly channel for feedback and information to senior management. I enjoy helping them find training opportunities and teaching them whatever I can. I enjoy designing projects and talking to local partners about their ideas. I enjoy interacting with my colleagues and finding our way around challenges. I do not like cluster coordination meetings, UN workshops, UN turf wars over things like CERF allocations, leadership who are fixated on competition with other agencies and who are jealously protective of information rather than being collaborative and open. I do not like the bullshitting and manipulation of facts that is involved in the reporting process. I really hate the 're-coding' of massive amounts of funding as projects come to an end; and equally the rapid, massive purchases that can occur in order to spend an underspent budget. I don't like the constrained timelines for longer-term development projects (social change in 18 months? really?), the fact that donors refuse to provide funds for training of staff, or the patronising attitude of iNGOs and UN towards local NGOs."*
> – 26-30yo white female expat aid worker

One main point made above is that social change -and that is what development work is in essence- cannot be rushed. I would hazard that most in the development world would say "amen" to her point.

Finally, this last one is a sideways comment on aid work, critiquing the fundamental nature of the sector and arguing what most of us know already, that, in the end, change comes from within the community.

"I don't consider myself a humanitarian aid worker (so the question above is a bit awkward). I really didn't like what I did in a traditional humanitarian organization - it was so disconnected from any sort of reality I could grasp, even though I was "in the field" every day. So I quit and began to work with a much smaller group, doing development work at a much smaller scale in [section of city], *where I was living at the time and had a connection to. This was so much more grounding and rewarding because when things went well, I actually felt it in my everyday life, and when things went wrong, I also felt it. Being connected to your work in that way is so much healthier than the "humanitarian" work I was doing before, because these places only existed during the working day and we were really not connected to the consequences. But when I worked in and with communities that I had developed relationships with, I understood how long change takes and how much it has to be owned and driven by people like my neighbors, and it helped me lose the sense of needing to be in control that so many humanitarians have (hence why many of them get stressed and smoke lots of cigarettes). Now, my work is less "sexy" and "exciting" than it was in the "humanitarian days", but it's so much more real."*– 18-25yo white female expat aid worker

Last thoughts

What I see *in toto* as I read all of these responses is, above all else, the words of those who care deeply about what they do and about those with which they work. They enjoy living their convictions and thus endure the frustrations inherent in their jobs.

One aid worker, Karen, a twenty-something aid worker currently in Iraq, offered these achingly timely, on point – and humorous – words summarizing much of the above.

"There are issues facing workers in this job that are so serious and so important that it needs the whole industry to stand up and shout about it. Clinics being bombed in Afghanistan and Yemen, the rapes and killings in Terrain in South Sudan that recently came to light, and the longer running attacks there, kidnappings and attacks in Syria, the death of Jackie Sutton in an airport and the underlying issues that exposed; I could go on, and on, and on. It is reassuring to see so many thinking about, highlighting, and working on addressing these issues, even if progress is too slow and the process seems painful.

At other times, however, it is the little things that get to me. The sleepless nights not saving lives, but writing reports, the grubbiness, the endless meetings seemingly only for the sake of meetings, and the underlying worry, that I'm not good enough, that I'm not

strong enough to support my team, my staff, to help the people I'm here for, that I don't understand the UN, the context, the problem well enough. The small things are the ones I don't talk about, because I feel it reflects badly on me. However, earlier this year I learnt that most people have these same fears and concerns to a greater or lesser extent, and that a vital coping mechanism in this industry seems to be moaning (*insert griping, whining, whinging depending on where you are from). And more importantly humour, frequently black and sometimes strained, and occasionally the laughter is very close to tears, but it helps.

I was on a tough deployment, not in terms of place (I had hot running water and access to both chocolate and a climbing wall), but I was having a bad few months. It was all the usual suspects, too many all-nighters pulling together proposals, too many HR gaps, and concern for my team burning out, precarious funding, missed R&R, and that awful decision of who of the many in need you will help. All of my least favourite things.

So with that in mind I came up with the below. By humming it to myself as I sat up late with yet another proposal, and swapping lines with friends in distant places I was able to moan and laugh and let off a little steam, and then get back to the work that I am fiercely proud of.

My least favourite things

(To the tune of "My Favourite Things" from The Sound of Music)

Writing reports and proposals for ECHO;
Drivers who lie and say they know where to go;
Poor internet signal so skype never rings,
These are a few of my least favourite things.

Staff late to meetings, and cluster conventions;
Stupid ideas hailed as latest inventions;
Poor coordination and all that that brings,
These are a few of my least favourite things.

When its leave time,
When there's cheese and wine,
When I'm feeling glad,
I always remember my least favourite things,
And then I just feel so bad.

Political problems and ignoring refugees,
Aid about donors and not beneficiaries,
Authorities playing games of kingdoms and kings,
These are a few of my least favourite things

Huge master budgets that are missing expenses,
Work overload that leaves you feeling pensive,
Cold bucket showers with water that stings,
These are a few of my least favourite things.

When AC works,
When TV works,
When I'm feeling glad,
I always remember my least favourite things,
And then I just feel so sad.

Kisses not handshakes used by strangers as greeting,
Especially occurring at long drawn out meetings;
Packing for missions, who knows what to bring,
These are a few of my least favourite things.

When the sun shines,
Not too hot mind,
When I'm feeling glad,
I always remember my least favourite things,
And then I just feel so fucking pissed off..."

11 HOW DO YOU EXPLAIN YOUR JOB TO NON-SECTOR PEOPLE?

"I definitely understand why dating within the aid worker population is appealing. Conversations with laymen are hard. I think I only try once in a while, usually when I'm unusually overwhelmed or frustrated and it kind of comes pouring out. But it's exhausting, because you realize how many words you need to use just to catch the person up on why something is as vexing as it is. It's such an intricate environment."
— 31-35yo white female HQ worker

"Entirely depends on the person, and their previous knowledge level and the degree of real interest."
— 61-65yo white female expat worker

"As long as I return alive, that's all she cares about. Fine by me. It's better she does not know."
— 51-55yo white male HQ worker

Sharing

With whom do you share details about your life as an aid worker? Under what circumstances? At what level of detail? How do you simultaneously honor the intense privacy -yours and others- of your field experiences and at the same time your deep need to share fully with intimates "back home"? What do you tell and what do you hold back? How do you deal with the inevitable need to put into separate compartments the roles that you play at work and at home?

The topic of this chapter is, in the end perhaps, efforts at mental hygiene as aid workers grapple with living out complex professional roles while at the same time attempting to have 'normal' social and family lives.

Below I focus on the questions 33-38 on our survey which asked respondents about the challenge of explaining the nature of their job to those around them, namely friends, lovers, family and children in their lives. The 1048 total narrative responses were fascinating to wade through. While many were short and minimally responsive, there were countless comments that shed useful and nuanced light onto our research questions about how aid worker's explain their jobs.

Explaining your job

Aid workers have a job frequently misunderstood by the general public; stereotypes abound, some positive, others not so much. How many times have you heard, "Thank you for all you do!" "Wow, you get to travel to exotic places!" or "Oh, you are one of those arrogant bastards trying to export Western lifestyle in all parts of the globe."?
But is this situation unique to aid workers? Likely not. Here is what a couple respondents pointed out:

> *"It's impossible to really understand without having the context. There are things my friends try explain to me about their lives that I have equally no context for - and is equally difficult. So I see the same issue on both sides."*
> – 36-40yo white female expat aid worker

> *"I would never expect people to be as well-educated on all the various aspects of aid work -- including all the criticism, rather than the "do-gooder" stereotype, which makes me uncomfortable. Just like they would never expect me to understand the ins and outs of their professions. It's just that their professions may not be as controversial or receive so much media attention. Specifically, I work on a very awkward area of maternal health -- women with obstetric fistula leak urine and sometimes feces from their vagina. It's not dinner conversation (which is part of the reason it's so marginalized even within global health circles -- people don't want to talk about it because it's embarrassing). So I usually say only very generally what I do and try to be very gracious when people talk about "all the good work being done in Africa" or whatever. I'll only go more in-depth if I can gauge a genuine interest that they want to hear more of the real stuff."* – 31-35yo white female HQ worker

This next aid worker gives an example that I can personally relate to as a university professor whose own spouse continues to ask "What are you doing when you are not teaching a class?"

> *"It could also be interesting to compare these answers to those from people doing*

other kinds of jobs. I guess complex work is always difficult to explain. I guess many people *think* they know, for instance, what a professor does, but many would be surprised to learn how little time is actually spent teaching or doing research as opposed to other tasks such as writing grant proposals, acting as editor or reviewer for some journal, organising conferences, responding to emails, etc. What makes aid work different is that many of the existing stereotypes and preconceptions have a negative connotation (white saviour, proselytism, exporting Western democracy / capitalism...). This means that aid workers who want to explain their jobs need to dismantle prejudice, whereas the professor from my previous example can honourably get away with "yes I do teach undergraduate classes among other things". Also, 'aid worker' is terribly generic and lumps together the war surgeon (something not too difficult to explain, albeit extremely difficult to do) with the fundraising or the monitoring and evaluation officer (less easy to explain)."

Fair enough. The cultural and social worlds we inhabit often are very different one from another and we all often make the mistake of assuming a sharing of understanding where that is not the case. Getting into the details of any occupation can be a rabbit hole of nuance and complexity, but perhaps aid workers have it a bit more difficult because of the added layer of shifting contexts. Indeed, aid workers are occupationally different from most jobs in that they frequently must transition from one cultural content to another.

One female expat aid worker went even a little further noting that,

"Beyond just culture, I get a LOT of questions re: why we're giving the money away and not spending it at home … we should be more isolationist, yadda yadda … perhaps unsurprisingly (not surprising to me anyway), this feeling comes almost exclusively from my Republican friends. No judgment, BUT … difficulty explaining your job goes well beyond cultural context."

But why would you want to explain your job? The answer is simple: we are a social species and our mental health and happiness are in large part dependent upon having family and friends with which we can express and share emotions. The natural urge to share one's life with intimates is stressed by the aid worker's job. The voice below is describing a situation where, I suspect, unwanted barriers are being created.

"None of my family or friends back home have ever done aid work before and many rarely travel overseas. Thus most of them don't seem to be able to

*understand why I work overseas in one of the most violent and stressful
contexts. This lack of understanding often creates a gap which makes it hard
for them to contextualize the work and lifestyle in country. Sometimes this
means they avoid asking too many questions."*

— 31-35yo white male expat aid worker

Parents, siblings, in-laws

Q33 asked, "Which statement below best describes your ability to explain
to non-aid worker non-significant other adult family members the nature of
your job?" Rising above the awkward wording in the question were 426
respondents offering some comment regarding difficulty explaining their
job to parents, siblings, in-laws and others close to them. I'll preface this
section by pointing out that there was a subtle but, I feel, telling difference
in how men and women responded. The results below indicate that women
tend to have a much more trouble than men explaining their job. The
differences highlighted in blue are statistically significant.

	I have no difficulty explaining virtually everything about my job.	I have some difficulty explaining my job, but it can be done.	I have some difficulty explaining my job, and can only articulate a general sense of what I do.	I don't even try to explain my job.	Total
Q4: Female (A)	11.73% 65 B	39.17% 217	38.45% 213 B	10.83% 60	69.51% 555
Q4: Male (B)	20.33% 49 A	39.42% 95	31.12% 75 A	9.13% 22	30.31% 241
Total Respondents	114	312	288	82	796

That the quantitative male and female responses differed is evident,
but having pored through the narrative responses – first female then male
the – "why" lingers unanswered in my mind; no clear thematic differences
are evident in the narrative responses.

Difficulty of explaining depends on the audience and on what job
you have

In looking for themes in the narrative responses it was clear that
the level of difficulty and frustration with communicating about the job was
directly correlated with (1) the nature of the aid/development work being
done and (2) the level of education and/or cross-cultural literacy of the
people the aid worker was trying to communicate with. These first two
illustrate clearly that explaining the job is clearly not "one size fits all."

"It's too complicated to get through the layers of assumptions, stereotypes and cliches; most of my family seem to think i'm on a vastly extended gap year, in a comic relief sort of way. They don't know the kind of money and resources i oversee or the complexities of the work. I think too if i described to them what i actually work with, they wouldn't be able to hear it as it is hard to think about directly. For some of them, the response is 'well, you chose it' if i mention any difficulties. For others, there's almost a resentment connected to 'oh you're so worthy' which i don't completely understand. A couple of my close family know what i actually do to a greater degree and are proud of me. Mostly i think people start with an assumption that they know what it is and it's too hard and too boring to get into why it's not that. In addition, my technical area of violence against women is not something people generally want to think about or talk about too much – and there are also a lot of assumptions about this too." – 41-45yo white female HQ worker

"This depends on the person. In general, I try to gloss over the bad stuff and just focus on the good stuff. Or if I talk about the bad stuff I complain about the food or not having any personal space and I leave out the dead babies unless someone asks a direct question." – 31-35yo white female HQ worker

If the family/friends back home have similar experiences or are otherwise cross-culture savvy, explaining the job can be easier.

"The difficult is more on the technical side as I come from a family that includes development workers, although not humanitarian aid workers, so the motivation is not difficult to explain nor is the sacrifice on family time, personal safety, material comforts." – 41-45yo white male expat aid worker

"My family has tried a lot to understand what I do. My parents even took a SPHERE training course and get often ask me if I am keeping up with standards when I am on the field. They also understand the Faith component of my motivation to work. But it's the relationships and the tension, the raw side of the responses that people don't understand. They don't have the frame of references to understand the extreme pain, poverty and insecurity seen on the field. But they try and I love my family and friends for that."
– 26-30yo white male

If your job is in medicine or communications explaining is pretty straightforward.

"Since I work in field communications, it's not as difficult to explain that I help in the process of obtaining stories of the people who benefit from our programmatic work. If I need to explain the development models in more depth,

that could be harder depending on who I'm speaking to and their level of interest and comprehension, but I've done it long enough now that it's quite second nature." – 31-35yo non-white female, HQ worker

Persistent misconceptions and oversimplifications

There were many responses voicing a frustration that despite best efforts otherwise misconceptions and oversimplifications, most framing the work as simplistic and/or charity, persisted. Others marginalized the work by reframing the mission of the sector, as in this first example.

> *"My adult family members question the difference between development work and the invasion of Afghanistan, feeling both are western imperialism - one just happens to be at gun point."* – 26-30 non-white female HQ worker

The next few are typical in describing the entrenched stereotypes of aid workers.

> *"For years, I basically said, 'no, I do not hand out bowls of soup.'"*
> – 41-45yo white female, HQ worker

> *"I have difficulty explaining that I am not a white savior protecting the orphans of Africa from dreaded disease and war."*
> – 26-30yo white female, HQ worker

> *"I am a funding policy adviser. My role is to advise donors and advocate for best funding practise on behalf of a membership organisation of international NGOs. My mother thinks I rattle tins at supermarkets to get coins to give to starving Ethiopians."* – 31-35yo non-white female HQ worker

> *"'So you dig well for Africans, right?'... 'No, darling brother, I am a fundraiser. I work at a desk and deal with bureaucrats all day'... 'Cool. So how many wells did you dig this year?'... and repeat."*
> – 26-30yo white female, HQ worker

> *"I'm not a nun. I don't distribute soap."*
> – 26-30yo white female, expat aid worker

These next few voices, I am sure, speak for many. I love the "bridge-building" imagery in the third one.

> *"I'm tired of the whole, "oh you're in charity work?" the platitudes about helping the needy, and the inevitable insta-generalizations about people from the*

place I'd most recently traveled to." – 36-40yo non-white female HQ worker

"It is all but impossible to explain that aid isn't always good and that the UN can't solve shit. We're not heroes and most of us are career bureaucrats just like any other work. But people hear "Africa" and know I must have saved thousands of starving babies, even if I don't work for a nutritional program."
— 31-35yo white female expat aid worker

"It's a long bridge to build from where I work to "every day" life in the US. It takes time, which sometimes people don't have, but people seem genuinely interested and listen. That's all I can ask. Sometimes I get bizarre and bigoted questions, but as you know Americans are generally clueless about the world."
— 36-40yo white female expat aid worker

Many specific jobs just don't translate well, so some aid workers resorted to comparing the job to something with which the family member might have some referent.

"First of all it is very difficult explaining the difference between charity and aid/development and especially when it comes to long term community development. Non-aid workers do not really grasp all the theories that go behind why or how we do things. Second of all, my work is strategy and M&E and so am not really a front-line staff so that makes it even more difficult. I sometimes try to compare it to "auditing" but even that is not even close to what I do."
— 31-35yo non-white female, expat aid worker

The accumulated frustration of trying to explain the job generates various responses. The first example provides with a nice visual.

"They don't really get it, so I keep it simple. They think I am in Africa working with kids. Its a lot more complex than that, but taking time to explain details would be enough to make me want to jam a fork in my eye."
— 31-35yo white female expat aid worker

Are you a spy?

There were many interesting themes but one that I thought was both amusing and telling is that more than a few mentioned that their family or friends suspected that they might be doing something other than aid or development work, namely that they were secretly CIA. These suspicions are legacies of the Cold War, but they also point out the questioning cloud that can hang over this line of work.

> *"Lots of people in my family though I worked for the CIA! All they knew was that I travelled a lot to weird places. It got easier to explain once I started working for an organization that was more focused, and only one major, relatively specific purpose in mind, rather than some of the large development orgs that do just about anything and everything."*
> — 31-35yo white female, HQ worker

> *"My job these days is fairly straightforward. My previous job (involving democracy development) was nearly impossible to describe and my family all thought I was a spy. Humanitarian aid work is far more straightforward."*
> — 36-40yo white female expat aid worker

> *"They often think that I am, in fact, a spy."*
> — 46-50yo white male HQ worker

Selective telling: choosing not to share exactly what you do

In some cases aid workers choose not to share job related details. In sociology we call this 'selective telling,' and the most common reason found within our responses for this less-than-complete descriptions was, essentially, that some details are too stark, intimate and private, only to be shared with those who have seen the same. Here are some examples.

> *"The humanitarian aid worker experience is very hard to describe to others. Field work operates at such a constantly high level of intensity that even normal seeming activities become something else, which is nearly impossible to explain. The challenges and tragedies aren't even worth explaining, because they are based in a completely unrelatable framework."*
> — 18-25yo white female expat aid worker

> *"I am generally able to articulate what I do in practical terms but perhaps not to explain the emotional impact on myself - particularly in terms of what I see, the environments within which I operate and how they change me as a person."*
> — 31-35yo non-white female expat worker

Selective telling is a common defense mechanism for avoiding controversy or conflict.

> *"There's a catch-22 in aidland - if you tell the outside any of what we fear/doubt on the inside, the field gets undermined... who wants to give their aid dollars to someone who's not entirely sure what it does, or whether it's aid itself*

(and the relief it provides from pressure for systemic change) that is a fundamental part of the problem?"
— 41-45yo white female HQ worker

And, finally, showing the social grace to preserve civility and maximize useful understanding is another reason for selective telling as voiced so well by this next female aid worker.

"Other than that, I just wanted to add that I am one of those people who refrain from sharing too many details of her work: just too complicated to explain, and most of the times I'd rather avoid ruining a nice evening out by starting a debate on, say, the root causes of corruption or the role of country X in the Syrian conflict. What usually works is if I find ways to relate my experience to what the other person does: e.g. I explain that I write grants to people who are familiar, say, with research grants (even though grant-writing is usually just a small part of my duties), or I talk about procurement and subcontracting to someone who deals with these issues in their company, etc."

The Lord

And, for comic relief – or not – we had a response from Aid Worker Jesus. I personally have a bit of doubt about this "free will" thing. See here.

"My father created the heavens and the earth. Not a sparrow falls that he does not see. He gifted all mankind with the gift of free will. Nonetheless it is still impossible to explain participatory appraisal methods without devolving into debates about PFIM and the like in the time between now and judgment day."
— 71+yo non-white male

Before leaving this section I'll share a response that got my attention. In response to this obviously angry person I'll gently say yes, I do care to understand.

"They don't understand and probably don't care to. AND, btw, neither do you, for asking such a fatuous, facile, fucking stupid question."
— 66-70yo white female expat aid worker

Significant others

Q35 looked at sharing with life partners and lovers asking, "Which statement below best describes your ability to explain to non-aid worker significant other the nature of your job?" Though many reported having the luxury of their partner also being an aid worker or in a similar job, many offered comments illustrating a range of understanding and acceptance. Of note is the fact that many used this comment space to point out that they were without a significant other. This respondent, methinks, speaks for many:

> *"Um, what if I don't have a "significant other." You bastards. Didn't think of that did you? When I was dating aid workers (which happens) I didn't have any trouble explaining 'what I did' but the relationships were so dysfunctional that explaining our jobs in tidy sentences was the least of our problems. I dream of dating somebody who knows nothing about what I do..."* – 41-45yo white male HQ worker

On the dating front, I saw this comment frequently in various wordings,

> *"Since becoming an aid worker I have only dated aid workers, diplomats, military, or related. They all get it. I can't really imagine having a significant other who has not been in such a sector."* – 36-40yo white female expat aid worker

	I have no difficulty explaining virtually everything about my job.	I have some difficulty explaining my job, but it can be done.	I have some difficulty explaining my job, and can only articulate a general sense of what I do.	I don't even try to explain my job.	My significant other is an aid worker.	Total
Q4: Female	21.37% 109	33.53% 171	19.02% 97	7.25% 37	19.02% 97	68.32% 511
Q4: Male	23.95% 57	32.77% 78	14.71% 35	7.98% 19	20.59% 49	31.82% 238
Total Respondents	166	249	132	56	146	748

This respondent represents the views of many aid workers:

> *"Part of being an aid worker is not really understanding what 'significant other' means - or only dating in the sector - both of which being equally confusing. in the sector, it's hard to detach from work - and it's a relationship (vacationship or locationship) built around coordinating R&Rs and understanding each other's acronyms. outside the sector it depends on how much of an interest he takes in my work - hopefully a good amount, but not always the case. more often than not it remains a mystery."* – 36-40yo non-white female expat aid worker

These next quotes illustrate a common "holding back" theme.

"My on again off again boyfriend thinks I do this job for the ego boost (I try to explain that I spend a fair amount of time hating myself and trying to un-see what I've seen). He wants me to quit..." – 26-30yo white female expat aid worker

"My partner worries about my exposure to danger, so I censor most of what I do." – 31-35yo male expat aid worker

And finally for comic (?) relief, here is another response given by AidWorkerJesus, "I'm not allowed to comment about my significant other, despite the allegations in certain racier pages of the non-canonical gospels."

Children

Q37 drilled into the task of explaining the job to children asking, "Which statement below best describes your ability to explain to non-adult family members the nature of your job?" There were many who felt that it was impossible and/or inappropriate but also many who felt that children could sometimes understand more easily than adults in part because they were free of preconceptions.

	I have no difficulty explaining virtually everything about my job.	I have some difficulty explaining my job, but it can be done.	I have some difficulty explaining my job, and can only articulate a general sense of what I do.	I don't even try to explain my job.	Total
Q4: Female	10.52% 57	28.78% 156	28.23% 153	32.66% 177	69.70% 543
Q4: Male	16.03% 28	31.22% 74	22.78% 54	29.96% 71	30.42% 237
Total Respondents	95	230	207	248	779

The five quotes below illustrate a common thread I have noticed throughout the narrative data. Aid workers are very sensitive to the fact that what they do is frequently misunderstood and reframed improperly in ethnocentric/Westerncentric terms.

"Nieces/Nephews understand that I travel a lot to help people. I focus more on natural disasters (earthquakes, cyclones etc.) to avoid explaining complex conflict (i.e. CAR) and to discourage sub-Saharan African bias." – 31-35yo white female HQ worker

"Out of fear of instilling a "help the people with charity" mentality in my

younger relatives, I just try to emphasize that people help themselves more than I help anyone." – 26-30yo white female HQ worker

"Way too complicated. "Helping poor people in Africa" is about all my teenage nephews could compute, and I refuse to talk about my job in that way." – 41-45yo white female expat aid worker

"Not sure they're interested. I also don't care to glamourise this work in case they feel it's something that can get into through voluntourism." – 31-35yo white female expat aid worker

"It's easiest when I describe to people that we help governments in developing countries to support their Ministries in e.g. Health and Education perform better, collect data, deliver services, etc. Family can relate to Government Ministries doing real and important and complicated work. That way, it's not about pencils and goats and they can understand this isn't little charity projects - it's professional work and yes third world countries have functioning States like you do." – 36-40yo white female HQ worker

This next statement captures the same sentiment and expands on the ongoing challenge of aid workers to frame the social reality of their world in the most accurate and unbiased manner possible. Part of the task involves understanding and then working to change the 'mental models' of others.

"There are different mental models that we all have regarding interpretations of aid work and I find it difficult to relate to others' mental models or bring people into my mental models. This prevents meaningful discussions or prevents moving past surface level conversations. This is exasperated by increased levels of idealism amongst youth that I find difficult to relate to." – 26-30yo white female expat aid worker

Other comments illustrate that some kids can understand more than some might think though some may not be ready for deeper appreciation.

"It's easier to explain to kids that things are complicated because they haven't yet formed opinions. They can manage complexity better than many adults." – 31-35yo white female expat aid worker

"I think that when my niece, and inshallah my own kids, are older (10?12?) I will start to have some of those conversations. For the moment, at age 5, it's all about Disney princesses. Maybe we should write to Disney and get them to

make a film about aid work!" – 31-35yo white female expat aid worker

"The easiest is to whip out my phone and say, 'yeah look at the photo of that elephant, I took that. Now check this photo of a starving kid, I took that too, now eat your veggies.'" – 31-35yo non-white male expat aid worker

The last respondent I'll highlight raises a very critical question about who can handle the full truth. Most parents struggle with the issue of how long to preserve the age of innocence, and no parents are in a tougher situation than those like the woman below.

"I work a lot on gender violence issues and have a real difficulty addressing this with my children, especially with my daughter. I don't want her to be aware of how dire the discrimination of women can be. I don't want it to affect her identity." – 26-30yo white female expat aid worker

Concluding thoughts

One takeaway from this section of the survey is that being an aid worker is complicated, both the actual job but perhaps even more so sharing of the details of the job. Sharing the life and death intensity, the stark, raw reality of some of what is experienced can feel wrong at times, and putting some memories into words can seem incomplete. No description regardless of the verbal skills of the aid worker can do full justice to the complex nuances of sights, sounds, smells, and emotional highs and lows. In the words of one respondent, "You would have to experience the fear and hopelessness first hand to get the whole picture." Another respondent noted,

"That is one of the main problems we have. After being away for years your mentality, values and personality changes. You disconnect from your old habitual community and then it is difficult to communicate as we ended up on two different planets: usually I am not interested what they tell me because the topics they touch are not interesting to me and other way round." – 36-40yo white male expat aid worker

Transforming an experience with innumerable dimensions into words – necessarily a linear description- means destroying -and hence disrespecting – some of the content. There are some details which cannot and perhaps should not be shared with outsiders. You had to be there or, at least, have been somewhere similar, and that means with those who you've lived within the team house or other aid workers, in the same "compartment."

As a final thought, as I reflected on all of the narrative responses above I was brought back to a statement by James Dawes in his book *That the World May Know*. He writes, "This contradiction between our impulse to heed trauma's cry for representation and our instinct to *protect* it from representation – from invasive staring, simplification, dissection – is a split in the heart of human rights advocacy." (emphasis in original)

Postscript

Here are some questions that went through my mind as looked at the many hundreds of narrative responses to our three open-ended questions asking about how people explain their job to those outside of the sector:

- When the situation calls for it, how do aid workers explain their job to friends, lovers, family and children in their lives?
- Is the need to explain based mainly on affective/emotional needs or are there purely instrumental reasons for disclosing?
- To what degree do the preconceptions people have about the aid work sector impact the ability to explain their job?
- To what degree is the aid work job too complicated to explain effectively?
- To what degree does the nature of aid work impact the tendency for aid workers to compartmentalize their lives?

12 YOU'RE FIRED! NOT A PHRASE HEARD OFTEN IN THE SECTOR

"We do need to become more effective and efficient at what we do.... and get better at firing well-meaning people who are not competent at their work...."
— 36-40yo non-white female expat aid worker

"Ha ha. I work for the UN. Nobody gets fired."
— not-to-be-identified respondent

"I have worked with too many colleagues — senior managers included — who were not qualified for the jobs they were hired to do. I wish the development and aid industry would take on a more private sector approach when staff clearly are not performing in their jobs - despite coaching, training, investment etc. It makes me angry that public funds from taxpayers or donors are wasted."
— 36-40yo white female local aid worker

"Fired? Really? Does this happen? I wish more would be fired, the incompetence in this sector is one of the reasons I will probably lose confidence in the system."
— 36-40yo white female HQ worker

"My position does allow me a line of sight to the HR processes in some of the terminations at my org. All of those reasons explain why people I know of were fired: those that were promoted too high too fast and aren't competent in their current roles are often 'downsized,' those who chronically bump heads with their superiors are often 'downsized' (whether personality clashes or differences of philosophy), and I've seen an (otherwise) good employee drive drunk once using the company vehicle (and then lie about it!) 'resign' in the middle of the investigation. In my org, at least, many more employees are 'downsized' or

during a 'restructure' their job description changes, and they're asked to reapply and don't get it. Not too many are outright fired (due to legal liability that would open us up to). Others simply don't have their contracts renewed when they expire."

– not-to-be-identified respondent

Where we're headed

Below I both present more data -mostly qualitative- and also offer some analysis, comment and opinion regarding getting fired – or not – in the aid worker world. First, validating the title of this chapter, here's what our respondents noted in Q44. That tiny slice of the pie chart below represents the .52% – less than one percent – getting fired.

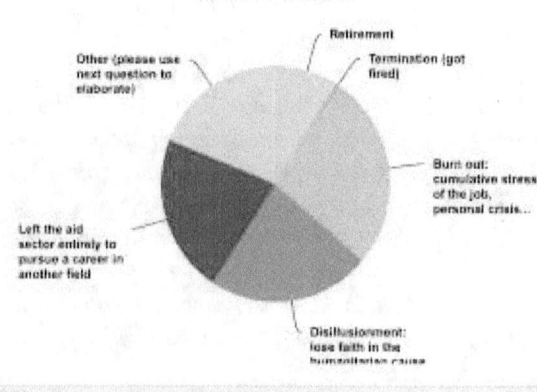

Many (most?) humanitarian aid workers will ultimately become ex-humanitarian aid workers. Excluding those few -but tragic- that will die in service, which below do you think is the *most* common reason why humanitarian aid workers choose to leave this line of work?

Answer Choices	Responses
Retirement	8.93%
Termination (got fired)	0.52%
Burn out: cumulative stress of the job, personal crisis related to on-the-job experiences, etc.. become too much to continue	25.78%
Disillusionment: lose faith in the humanitarian cause or mission overall, lose confidence in your organization or the overall humanitarian system	22.30%
Left the aid sector entirely to pursue a career in another field	21.39%
Other (please use next question to elaborate)	18.89%
Total	

Some thoughts on the "big picture"

Gross generalization: this sector's work-force profile is the way it is because of the nature of the work and the unique – and recent – exponential growth in both the size the number of aid entities in the last 20 years.

For present purposes we can go with the most basic taxonomy: the for-profit and not-for-profit organizational entities. In general, in the for-profit sector there is very little patience for incompetence and, given chronically high under- and unemployment factors, – that is, it is a buyer's market – it is understood that lack of performance will get you fired. The bottom line is the bottom line. An important related factor is that measuring output/performance is, at base, very simple in the for-profit world; again, the bottom line is the bottom line.

In direct relation to the difficulty of quantifying performance – measuring with some fidelity the value-add of someone's activities on the job – the nature of the firing process gets more complicated.

In the non-profit world the deliverables tend to be inherently more nuanced, difficult to quantify and frequently are, and are intended to be, long term results. Yes, some tasks are easier than others onto which to attach metrics, but there are so many tasks the outcome of which is (1) long term/beyond the contract period of the worker, (2) interconnected with myriad other factors that make it difficult to discern clear linear cause-and-effect impact, and (3) are part of a team effort that make individual contribution hard to parse out.

The not-for-profit world includes many organizations such as those in the humanitarian aid world but also, for example, higher education. As an academic I am keenly aware of the promotion and tenure process and know well the battles that are fought over what "counts" toward same. Indeed, in my world, unfortunately, not being able to make that which is real measurable, we tend to make that which is measurable real. Translation: publish or perish because you can't measure service and "good teaching."

The nature of the humanitarian aid world

There will always be those who feel they belong in the humanitarian aid world in whatever role because they feel compelled to "help." I stand by my assertion that this is a basic human need; we are wired to feel empathy (mirror neurons, anyone?). As one respondent put it, *"There will always be disasters, there will always be poverty and there will always be some people who feel impelled to try and make a difference."*

Given the questions we asked there is no way to tell if our respondents associated with at any specific aid organization – with the major exception knowing that 6.5% of our respondents work "somewhere in the UN System" – but my guess is that very few if any were with MSF.

The MSF reputation in the aid world was clearly elevated – and affirmed? – in 1999 when they received the Nobel Peace Prize, and my sense is that though they coordinate with other organizations on important matters (e.g., cluster meetings) there is a clear demarcation between "us" and other aid organizations. On a smaller scale, in Haiti Partners in Health might be seen in a similar light.

The reason I am pointing this out is that I believe that what these two organizations have established is what the rest of the industry appears to lack, namely higher than typical entry and renewal standards for all associates. These two, MSF and PIH, are outliers in that both are medical and health-focused niche agencies. They've focused on specific sectors (medicine, community health) that are quite technical and for which the standards of qualification are well-established and globally regulated, and so firing someone for incompetence (malpractice in the medical world) would be relatively straightforward for both. That said, management of HR is not without its challenges, as they have significant turnover rates as well. Take a look at the article "The impact of humanitarian context conditions and individual characteristics on aid worker retention" by Valeska P. Korff et al. for specific research comment on this topic.[1]

There is a non-existent – or at the very best, weak – culture of firing in the sector within many organizations. As evidenced by our respondents comments, that this should change is without question. But how do you create and sustain a "culture of firing?" Perhaps you start at the source of the problem. Organizations are systems, and systems can only function as well as their weakest component. As one aid industry insider put it, "fear of adverse public opinion drives ass-covering HR policy and process."

Reasons why people do not get fired

A reading of all the narrative responses yields the following observations. People do not get fired because (1) a warm body that can function minimally is better than an empty desk; something is better than nothing (*"Lots of people think their very presence is valuable, because poor people need all the help they can get or something."*, (2) metrics for performance are unclear and hard to measure, (3) it is much easier to just let a contract run out and not renew, i.e., passive firing (said one respondent, *"Honestly, it can be hard to be fired. Many people simply don't have their contracts renewed."*), and (4) the firing process can be time consuming and, ultimately, more trouble than it is worth for the supervisor. Another reason suggested by a long-time industry insider is the extreme risk-averse nature of NGOs, especially established household charities is the underlying cause: they're very afraid of litigation, especially litigation that gets dragged out into the public, paints them in a poor light, and costs them donors. The necessity of kowtowing to the needs and expectations of donors is indeed a common frustration among aid workers.

Some data

Q48 asked "Some humanitarian aid workers leave because they are fired. Which below do you think is the most common reason humanitarian aid workers are fired?" Here are the data:

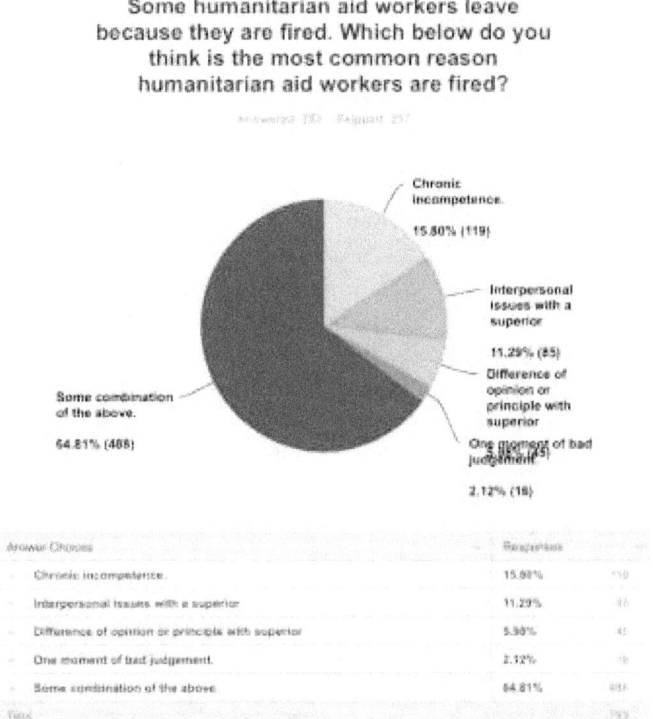

Some humanitarian aid workers leave because they are fired. Which below do you think is the most common reason humanitarian aid workers are fired?

Answer Choices	Responses	
Chronic incompetence.	15.80%	119
Interpersonal issues with a superior	11.29%	85
Difference of opinion or principle with superior	5.98%	45
One moment of bad judgement.	2.12%	16
Some combination of the above	64.81%	488
Total		753

Reasons for firing someone are rarely simple. That 65% of the respondents answered "Some combination of the above" seems logical and telling. Though our survey respondents guessed that less than 1% of people leave the sector because they are fired, I find it interesting that 366 respondents took their time to offer narrative thoughts on Q49 "Please use the space below to elaborate on the question above concerning what you think is the most common reason humanitarian aid workers are fired? Most, though, did use that space to vent about why people *were not* fired.

Aid worker voices on (the lack of) firing in the aid sector

A robust number of respondents – 372 – chose to complete the open-ended question Q49: "Please use the space below to elaborate on the question above concerning what you think is the most common reason humanitarian aid workers are fired?" Here are some of their responses, most illustrating the reasons I listed above.

This first one hits on a dominant theme in the responses, namely that the structure of the sector can make personnel issues complicated and easy to ignore and/or deal with ineffectively.

> *"I don't think nearly enough aid workers get fired for chronic incompetence. If it was up to me there'd be more of it. The problem with people on 3, 6, 12 month contracts is people are too busy / not good enough at management to performance appraise, and tend to just let people's contracts lapse, or let them move on – no one reference checks properly, or does informal checks, and it means genuinely dreadful aid workers get employed again and again. This does real damage to the NGO sector. The UN is probably worse by the experience I have had of those agencies – so well paid, and benefits so good that complacent, disenfranchised people stay in jobs otherwise their kids would have to come out of boarding school/ they'd have to give up that holiday house and the enormous DSRs. It's dispiriting. I'm sorry if that doesn't quite answer your question, but I have not really seen many people fired. The only one was a bad judgement on security brought on by incompetence and inexperience. Sometimes also people are promoted way too quickly and lack any depth of knowledge on a context which can lead to some very naive decision making."*
> – 31-35yo white female expat aid worker

The several responses below point to a major theme, namely that there is (a perception of) a great deal of incompetence in the sector, and it is tolerated or at least not dealt with head on.

> *"Incompetence generally doesn't get people fired on its own (not unless it results in some really major fuck up), but incompetence coupled with interpersonal issues with a superior is definitely going to put someone at real risk of losing their job. Interpersonal issues really come to prominence in shared housing."*
> – 26-30yo white female expat aid worker

> *"Unfortunately, incompetence is more rarely the cause of losing your job as a humanitarian worker, than politics around principles, opinions or personality differences within the team (not necessarily a superior)."* – 26-30yo white female expat aid worker

"Chronic incompetence is the least likely reason...." – 36-40yo white male HQ aid worker

"I think it's incredibly difficult to fire people in this field and most who are fired are for issues to do with supervisors. Not incompetence. That's usually encouraged or promoted (seriously..)." – 31-35yo non-white female expat aid worker

"Honestly, not enough aid workers are fired. I have seen seriously incompetent workers go from one agency to another because apparently nobody EVER gives a bad reference - even if a guy is a barely functioning alcoholic that regularly uses prostitutes and goes around in the NGO t-shirt!" – 26-30yo white female expat aid worker

"Man, if people got fired from humanitarian aid jobs because of chronic incompetence, the industry would be a better place. I think most people get fired out of a combination of interpersonal issues with superiors or funders, combined with a sense that they're not quite what the organization needs." – 36-40yo white male in regional office

"It really has to be chronic, chronic incompetence as the sector seems to recycle poorly performing workers all the time." – 26-30yo non-white female expat aid worker

"Incompetence plagues this sector. Many people get jobs through personal connections with little or no relevant experience. Training is generally poor and opportunities to learn come from other people with academic and developing world experience only. We need more people transitioning from senior private sector roles ideally to up-skill the development labour force." – 31-35yo white female expat aid worker

These next two highlight the perception that even when the situation calls for it, firing just does not happen.

"Unfortunately, it is not for reasons for which firing should occur (eg. sexual misconduct, abuse of minors, fraud) but for failing to successfully navigate relationships with a boss. I have never been fired, by the way, but seen many occasions where it unjustly occurred, or unjustly did not occur." – 41-45yo white female expat aid worker

"I would guess that the most common reasons would be interpersonal issues and a difference of opinion. Aid workers have strong personalities and strong opinions...and sometimes superiors have plenty of pride. A moment of bad

judgement could also lead to being fired." – 26-30yo white female expat aid worker

This next one points to an issue about lateral moves after being fired. Why this happens is a critical question.

"The question is whether the fired get re-hired in the industry. Which - the only thing I did not anticipate or expect -happens so frigging commonly in intl. agencies." – 31-35yo non-white female HQ worker

This next sentiment is critical as well, and points to the all-too-frequent "field promotion" phenomena.

"Mostly underqualified people given too much responsibility." This extended comment is from a (female) industry insider and affirms the point I make above about the "weakest link within any system/organization" problem.

"I often argue that Human Resources is one of the weakest departments in most aid organisations. Most, if not all, of my consultancy assignment came from personal relationships. I think I am fairly good at doing my job, but was I really the best candidate for those positions? There is no way to know. This is true for most – if not all – of my colleagues, and I am yet to meet anyone who got the job after applying to an open vacancy.

The problem is that it is not just excellent people who keep being offered dozens of assignments. Some of these people who are hired again and again are so blatantly incompetent, they should stop working in the aid sector, period. Others are just not the right person for the job. Posting people with limited English knowledge to English-speaking countries? Check. Asking an anger-prone, no-bullshit type of person to suddenly master the art of diplomacy? Check. These people might have been great in another context, but they are out of place now. Bear in mind I am talking mostly of people on short-term contracts: the issue is not really about firing them, but about not offering them new assignments after a dismal performance. And even in cases of staff on permanent contracts, it should not be too difficult to imagine a way to prevent them from being given roles for which they lack basic skills.

One of the problems, in my view, is that HR departments often deal only with the bureaucratic aspects of hiring staff. They send you the contract, they make sure you fill in and sign all the right forms and attach a recent medical certificate, and that's about it. Hiring decisions are actually made by managers who do not necessarily have the skills, mindset and training to spot the best candidates. Another issue is why aren't performance evaluations taken into consideration? I guess that either hiring managers don't bother reading them, or supervisors fail to disclose their staff members' failures."

This male aid worker affirms the above and underlines some additional points related to staffing in a fluid and demanding sector.

> *"I've seen the reason for termination given as incompetence, but that was never the reason in reality. And incompetent people in all positions tend to get passed around unless they're really bad (can only thing of one that eventually got permanently sideline, but it took lots and lots of drama creation from their side, so maybe it was more the interpersonal issues). The reality is, in most specific situations this industry needs warm bodies and a pulse is worth more than an appropriate technical background. Plus there are a lot of really, really maladjusted folks kicking around this industry. Normally shocking incompetence usual goes under the radar or can be excuse by ever-present extenuating circumstances. Sometimes doing a performance evaluation or reference check would just take too much time out people's busy schedules. It's very common for people to get no reference check at all, or a reference check is used as a reason to exclude someone. Considering the kind of environments people are expected to work together in, I'm surprised that even pure self-interest doesn't lead to more due diligence."*

On another note, there are, at the end of the day, many reasons why an aid worker might engage in aberrant behavior that may or may not lead to being fired. That this line of work can be emotionally and physically brutal at times is a fact. As one aid worker pointed out,

> *"It [aid work] is a field where there is little work-life balance and the cumulative stress over the years leads to many of the things listed above. International aid folks are known to be pretty eccentric, traumatized, unbalanced, and needing for mental health support. All these things make it more likely that they will make bad choices which lead to being fired."*

The data indicate that people do, rarely, get fired because of gross inappropriate behavior, to be sure, but it appears that personality clashes, especially with superiors, is a more common reason.

I was a bit surprised how strong the "incompetence does not get you fired" thread was throughout the 372 responses, but there you go. Having said that, as I look at other sectors both for-profit and not-for-profit one can find similar dynamics at play. Despite Donald Trump's popularization of the phrase, "You're fired!" in many sectors it is just not that common. In the US at least, people are forced out, leave as they see the writing on the wall, get transferred, downsized, "made redundant" in all manner of creative ways, etc. – all the reasons permutations mentioned above in our aid worker data – in lieu of getting the proverbial "pink slip."

Is the aid sector really all that different? Certainly we do not have the data for any conclusion along that line but I offer the conjecture that any exceptionality is a matter of degree, not of kind.

Human Resource officers take note

Aid workers are frustrated by many aspects of their employment, especially when it comes to dealing with the consequent actions of incompetent coworkers. This is certainly evidenced in the data from Q's 48 and 49 and, of course, cannot come as a huge surprise to anyone in the sector. For me the take home from a HR perspective from the above includes at least considering these action points:

- Let proven competence relevant to positions drive hiring decisions.
- Have more extensive exit interviewing of all employees (make it a condition of final pay if necessary) and use those data effectively to make hiring and care-and-feeding policy decisions.
- Do not promote beyond credentialed expertise; sometimes nothing is better than an incompetent something.
- Consider more extensive psychological/personality testing of potential hires.
- Make more public and obvious rubrics/expectations for performance. There must be open and transparent terms of reference and standards of performance. And, critically, all in the chain of command must be held accountable for them.
- Use every new hire, lateral move or promotion as an opportunity to move your organization in a positive direction, especially regarding weeding out the marginal and those who fail to grasp and hold true to the core missions of not just your organization but to those the aid sector in general.
- Network with your HR counterparts across the sector to work toward more standardization of hiring criteria.
- Make knowledge transfer a major priority by demanding overlapping deployments.
- Start in the interview process by messaging a more demonstrative "culture of firing" (as mentioned above) and reinforce this rhetoric with action.
- And, finally, this last one from an industry insider who prefaced this suggestion with "...JD/TORs/SOWs are usually very badly written; HR risk-averse, cover-your-ass procedure makes it very difficult and process-intensive to outright fire someone."

- Grow a pair: lose the hyper risk-aversion. If someone underperforms or is incompetent, document it, fire them, and move on.

A warning of a coming demographic change SEP

The work force in the US and in much of the rest of the Western world is aging, and this demographic shift will have an impact on the aid sector in the not too distant future. This can be seen as good news. Organizational cultures with low staff turnover are slow to change, but those with rapid turnover can use this dynamic to bring about desired cultural change. In short, this can be seen as a moment of crisis for the aid sector. We have all heard the cliche that the Chinese character for crisis is the combination of danger and opportunity, and perhaps now is a time for the entire sector to devote some time looking into the future and planning for how to be more robust, effective and, at the very least, find a way to weed out the incompetent. There is too much at stake to do less.

This parting thought by one respondent sums up much of the above and offers a glimmer of hope for the future.

> *"There is no clear route into the sector to ensure the best of the best are employed and given opportunities. It is essentially a cowboy industry where people are employed because of friends or for soft skills, or because of many years' experience which does not necessarily equate to brilliance. As the sector slowly by slowly becomes more professional, incompetency is more noticeable and less tolerated."* – 26-30yo white female expat aid worker

NOTES

1. Valeska P.Korff, Nicoletta Balbo, Melinda Mills, Liesbet Heyse, and Rafael Wittek, "The impact of humanitarian context conditions and individual characteristics on aid worker retention," *Disasters* 39 (2015): 522-545.

13 WHY DO AID WORKERS LEAVE THIS LINE OF WORK?

> *"Don't believe this should be long career."*
> – 26-30yo white male expat aid worker

> *"I think that the aid sector would ultimately benefit from a HR base that has a wider variety of experiences. I don't think staying in the sector my whole career is healthy for the sector or for my intellectual development."*
> – 26-30yo non-white female HQ worker

> *"I feel that I will always be connected to this line of work in one way or another. If it is not working internationally as an expat, then I will most likely be working locally for various NGOs in my home country or city. If not that, then I see myself pursuing a PhD where the topic of research will be related to humanitarian work."*
> – 36-40yo white male

Overview

In the last chapter you read many aid worker voices about the topic of getting fired. As we learned from the data, the perception is that getting fired in the literal sense happens very infrequently and getting "let go" – as in not having a contract renewed – is more common. That said, the humanitarian aid and development sector has a fluid work force, in general, and staff come and go for all manner of reasons.

Our survey included four questions attempting to drill down into what these reasons might be.

In Q44 we asked "Many (most?) humanitarian aid workers will ultimately become ex-humanitarian aid workers. Which below do you think is the *most* common reason why humanitarian aid workers choose to leave this line of work?" and then in Q45 we followed up with an open ended question asking the respondent to give their thoughts as to "why humanitarian aid workers will ultimately become ex-humanitarian aid workers."

Q46 was a forced choice format asking "Many (most?) humanitarian aid workers will ultimately become ex-humanitarian aid workers. Excluding the unlikely and tragic possibility that you will die in service, if you do so by choice which below do you think will be *your* reason for leaving this line of work?" and the results are below. In an additional follow up question Q47 we asked "Please use this space to elaborate on your answer to the above question asking about your reason for leaving this line of work?"

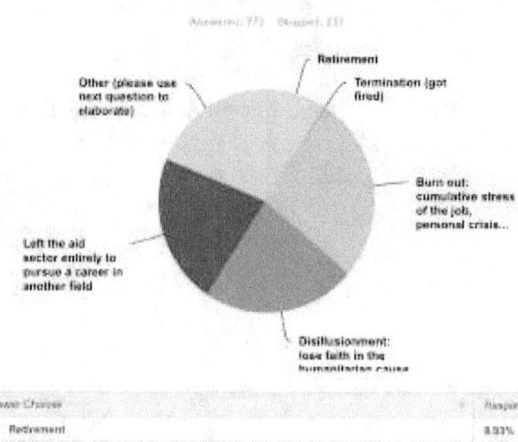

Many (most?) humanitarian aid workers will ultimately become ex-humanitarian aid workers. Excluding those few -but tragic- that will die in service, which below do you think is the *most* common reason why humanitarian aid workers choose to leave this line of work?

Answer Choices	Responses	
Retirement	8.93%	49
Termination (got fired)	0.52%	1
Burn out: cumulative stress of the job, personal crisis related to on-the-job experiences, etc. become too much to continue	25.78%	267
Disillusionment: loss faith in the humanitarian cause or mission overall, loss confidence in your organization or the overall humanitarian system	22.30%	171
Left the aid sector entirely to pursue a career in another field	21.99%	170
Other (please use next question to elaborate)	18.89%	146
Total		721

Here again (this was included in the last chapter) are the data for Q44. Given that the respondents represent varying levels of longevity on the industry, many with just a few years, the responses below are based mostly on impressions. The forced choice responses we offered are not necessarily mutually exclusive and so the qualitative data from the follow up questions yields our best source for the 'real' reasons people might leave the sector. Analysis and comment on the two open ended questions is below.

Data from Q46 – "Many (most?) humanitarian aid workers will ultimately become ex-humanitarian aid workers. Excluding the unlikely and tragic possibility that you will die in service, if you do so by choice which below do you think will be *your* reason for leaving this line of work?" – below are presented in a table format to emphasize the difference between those who identified as male as compared to those identifying as female. As you can see, the same forced choices were used but now, breaking down for gender, we see something interesting. Those numbers in pale blue indicate statistical significance, and five of the six choices fall into this category, raising the question about why female aid workers feel differently about why they or others might eventually leave the sector. We can discount the "Termination (get fired)" answer, but the others are worth a look. In words, here is what we see below:

- Males are significantly more likely to see themselves as "lifers," retiring as aid workers.
- Females are significantly more likely to think they'll leave because of "disillusionment" of some sort.
- Males are significantly more likely to think they will leave to pursue another career outside the sector.
- Females are significantly more likely to indicate they have "other reasons."

That's the "what." The "why" lies within the narrative responses.

	Retirement	Termination (get fired)	Burn out: cumulative stress of the job, personal crisis related to on-the-job experiences, etc. become too much to continue	Disillusionment: lose faith in the humanitarian cause or mission overall, lose confidence in your organization or the overall humanitarian system	Leave the aid sector entirely to pursue a career in another field	Other (please use next question to elaborate)	Total
Q4 Female (A)	16.67% 56	0.60% 0	15.31% 75	20.93% 158	26.68% 149	18.41% 96	69.82% 516
Q4 Male (B)	23.32% 52	0.90% 2	18.31% 27	13.00% 29	48.81% 91	11.66% 26	30.18% 223
Total Responses	138	2	102	137	350	121	739

Thoughtful responses related to disillusionment

Many key points are made by the four respondents below perhaps the most important of which is the generalization – borne out by the responses to Q31 (discussed in chapter 10) – that a majority of people enter and stay in the sector for humanitarian-related reasons; they care about others. When the choice to leave the sector is considered, the reason is not that they no longer care but rather that life priorities have altered. Many feel that they can live out their impulse to make a difference in other ways.

The second comment makes an interesting point about career trajectories. She makes an argument with which I do not disagree, namely that the sector can be inherently frustrating for many reasons, one of which is the incompetence or lack of compassion by those in high-level position. Several additional key reasons include (1) the gap between what *needs to be* accomplished and what *is* accomplished is often pretty wide, and the understanding of that gap gets clearer the longer one stays in the sector, (2) massive, large scale change is impossible through the sector alone; macro level economic and political change must come first, and (3) though more related to development work than to aid work, there is a creeping sense that the very *raison 'd etre* of the industry may be flawed and that, writ large, effective and sustainable change can only come from within. Listen to these voices.

As to why she might leave the sector this woman speaks of the disillusionment with her situation and by inference perhaps the entire sector, affirming my point above.

> *"For myself it will be the risk and the growing appreciation that change must come from within, working recently in South Sudan I realised the fragility of the human condition and how ultimately pointless all this development is if the conditions and structures are not in place to maintain peace from the grassroots."* – 31-35yo white female expat aid worker

This next woman reflects along the same line though even more cynical.

> *"It is questionable if we are doing any good, a lot of what we do as expats could be better done by local staff. We take a lot of money out of local economies and distort them with how much we are willing to pay for goods and services. In places like Cambodia, I question if we are doing more good than harm."*
> – 26-30yo non-white female, HQ worker

Next an honest, insightful big picture look:

> *"This is a sector filled with people who need to believe in their work and believe that they are accomplishing something (not necessarily "saving the world", but*

at least doing something productive and that they feel is worthwhile). by nature, i think this is therefore a group more prone to disillusion than other others (bankers, lawyers, whatever). no doubt, the aid world is deeply flawed, but people working in fields where they don't need so badly to believe their work is worthwhile and being done well are less likely to get fed up and leave. as well-intentioned, experienced aid workers get too frustrated/burnt out to remain in their chosen career, it also means that a lot of the people who stay and move up the management chain are those who either don't care about the problems or aren't willing to address them because they have too much to lose. this creates further disillusion with people who want to do their jobs well. burn-out is certainly also an issue, but there are an awful lot of burnt-out aid workers who keep working in aid whether or not it's good for them or anyone else."

— 31-35yo white female expat aid worker

And now this one, even more personal.

"I think it's often a combination of many things and i can see this coming for myself - wanting more stability, being soul-tired of being 'foreign', being tired of the same conversations, over and over (all those 'lessons learned' being left in a folder on a shelf somewhere), needing to earn more money, not wanting to be old in the field, wanting more balance in life so that work is not so all-consuming, becoming more cynical. More positively, one of the things that i love about this work is that everyone has dreams and ideas about what else they would like to do - usually it's still something connected to making the world a better place, but i love that no-one thinks this is it and there aren't other possibilities as well, one day. I don't see this in non-humanitarian industries - it tends to be a rare and notable thing when people retrain and do something different and i love it that we generally have other ideas too."

— 41-45yo white female HQ worker

Where to if not the aid sector?

Over and over again in the hundreds of written responses I found statements affirming that aid workers are "different" as a group and that they do want to live what they consider to be meaningful and humanitarian-focused lives, many sounding like this woman, *"And transition into domestic social justice work."*

Many permutations of this same sentiment came out in the data, some offering the thought that they could remain positive agents of social change near home and others indicating that the sector was shifting in ways that would take them home regardless. Here are a few that voice a sense that the sector may be changing toward the private sector.

"I think the humanitarian sector is valuable and needed but I also think private sector will ultimately be the catalyst of growth."
— 26-30yo white female expat aid worker

"CSR [corporate social responsibility] is the way forward."
— 36-40yo non-white male expat aid worker

"I think I will always be involved in development, one way or the other. Development isn't only about working for an NGO, but can come from private sector or other means." – 36-40yo white female expat aid worker

Aid workers, like workers in any industry, regularly at least consider career moves as a matter of course; we all think ahead to the 'next step.' To what extent is this sector different than others? Perhaps some clues can be found below.

Family and relationships a big factor

Many – both males and females – gave relationship related reasons why they will leave the sector. This first one from a female expat speaks, I think for many.

"Eventually I will want to have a dog, and I'll have to pursue a more conventional job in my home country for this. Also, my partner will want to go home." – 26-30yo white female expat aid worker

Here are a few more representing this general sentiment, the last I feel confident will resonate with many females.

"In order to start a family of my own and to be closer to support my aging parents." –26-30yo white female expat aid worker

"It would probably be for family reason and i will pursue another job that fits better the needs of my family." – 46-50yo (unspecified race) female

"[I] will want to settle and have children at some point and also do not want to become one of the insane and bitter people who have spent too long in the field!" — 26-30yo non-white female expat aid worker

"If I continue to get told that having a child is difficult in finding positions other than HQ I will quit trying at some point. Idealism doesn't put food on the table." – 31-35yo white female expat aid worker

"I don't know yet, but this game isn't much one for settling down and having a family. As chicks, we get to a certain age where the biological clock ticks pretty loudly and we have to weigh up our options of a steady job or moving on. We shall see." – 31-35yo white female expat aid worker

"I want to actually live in the same city as my husband for a few years before we have kids... his line of work doesn't exactly bring him to conflict-affected areas." – 26-30yo white female expat aid worker

"I've got a partner and dreams of seeing a garden through an entire season; it's hard to imagine getting lucky enough to get a secure an aid job that I can also have a stable home life in my city of choice. This is one of the 'second wave feminist' Lean In problems, but I hate to say I am totally facing it."
– 26-30yo white female expat aid worker

Finally, continuing the feminist thrust, this woman felt the need to end her note demonstratively.

"If you are a woman, you often have to leave to have a family. the humanitarian and emergency sector is entirely unforgiving to those (especially women) who choose to have kids. accompanied missions are hard to come by, you don't get them in tough places, and the work hours and travel needed prohibit family life. a woman can be a mother but she has to choose a different kind of job (i.e. a desk job in HQ) or if lucky an accompanied mission. OR she leaves. I am very lucky to currently have a stable job in an accompanied position working on humanitarian projects. This allowed me to have a baby. However, I am under NO illusion that my career prospects have considerably narrowed, and i will have to fight for the next accompanied mission. Or just give it up. Although I am flexible and do travel away from my family for some time, I refuse to choose a job that another aid worker can do, in place of my child. It's a young person's game, or a single person's game, and for the reason above, in the long term, it tends to be a MAN'S game."
– 31-35yo white female expat aid worker

Now for some other themes from the data.

Money and career options

These next few reflect numerous themes in the data, though I include them specifically to represent the mention of low pay that was echoed by many.

"I guess I hope I find a balance in life. I think Aid work is not the end all. It doesn't pay enough, and there are people close to home that need help as well. And then there is family and friends. Finally Aid work is evolving and the line

between the private sector and development is changing. I would like to think I will evolve as well and find a place where my skills and experience can be used before I get shot or burn out." – 26-30yo white male

"Money is a big concern. I spent most of my 20's making less than half of what my college friends are making doing non-aid work. If I am interested in having a family, this will be a big issue for me. I have already begun looking at options in management consulting and defense contracting... no reason but money to do those things, but I'm not sure how I could transition to any other fields at this point." – 31-35yo white male

"I am interested mainly in marketing and PR which is what I'm currently doing for my organisation. But if a more interesting or lucrative opportunity were to arise in another field, I would probably take it."
– 31-35yo non-white female expat aid worker

The mention above that "the line between the private sector and development is changing" is interesting and reflects a good bit what I presented in "Aid Worker Voices on the Future of Humanitarian Aid."

The wear and tear on body and soul of being an (expat) aid worker[1]

Some jobs in the sector – maybe most? – take a heavy toll, and that toll is tolerated by many for long periods of time, I conjecture, because most view this array of experiences and emotions as '#firstworldproblems' and just make an effort to just "suck it up." But these efforts can fail over time and eventually lead to consideration of career change.

"I am so fucking tired of the constant heckling, jeering, staring, groping, and living in fear. Every day I experience a moment during which I could easily die. I'm incredibly isolated. I'm unhealthy. I'm ready to be happy and healthy and surrounded by people who love me in a place where I fit in."
– 18-25yo white female expat aid worker

"Having already experienced burnout in this field, I'm carefully on watch for it happening again and working against that. If it every starts to head down that path again, I will leave. I will not compromise myself or those close to me in such a way again." – 41-45yo white female HQ worker

"Wanting to have light 24 hours a day, safe clean water, no need to have house security measures, good health services, usage of functional public transport, fully stocked Supermarkets and just being one more person on the street, not having the 'Expat' label on my back."

– 31-35yo non white female expat aid worker

Not even imagining a career change

Though the prompt asked respondents to image what might lead them to become "ex-humanitarian aid workers" many were not ready to even consider this option. The responses below indicate the range of reasons.

"I love everything about this job (I am 28 and single!) and I suspect over the years the nature of work will change but I will stay in this sector."
– 26-30yo non-white female HQ worker

"I like my line of work, I like change every few years, my family is on board and we enjoy this (privileged) lifestyle. We find the schools are superior than those at home (except for the ones we'd have to pay through the nose for). We enjoy the travel, meeting other cultures, living in amazing places...instead of visiting them for just a week." – 41-45yo white female expat aid worker

"Can't see myself back in a normal job, or back living in the West. Lack of money is not a problem – mostly."
– 41-45yo white male expat aid worker

"I would hope to make it to retirement but am not so unrealistic to think I can keeping working like this for another 20 years. Will probably negotiate a job at headquarters with limited travel in the next 5-10 years and hope the pension matures to something that will keep me warm and fed anytime thereafter."
– 46-50yo white female expat aid worker

Concluding thoughts? I continue to be struck at the forthrightness and thoughtfulness represented in what aid workers wrote. Here are a few to end this section, each waxing philosophical on the nature of the their lives and work.

"I have already pretty much lost faith in the humanitarian system, and don't feel ethically good accepting most of the job opportunities available to me. They mostly seem like they may potentially put me in a situation where I would have to exploit a community for the sake of a donor, and I am just not ok with that and don't even want to be put in the position to do such a thing. So I may have to look for a job in another field where I can make my money with less moral ambiguity and then do my own 'development work' on my own time and my own dime." – 18-25yo white female expat aid worker

"Even though I say I am pragmatic, I am also increasingly weary and just disappointed in our industry for not being *better.* I am more often disappointed these days than inspired and think our industry is on a path toward self-destruction if we don't get our acts together. There are many more players today who want "in" on the development project, and we stodgy INGOs seem to resent that we don't have a corner on the market anymore. I think the age of the "big INGO" is increasingly going to be challenged by actors that are younger, bolder, more nimble and lean, innovative, etc., and at some point I will probably want to jump ship rather than go down with it."

— 31-35yo non-white female expat aid worker

This next one points to the fact that many aid workers are in relationships and career choices are a negotiated dance with partners, family and so on.

"I do think people face a personal crisis or moment of choice, career wise or life-wise. For me I think what I like about the job (living new places, working for an organization I - with some caveats, but fundamentally - believe in) can be achieved in not-humanitarian work, more general development work and the like. I want to keep living abroad and working for international institutions, maybe that means more humanitarian work, maybe it means something else. I have a partner with the same goals, which helps a lot - but it also means maybe my choices will be dictated by his next job."

— 26-30yo white female expat aid worker

Yeah, one's journey through life is complicated and impacted by many forces, some under our control and others not so much. That the aid worker's journey and life trajectory is more complicated than most seems to be very apparent from the voices reported above.

14 THE RELATIONSHIP BETWEEN THE "HOME OFFICE" AND THE "FIELD"

"Well, HQ is HQ and the people there are just different. Not necessarily ill-intentioned or stupid (although it seems that way at times), just different."
-26-30 yo white female expat aid worker

And now more on the survey results...

Yes, I am aware of the increasing blurring between what can be called "home office" and the "field" and also that many aid workers are neither and both at the same time. That said, here are some interesting results from our survey questions that simply asked for an overall perspective. Below we look at both the quantitative and qualitative results from three questions, Q50-52.

Q50 results below indicate a pretty negative view of the relationship. Our results indicated a microscopic 1% indicating that "The field and the home office are completely in sync regarding important matters like priorities and processes." A hefty 40% indicated these two realms were "rarely in sync." Why is this? One broad-strokes answer is the truism that as bureaucracies get larger – and a good percentage of our respondents are from "big box" organizations – communication and coordination are structurally more complicated and, hence chronically compromised or at the very least challenging.

Here is one narrative example to illustrate:

"Generally it's all down to regular communication and putting faces to the names. The home office sometimes push "top-down" priorities that they want to

see be coherent across all active programme-countries, and sometimes need to step back from their perfect plan and accept that it can't be copy/pasted across different sites. On the other hand, I have seen the field staff exaggerate how "badly understood" they are by the home office (sometimes to excuse a lack of progress...it's so easy to blame things that the home office "just don't understand" about the conditions. But sometimes, it really is just due to bad field-management!..that makes it hard for the home office to know the difference)." – 26-30 yo white female expat aid worker

This next respondent nails my point:

"This [lack of sync] *applies to all organisations with HQ and regional offices, not just aid work."* – 56-60yo white female expat aid worker

So, here is the quantitative data from Q50 and Q51:

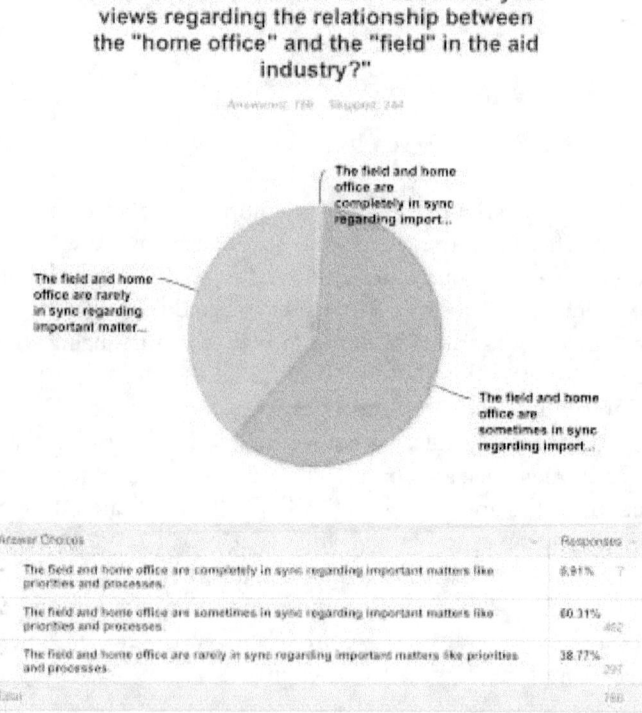

Which statement below best describes your views regarding the relationship between the "home office" and the "field" in the aid industry?"

Answered: 759   Skipped: 244

Answer Choices	Responses
The field and home office are completely in sync regarding important matters like priorities and processes.	8.91% 7
The field and home office are sometimes in sync regarding important matters like priorities and processes	60.31% 452
The field and home office are rarely in sync regarding important matters like priorities and processes.	38.77% 297
Total	760

Q51 results are interesting in that it gets a bit more personal, our question asking about the current organization of the respondent. The "rarely" response, like Q50 above is still low at a paltry 9%....less than one in 10. The "rarely" response is still high, but now that the respondents are talking about their own organization the number is 29% (as compared to the 39% reported about the relationship in general in the industry.

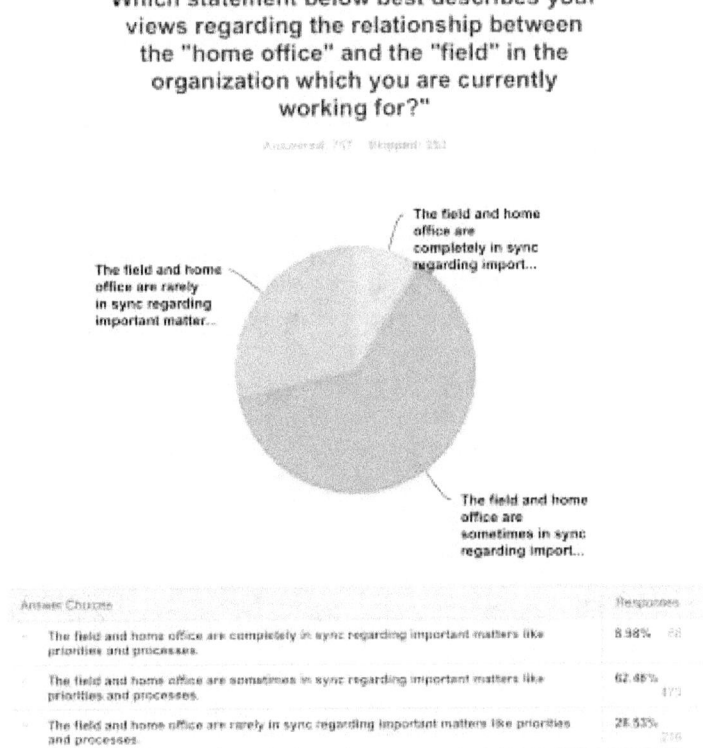

Which statement below best describes your views regarding the relationship between the "home office" and the "field" in the organization which you are currently working for?"

Answer Choices	Responses	
The field and home office are completely in sync regarding important matters like priorities and processes.	8.98%	68
The field and home office are sometimes in sync regarding important matters like priorities and processes.	62.46%	473
The field and home office are rarely in sync regarding important matters like priorities and processes.	28.53%	216
Total		757

Here are some specific narrative responses that flesh out the numbers above.

First these two from what I would call a reality-based perspective:

> *"Much of the decision making is done in the field and since the vast majority of employees are very competent, this works well. The biggest source of feeling "out of sync" is in regard to human resources- both being able to staff the field adequately and taking care of people when they leave." –* 31-35yo white female expat aid worker

161

"Time zones, language/cultural barriers, personality differences, technological skill- these are just some of the challenges to attaining complete alignment between the 2 types of offices." – 18-25yo non-white female HQ worker

You can sense the frustration in these next three:

"We are regularly left out of home office conference calls and group emails that include all other country offices in the region. I don't know whether the home office forgets to include us or is being passive aggressive. Either way, we are a mess. The leadership of my country office criticizes our regional office and our HQ/home office regularly. It seems like the feelings are mutual." – 18-25yo non-white female expat worker employed within the UN system

"Put simply, there is an immense disconnect between reality and policy. Also, I often feel or am made to feel inferior by the hierarchy in which final decisions must go through HQ and are decided by people who are totally removed from the contexts. To make decisions, you must spent endless hours justifying a decision before you can make it. Can't imagine what national staff must feel like (hence the indifference, I suppose)." – 36-40yo white male HQ worker

"Damn emails. the world was beautiful before emails and the immediate responses needed by someone at HQ. that's why I like to work in the field where I can decide that the internet 'didn't work for several days.'" – 56-60yo white male expat aid worker

These next two are particularly insightful and speak to issues that most in the sector will recognize:

"In my experience, the relationship between the field and home office is good when there is a close dialogue and working relationship between the Country Director and the Regional Director that the CD reports to. This being said with increasingly multiple reporting or accountability lines, I am not sure that the above really applies... It's always a difficult balance, especially in high profile emergencies, between the field having space and support to make decisions and the home office feeling that its interests are being met." – 46-50yo white female HQ worker

"This is the result of having very high turnover at all positions including high level management ones. Some people came with centralization ideals, others with decentralizations. Result: we find ourselves with two layers that develop themselves regardless of the other. Processes, procedures and responsibilities are often blurry. "Home office" works 4.5 days a week from 8 to 4pm, "field" is

6.5 days a week from 7 to 8pm. "Home office" is gangrened with political and career building moves. Often, the field ends up flipping the finger and taking over everything. "Home office" then try to finds itself a justification to exist in terms of informal support line. Once in a while they get hormones rush, and they go top-down very strongly. At field level, you then choose your battles. Field has a strong feeling that they don't need the "home office" to operate. The "home office" thinks that they are the captain of the boat. The whole thing could be a giant case study to analyse for a final exam in management." – 26-30yo white male expat aid worker

Indeed, this is a problem of organizational management, but though we can react to communication and sync issues as they arise, the bigger picture is that the problems identified about are inherent whenever organizational size increases. The truism in the business sector that "big fish eat little fish" – and hence that there is a force toward the domination by bigger business entities – is somewhat also true in the aid sector, if only because the economy of scale. That and, well, Max Weber was right in pointing out the bureaucratization inevitably leads toward quantification and depersonalization and to the overall phenomena of organizations acting in the interests of survival as an entity and straying from original mission.

The point made in the last respondent's comment that there is "*...very high turnover at all positions including high level management ones*" cannot be ignored as a major factor impacting the overall efficiency level of aid organizations. Two obvious impacts include (1) training new personnel takes time, energy and both human and material resources and this constant drain inevitably impacts overall system performance and (2) institutional memory is constantly being lost as personnel come and go, hence the sense that some organizations are always recreating the wheel. To be clear, these issues are *not* unique to the aid industry.

To go back to the sociologist Max Weber for a moment, he invokes the image of the *stahlhartes Gehäuse* or "iron cage" in his ruminations about the inexorable rise of bureaucratization in the modern world.[1] Were he alive today he would look at the aid world and say "it is what it is" (or some German phrase meaning as much). Big bureaucracies will always be necessary and indeed the only way forward for social organization but they will always be inherently hampered by their size: the bigger they get the less efficient they become...for many of the reasons touched on above, and more.

When I talk about the "iron cage of rationality" with my students I trot out an aphorism I coined may years ago to explain one important dimension of the problem of bureaucratization, this one especially relevant in the aid world when examining the need to "show results." Merging a thought by Blaise Pascal "And thus being unable to make what is just strong, we have made what is strong just"[2] with my understanding of Weber I came up with "Not being able to measure that which is real, we tend to make that which is measurable, real." Where was the drunk looking for his watch? Under the lamp post. Why? Because that is where the light is best. Hence we forever spin our wheels constantly inside our iron cages. Sigh.

So I'll end not with comments from our respondents but from my muse Max Weber. To wit,

> *"When those subject to bureaucratic control seek to escape the influence of existing bureaucratic apparatus, this is normally possible only by creating an organization of their own which is equally subject to the process of bureaucratization."*[3]

Yes, creating your own organization (MONGO) does seem like a good idea at the time....

The take home point from the above is that only by aggressively, tirelessly and creatively addressing the structural challenges that are inevitably and inherently produced by any bureaucracy we will be faced with the future that Weber foresaw:

> *"Not summer's bloom lies ahead of us, but rather a polar night of icy darkness and hardness, no matter which group may triumph externally now."*

NOTES

1. Max Weber. *The Essential Weber: A reader*, ed. Sam Whimster (New York, Routledge 2004), 33.
2. Pascal, Blaise. *Pensees and the Provinical Letters*, trans. W. F. Trotter (New York, Random House 1941), p. 103.
3. Max Weber. *Economy and Society*, trans. and ed. Guenther Roth, Claus Wittich (New York: Bedminster Press 1921/1968), 224
4. Max Weber. *From Max Weber: Essays in Sociology*, ed. H. Gerth, & C. Wright Mills (New York: Oxford University Press 1946/1958), 128.

15 AID WORKER VIEWS REGARDING MONGOS

"I think that if every overly bright, well-dressed 20something would just get together and co-run the skinny jeans appreciation society in their respective countries, the rest of us could put all that money and press to actual use."
– 26-30yo white female HQ worker

"Deep breaths.   Too many."– 41-45 yo female HQ worker [extra spaces for emphasis in the original]

"They are petty indulgences normally of middle class white people who want to help someone and feel better about their privilege."
– 31-35yo white female expat aid worker

Aid worker views regarding MONGOs (My Own NGO): mostly negative

The 2014 kidnapping of two young Italian women in Syria underscores the fact that being an aid worker comes with risks. There may be something specifically about this particular episode that merits a deeper understanding, and a start might be to examine aid worker voices about the kind of organization to which these young women were associated, namely a very small, new, self-started NGO.

What kinds of organizations are best suited to doing aid work? Does size of the organization matter? Is there variance of opinion between developed countries and how they view smaller NGOs and developing countries and their views? How do our survey respondents feel about smaller humanitarian aid entities and what are some of the positives and negatives from their perspective? These are some questions that I examine below using our survey respondents views to illustrate and, hopefully, provide a deeper perspective.

Overview

Aid workers' views on MONGOs can be found, such as a blog post by aid worker Lee Rainboth entitled "Whatever you do, don't start your own NGO" but there is very little data that I have been able to find on this question.[1] Let's turn over this rock and see what we find.

We had 479 (of 1010) people respond to our open-ended question regarding MONGOs. Here is the prompt for Q58: "What is your general view of so-called MONGOs (My Own NGO) or other smaller humanitarian aid work entities?"

I went through every response and tagged each as "positive," "neutral" or "negative," and the results indicate clearly that MONGOs have a mixed and mostly negative image among aid workers. Here are the results of my tagging:

- Overall positive: 11%
- Neutral/mixed: 46%
- Negative: 43%

The short of it

The vast majority of respondents had a very negative view of MONGOs, with "negatives" outnumbering "positives" by almost four to one and most of the responses that I tagged "neutral" pointing out that there were both positives and negatives to be argued, stressing the negatives of those organizations which are not "done right."

As many of the "neutral" responses correctly pointed out, MONGOs are not a monolithic whole. An attempt to list and categorize types of MONGOs even within one country would be extraordinarily complicated, and doing a comprehensive listing internationally would be even more difficult certainly by an order of magnitude. The numbers of MONGOs is on the rise every year internationally and thus any list established would be out of date immediately.

Certainly one of the beginning points of any typology would be differentiating between those that have their origins in one country and have a focus in some other part of the world (a NGO based in the US dealing with homeless boys in a specific region in Honduras, for example), and those that are originate in the country where they function (e.g., a micro-finance scheme organized and run by locals in rural Zambia).

From the narrative survey responses I gleaned a number of differentiating characteristics. The list below are some of the most important factors and may be useful downstream as we attempt a typology of NGOs:

- Type and motivation of leadership
- Type of motivation of founder(s)
- Overall organizational structure
- Methods used in recruiting and training staff
- Western primarily (e.g., US and UK) originated and based vs locally/community organizations
- Degree of focus or lack thereof of core mission
- Breadth and clarity of and fidelity to mission statement
- Level of overall professionalism
- Whether or not aid or development focused
- Ability to make sustainable change/scalability
- Ability and/or willingness to communicate and work with others in the sector
- The length of time that they have been established
- The existence of an active governing board overseeing activities

Many of the "neutral" responses leaned negative but qualified their answer, tending to say, in short, some MONGOs can be great/effective if the leadership is good, there is a narrow, defined focus and they are run professionally. MONGOs that score high on all the variables above can have many positives:

- Flexible; can change and modify very quickly
- Have generally low overhead
- Can have very creative responses to niche conditions

Perhaps one of the more astute observations made by one respondent was that, after all, this is the way all aid organizations started (see Red Cross, MSF, etc.). The list of negatives that appear in both "negative" and "neutral" responses is long and damning, and I invite you to read the sections below for some great examples.

- Lack of professionalism
- Lack of standardization
- "White savior complex" underlying motivations

• Just adding to noise and confusion for beneficiaries, donors and the aid industry

• Poor/misguided mission
• Ego-driven leadership
• Just reinventing the wheel
• Inefficient
• Do harm in some cases
• Self-serving
• No accountability
• Prone to corruption
• Thinly disguised proselytization
• Overall give aid section a bad reputation

Many respondents touched on a current debate voiced succinctly in the comment made by an experienced female aid worker, namely:

"Humanitarian aid is a profession not a hobby."

In short, MONGOs: not so good except in rare cases.

A thought from my sociological perspective. As I have argued in other chapters I believe that it is human nature to have empathy toward others and to want to help somehow when one sees others in need. Indeed, that is what prompted Henri Dunant to do what he did in response to the wounded at Solerfino and later help establish one of the very first humanitarian aid organizations, the Red Cross. The urge to create MONGOs is there. What to do with individuals who act on it is the question we must explore in more detail at some point. Below I present representative responses from each of the three groupings.

Positive

"Great! I love the small initiatives, but I'd qualify it since it depends a lot on the origins, agency of the organization and what they're up to (since many depend on assumptions we give them that we say works, when it very well might be ivory-tower driven). We can't work with them because of rules from up top, but generally, I think they do our work better than we do."
— 18-25yo white female expat aid worker

"Have limited reach but have the potential to be better with adaptation, better at identifying nuances to local development, and may be better at small scale development." — 26-30yo white female expat aid worker

"Can be useful if service providers in niches. But no way to partner with at scale." – 36-40yo white male expat aid worker

"Some are quite nimble and do good local work and focus very effectively on social justice. However they can lead to too much fragmentation and some serve the egos of their founders too much." – 36-40yo white female HQ worker

"Often the smaller ones achieve more with fewer overheads and admin costs."
– 41-45yo white female HQ worker

"Some can grow to be great organisations as long as they learn from their mistakes and have clear leadership which understands the complexities of the isssues (sic) they are dealing with." –26-30yo white female expat aid worker

"There is plenty work to be done, problems, issues to be addressed (sic). Plenty spaces for MONGOs. And it is good as well to have a variety of organization." – 36-40yo white female HQ worker

"If they are local NGOs/CBOs, they can make very good work because they can understand and address the very local issues and problems. Creating an NGO in the US to do fantasy projects to rescue poor dying African children is ridiculous." – 31-35yo white female expat aid worker

Neutral

Some respondents just had no opinion, some gave both sides, some qualify their responses in very insightful ways:

"Can't write all off with one brush. If they are filling an actual gap that can be a good thing. The big boy NGOs are not necessarily flexible or nimble so small can be good. However the ones that show up without a clue are making things worse." – 36-40yo white female HQ worker

"They can be frustrating in the sense that they rarely coordinate "with the big kids" - i.e. they tend to go off on their own and don't connect or feed into the broader humanitarian system. However, if working in partnership, they can be helpful when working in isolated locations since they are sometimes the only ones willing to go and do work in tough places... especially National NGOs."
– 26-30yo white female expat aid worker

"(chuckle... I think I'm running a sort of MONGO at present, but we try not to act like it!) It varies, some can do good work if they have a specific niche that they can fill, often as a sub to a larger organization. Others are of questionable competence and can have an outsized regard of their own importance. If not well-focused ("I'm here and want to help!) they tend to be ineffective."
— 56-60yo white male HQ worker

"Specialized NGOs in particular sectors or communities or nations are only successful, effective and good when run by individuals who understand humanitarian principles and values and ways of working; those run by enterprising individuals or those who have money and "care" tend to make situations worse for everyone, including the people they are trying to help."
--36-40yo white male HQ worker

"Impossible to generalize. Yes, I tend to roll my eyes. But there are some that are really good, a lot better at responding to local needs than the large INGOs. There are a lot that are bad. But even a bad MONGO is probably not going to do a lot of harm (in a global sense). I could say the same about large NGOs. Some are good, lots are bad. MONGOs have a similar track record."
— 26-30yo white male expat aid worker

"Some are great and because they have very little resources they find innovative ways of delivering services. Others are terrible and completely undermine what the international aid community has aimed to achieved e.g. Standardisation, principles, good practices, do no harm, etc."
— 31-35yo white female HQ worker

"I think it depends on the experience and motivation of the person behind the NGO. If the person either has a background in development, or makes and effort to learn - and has the backing of the local community they seek to assist, then it can be a good thing. However, I think too many of these groups think 'NGOs are doing it wrong, so I can't learn anything from them'. Yes, there are many things wrong with the NGO system that can be improved. But the development system has also learned a lot of lessons the hard way that all NGOs can benefit from."
— 31-35yo white female HQ worker

"There is some truth to all sides of this debate."
— 31-35yo non-white female expat aid worker

"Find it very interesting and thing there is definitely a place for them in the sector as the more established and larger INGOs start to move toward professionalisation and expansion processes that often make them more

inefficient and less receptive to and understanding of needs on the ground. there is generally a fairly condescending and negative attitude of INGO and NGO to MONGO which is highly questionable given that none of us are exactly perfect... " – 26-30yo non-white female expat aid worker

"Usually no harm, little large-scale impact but nice to see people trying to help people. I don't feel the condescending outrage about this stuff that many of my peers do. If missionaries from Kansas want to hold AIDS babies for 8 weeks, as long as no one is interfering with treatment and care, and local communities don't mind, why not?" –31-35yo white male HQ worker

"This is extremely complex. People don't give unconditionally, even if they think they do. Some people will only contribute if they can maximise their own opportunities for self actualisation. MONGOs are not generally the most efficient way to give aid. They also often result in aid that is sub-standard. However, some people will only contribute to a response when they do it largely themselves. This is, to a certain extent, their right, as long as they meet agreed standards. Small NGOs also have the capacity to be very nimble and innovative, this shouldn't be stifled. Essentially there are both good and bad aspects and I don't have the time or energy to write the thesis that one could on this topic!" – 36-40yo white male expat aid worker

"Great in for small-scale community work in development settings. Horrible in large-scale relief/emergency settings." – 26-30yo white female expat aid worker

"I think MONGOs like small businesses begin when the larger NGOs or companies don't listen to a good idea. Of course there is that bit of hubris in being able to say back home I have my own NGO. I think a more realistic term would be "my own short term project" like most startups unless they are bought out (or funded) by a larger organization they won't last long. I think any large INGO would be wise to create a space for ideas and innovation in programming to be heard from all members of staff not only the grants and program development people. This would help the INGO to grow and develop better programs while keeping their staff from quitting to start their MONGOs." – 26-30yo white male

"I feel they can still have a good impact if managers/staff are extremely talented and have a clear idea of their mission, vision and goals. Otherwise, funds would be better used within bigger orgs." – 26-30yo white female HQ worker

"I don't think it's possible to clump them together. Some represent true citizen action and real empowerment within people's own communities and within their

own contexts. Others are purely ego trips that do more harm than good. The key is to understand the difference and support the potentially transformative ones that could potential become bigger players." – 26-30yo white female HQ worker

"Get the skill set and capability to work for an NGO before going MONGO on us. And being 19 and reading Kristoff doesn't count. Some small NGO's are agile and well managed and if they have the resources they can help, but there is a challenge in coordination and doubling of efforts."

– 26-30yo white female expat aid worker

"They're like hipsters: super easy to mock. But maybe just maybe we should reserve our mockery for the enormous for-profit development firms that regularly generate batshit clusterfucks on a scale no MONGO --not even a celebrity-run MONGO-- could ever match. That girl who runs a one-person NGO teaching yoga to ex-combatants? She's fun at parties and has no money. Let's talk about Chemonics. Snarking on MONGOs is fun, but let's be honest with ourselves: it's not serious." – 26-30yo white female expat aid worker

"THEY CAN BE MORE ESILY [sic] CORRUPTED"
– Anonymous response

"I think if they want to work to address to a particular problem in a particular place where no one else is working then it can be a good thing. If it's just 'water in africa' probably best to use people already doing that."

– 31-35yo white male expat aid worker

Negative

It has been argued that the aid industry has three parts: the beneficiaries, the donors and the aid workers (*you!*), and what the data shows is that MONGOs create concerns about all three of these prongs. Many of you felt that these smaller organizations harmed the entire industry for a variety of reasons. Other major issues included incompetence, corruption, ineffectiveness, poor preparation and questionable intent. Here are some examples of what you said illustrating the many negative views, some of which are very critical and offer no reason for the reactions, but others offering a bit of depth in their critiques:

"Small NGO is a waste of financial and human resources. It also create (sic) confusion among the beneficiaries and the donors."

– 31-35yo white female expat aid worker

"It is in line with the online age of personal worldwide connection. MONGOs are generally more efficient with their resources but lack the resources to demonstrate that they are effective. It is easy for a MONGO to fail which also brings down the reputation of the industry."
– 36-40yo white male HQ worker

"Most people I've met conducting this type of work are hardcore idealists who genuinely want to make a difference. However, they lack the realism and practical skills to further the organization from the backyard-project level. In fact, most of the time these are conducted by expats who are not always accepted by the local community, and they think good will is enough to make a change, but it evidently isn't. It takes extraordinary beneficiaries to meet them halfway, but most of the beneficiaries just don't care about that white person's crazy idea, they're too busy living their lives within their context, and the initiative will die out before it has any sort of measurable impact. The remaining MONGOs I've encountered are people stealing money and justifying it through creative financing." – 18-25yo non-white female HQ worker

"More prone to corruption, less likely to have strong mechanisms to ensure transparency and accountability, more likely to rely on unrestricted funding from private donors (which exacerbates the first two challenges), less likely to have any genuinely collaborative/democratic internal decision making processes."
– 26-30yo white female expat aid worker

"In my experience, some are really fantastic, but others are at best laughable and at worst causing harm. Those I have seen that are most effective is when the organization is truly community-based and is founded and run locally with a specific focus. Those founded by well-intentioned white people who 'just couldn't stand to see the suffering' are the worst." – 31-35yo white female expat aid worker

"When they originate from the West: hate them. I'm sorry, but we don't need another church group flying out to country X to build another goddamn orphanage. If it's a local organization supporting their own community then I'm all for it." – 26-30yo white female HQ worker

"MONGOs are wasteful because the majority of ones I know are incapable of recognizing that they are reinventing the wheel. They don't even know the next NGO down the road, and repeat efforts. Guatemala has tons of NGOs and many of them serve the same populations. There is a lot of serving the same populations over and over again with the same services. They often refuse to collaborate. The worst are international tiny NGOs that have no clue how

things work in country. They execute things badly and are very often uninformed of government policies and interventions in the field they work in."
— 26-30yo white female local aid worker

"I would like to sponsor an anti-NGO proliferation treaty. There are too many NGOs, lacking coordination, going after less funding, and all claiming to have the best solution, so they're less willing to learn."
— 36-40yo white female expat aid worker

"Noise. Their mistakes are blown up into 'sector problems.' They ruin it for the larger entities. Charity is not humanitarian work."
— 31-35yo white male expat aid worker

"Well, they are called MONGOs for a reason - b/c the focus is on "my own" and not the work they are doing. This is exactly the type of stuff aid organizations are training political parties about - to be about the stakeholder articulated needs and not your cult of personality."
— 41-45yo white female expat aid worker

"Can't stop them as some people are impelled to do something when they see a disaster or crisis. However, they are sometimes symptomatic of the lack of trust people have in the larger humanitarian organisations. We need to be better at explaining and justifying our overheads, added value and the economy of scale we can provide particularly in the big disasters. We absolutely have to do this in conflict arenas to reduce the number of people risking their lives going off in a small van with bit of clothing and a few medicines."
— 46-50yo white female expat aid worker

"In Nepal, there are more than 30,000 registered local NGOs. Many of these are MONGOs set up by idealistic foreigners with little technical knowledge and who lack familiarity with the Nepal context. These agencies poorly coordinate with other actors and often work outside the government systems. They often provide donated goods which are of low quality (e.g. Expired meds) and are not purchased on the local markets, thereby undercutting local businesses." – 36-40yo white female expat aid worker

"Ugh. Don't get me started. Unless they are LNGOs in which case, good on ya if you are making a small, clearly planned impact in your own community."
— 31-35yo white female expat aid worker

"KILL THEM ALL. Seriously, can we start weeding out the stupid and ineffectual?" – 26-30yo white female HQ worker

"Generally, I am highly critical and skeptical of USA-based MONGOs (I like this term!) as they generally have little background, experience, or understanding of the communities they're trying to assist. I also generally take issue with the "at least we're doing something!" attitude that is rampant among smaller NGOs and their supporters. I have a more positive view of fledgling local NGOs, in general." – 26-30yo white female HQ worker

"They are petty indulgences normally of middle class white people who want to help someone and feel better about their privilege."

– 31-35yo white female expat aid worker

"They should be banned, typically unprofessional, often distort markets, mostly don't know what they are doing, often doing harm."

– 26-30yo white female expat aid worker

Conclusions?

So, what is the take-home from all of the above? One thing clear is that aid worker professionals have a generally negative view of MONGOs, but I am assuming most of the people reading this chapter would say that's not a new insight (though we do now have some data supporting this commonly held perspective). That said, what does the general public know about these opinions? If they were more informed about much of the above listed downsides of MONGO's would they be more cautious about their support and perhaps support the "big box" organizations more?

As for the two Italian young women kidnapped by al-Qaeda who were later released, I wish the best for them. I harbor the thought that in a more well informed world – where aid worker voices are made more public and prominent – this situation might never have happened. Their intentions were good, perhaps, but the money they likely earned for al-Qaeda for their return only adds to problems in the sector.

The fact is that there are many books and web sites that encourage and instruct how to create and run your own NGO, and there is a constant flow of those with big ideas and skinny jeans coming from the global north to "save the world." That is, MONGOs are here to stay and will, I feel, remain a factor to be reckoned with. The question is how and by what body? Perhaps the Core Humanitarian Standards could be stressed more and established as an industry standard for any aid related activity? Perhaps there could be national or international laws established (or those established, enforced more aggressively) that monitor NGO activity for competence? Perhaps the secret handshake at the entrance to cluster meetings should be more intricate?

In other words, I think the data indicate some very fundamental issues with MONGOs and that these issues should be first more clearly articulated and then addressed at the highest levels.

NOTES

1. Lee Rainboth, "Whatever You Do, Don't Start Your Own NGO," The Green Mango Blog, Feb 6, 2015, https://thegreenmangoblog.com/2015/02/06/whatever-you-do-dont-start-your-own-ngo/

16 THE CRISIS CARAVAN: INTER-AGENCY COORDINATION

"Interagency coordination is far from functional and effective – it will never work as long as agencies exist in such disparate ways and they have their own funding, programs, priorities, personalities. Territorial and personality battles take up far too much of my time. I have to constantly undertake delicate diplomacy to get things done – but where is the shared vision and clarity of purpose?! "one UN" is a far-fetched fantasy as long as agencies continue to obsess over branding, turf-wars, and pissing contests."
– 36-40yo non-white female expat aid worker

The Crisis Caravan: Inter-agency coordination

Q56 touches on what has been euphemistically called the "crisis caravan." The results below indicate that well over half (53%) of our respondents thought that there were frequent or even constant problems related to inter-agency coordination and cooperation.

Here's the data on Q56:

How would you characterize the overall
inter-agency coordination and cooperation
among the humanitarian aid agencies with
which you are familiar?

Answered: 753   Skipped: 247

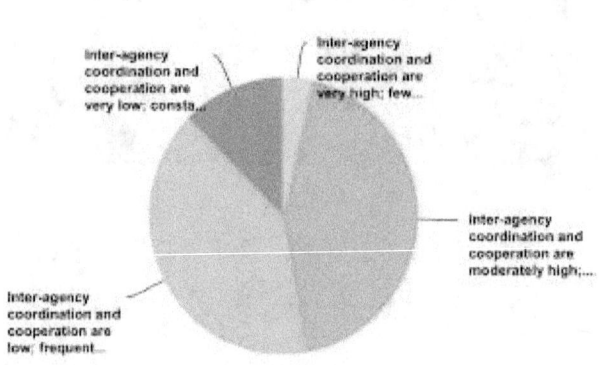

Answer Choices	Responses	
Inter-agency coordination and cooperation are very high; few problems	3.54%	27
Inter-agency coordination and cooperation are moderately high; occasion problems	43.64%	333
Inter-agency coordination and cooperation are low; frequent problems	40.37%	308
Inter-agency coordination and cooperation are very low; constant problems	12.45%	95
Total		763

Yeah, well, yawn.

The world is a complex mess and, of direct relevance to this question, there has been a constant and perhaps dysfunctional increase in the number of entities that are responding to humanitarian crises around the globe. At least 50 "big box" NGOs and literally countless smaller and/or MONGO organizations appear where ever there is a major humanitarian crisis. So, how many in the "crisis caravan?"

Too many to count is the most accurate number I can come up with. If there are communication problems within humanitarian organizations (as discussed in chapter 14) it stands to reason that of course there will be even more complex and distressingly pervasive inter-agency communication issues.

When Linda Polman wrote *The Crisis Caravan* she was looking backwards, writing about what was. No one sober looking back at 1994 and Rwanda or post-quake Haiti can disagree with her very critical observations regarding the big picture: seen from the advantaged perspective of frozen time and access to all of the "data," the crisis caravan seemed then – and perhaps seems now – quite a 'hot mess.'[1] But is it really? Our respondents seem to think so.

So, what has been, is being, and will be done to address this problem?

Has been and is being done

A couple answers appear immediately. First, two words: cluster meetings. Secondly, the Core Humanitarian Standard is the most recent demonstrative example of concerted and coordinated efforts in this sector to articulate and make public universally accepted standards for humanitarian responses. The Core Humanitarian Standard was created in 2010 as a result of the collaboration of the Humanitarian Accountability Partnership (HAP), People in Aid, and the Sphere Project, with the goal of increasing cohesion between aid organizations.[2] This and other efforts emphasize common standards that will, if adhered to, enhance coordination and cooperation.

What will be done

I've thought about this a bit and here's what comes up. We live in a world dominated by a species that is wired to desire justice (or at least fairness) and to have empathy for others. There will always be a steady supply of those who want to help others. And, given the trend in American higher education in the last 15 years toward more and more "service learning" programs and "social entrepreneurship" pathways, the stream of do-gooders coming from the US will not dry up any time soon. Just the opposite – bad news coming – I predict that there will be an even increasing number of MONGOs started in the coming years. More do-gooders and MONGOs means inevitably and inexorably that the "crisis caravan" will look even more chaotic in the coming years.

The well intentioned organizations and individuals working to enhance the sector and to address all of the "crisis caravan-esque" issues will continue working, innovating, messaging and, in the end, being always frustrated that their best efforts will never be complete or perfect. Their earnest work will be counterbalanced by the nature of the beast: more MONGO's, the inherent problems of communication in all and any bureaucracies, and, perhaps most distressing, the tendency we all have to "put out the fire closest to us." The world, as I noted above, is a complex mess, and so far there is no 'silver bullet' to be found, though many seem fixated on finding one.

Thinking in terms of the big picture is a luxury many of us don't have when confronted with the immediacy of current crises. Perhaps we are, and must remain -given the life and death urgency of the now- stuck in the weeds.

NOTES

1. Linda Polman, *The Crisis Caravan* (New York: Henry Holt and Company, 2010).
2. History of the Core Humanitarian Standard. https://corehumanitarianstandard.org/the-standard/history

17 CANCER OF CORRUPTION OR THE CULTURE OF CORRUPTION?

"One man's corruption is another man's wealth redistribution system. I find it hard to judge others on this." –26-30yo white female HQ worker

"Corruption is the biggest cause of poverty. If you are in aid, you deal with corruption." –36-40yo non-white male expat aid worker

"Corruption is there throughout the developing world (and the developed world but on a less blatant scale). We are often asked or hinted to pay bribes lest our applications for import, registration, visas gets put to the bottom of the pile. We don't because we have to account to our donors. But we did in one case buy drivers licenses as the 'process' was going to take about 6 months." –31-35yo white female expat aid worker

Difficult to define

How can we define, discuss and analyze the endemic social phenomena of corruption? How do aid workers understand and deal with corruption?

I will agree completely with the many who accurately point out that corruption is impossible to definitively operationalize and that cultural context, history, point of perspective, motivation, etc. are all factors. In fact I'll argue that the term itself is a semantic land mine charged with power/Western-centric thinking. Not the least of the complications regarding formulating one's opinion on this topic is the fact that in many cases what is unethical can also be legal and, critically, vice versa.

Defining corruption must include the fact that, well, it's a matter of definition, and we need to understand the forces driving that definition. To quote a German thinker of some note, "The ideas of the ruling class are in every epoch the ruling ideas..."[1] Just as the term child abuse did not come into common use in the West until recently (mid-20th century), I would argue that as a lived phenomenon is has existed for as long as there have been children. The same goes for corruption. My generic definition of corruption would be that it is a form of dishonest or unethical conduct by someone or some organizational entity entrusted with and/or structurally in a position of authority or power. Though since Greek times this idea has been bandied about, I submit that much like my example of child abuse, corruption has always been with us but not recognized, labeled or defined as such.

Begun in 1993, Transparency International has earned a reputation for generating both useful data on corruption internationally and in playing a part guiding policy changes[2] that address this issue head on. Their efforts have done much to raise the level of awareness about corruption internationally, though much remains to be accomplished both in terms of refining the measures and in being more inclusive in terms of differentiating the units of analysis that engage in corrupt behavior. The ubiquitous slippery slope between "business as it has always been conducted" and overt corrupt actions remains, and in many cases around the world there will be push back from those in power if "legal" actions are termed corruption.

Regarding corruption, the trope "no rules, just right" captures my perspective in that if by "just right" we mean that which is fair and just to all based on some universal understanding that the lives of all humans have equal value and should be treated fairly. I am reminded of various ethological studies, primarily among primates,[3] indicating that we have inherited a deeply wired sense of fairness and, by extension, that we are all capable of sensing abuse of power, i.e., corruption. Point being that corruption may not be entirely a cultural construct, adding yet another level of nuance to our understanding of this term.

This respondent added even another, critical dimension to the semantic soup concerning corruption.

> *"Corruption happens but does not affect me. Internal audits are quite strong and cases do happen. What is missing (for UN organizations at least) is the same vigilance against prostitution and sexual harassment."*
> – 31-35yo non-white female HQ worker

An argument can be made that popular culture definitions of corruption imply an almost myopic focus on misappropriation of money or materials, though most people would include favoritism, cronyism and nepotism. Is sexual harassment an abuse of power and thus a major form of corruption? Absolutely. Transparency International has a good – and growing – data base of information on this topic and in chapter 7 where I address the topic of how gender impacts the role of aid workers.

Survey says

Let's drill into what aid workers had to say about the issue of corruption, first looking at the quantitative data. We asked two closed-ended questions, first regarding corruption within their current organization and then in the context of the sector in which they are currently working. Here are the data in response to the question, "To what degree do you have to deal with corruption within the organization with which you are affiliated?" As you can see, about 70% reported having to deal with at least some corruption.

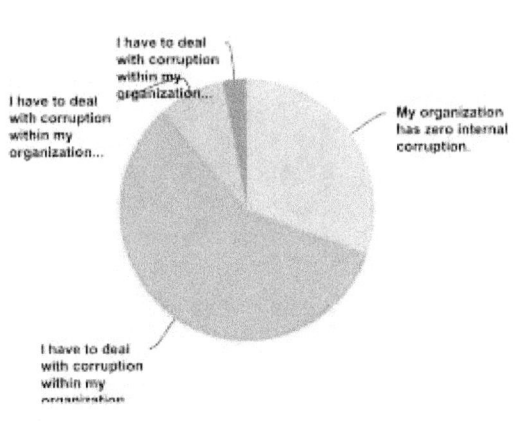

To what degree do you have to deal with corruption within the organization with which you are affiliated?

Answer Choices	Responses	
My organization has zero internal corruption.	30.45%	220
I have to deal with corruption within my organization occasionally	58.24%	438
I have to deal with corruption within my organization frequently	8.24%	62
I have to deal with corruption within my organization constantly	3.06%	23
Total		752

My wonder as I looked at these data was the mindset of those 30% that responded that "My organization has zero corruption." Digging into the data I found that among those who reported being affiliated with UN based organizations were only slightly less likely to report zero organizational corruption, and the percentages ranged very little among all the different affiliation groups. Given the broad definition of corruption that I outlined above, I frankly have no explanation for these results other than poor question construction. As one respondent put it, *"I work for the UN where unethical behavior is a constant."* Another put it this way,

> *"If someone's response is zero corruption, could you please publish the name of that institution so I can apply? Corruption exists within society and in situations of potential power abuse* [it] *flourishes..."*

The second closed ended question on corruption asked, "To what degree do you have to deal with corruption within the region you work?" As you can see below, the problem of corruption appears to be pervasive and serious, with 93% of the respondents indicating they have deal with corruption at least occasionally. That over a fifth of the respondents saying that they have to deal with corruption "constantly" is telling.

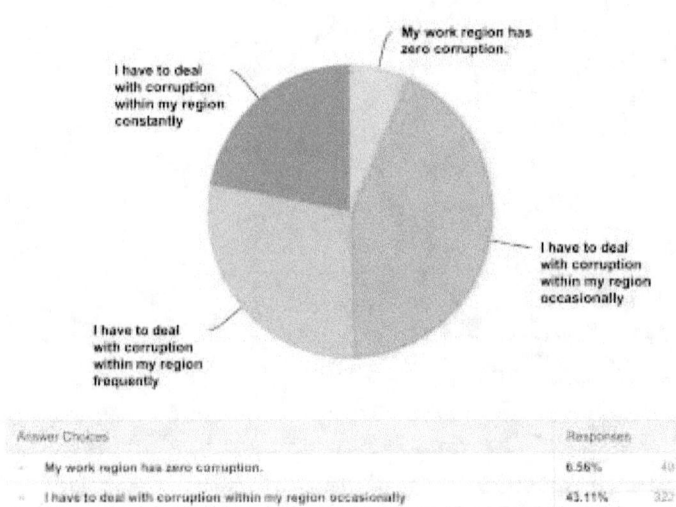

To what degree do you have to deal with corruption within the region you work?

Answered: 743 Skipped: 253

Answer Choices	Responses	
My work region has zero corruption.	6.56%	40
I have to deal with corruption within my region occasionally	43.11%	323
I have to deal with corruption within my region frequently	28.25%	211
I have to deal with corruption within my region constantly	22.09%	166
Total		747

Though the quantitative results are interesting, it is the narrative responses that paint a much more complex picture, one with many nuances.

Narrative voices on corruption

Just after the two closed ended questions on the survey discussed above the following prompt was given, "Please use the space below to elaborate on the questions above related to corruption." There were a total of 313 narrative responses, many providing some useful points of departure for our exploration.

Affirming the most recent rankings of Transparency International (TI), here are some representative responses getting directly to the point, indicating simply that dealing with corruption is a given within certain countries.

"Uganda...need I say more?" (TI ranking 139/167)

"I live in Cambodia. It's all corruption." (TI ranking 150/167)

"I work for an Iraq country office. Everything is corrupt." (TI ranking 161/167)

"It is embedded in the Liberian culture." (TI ranking 83/167)

"Somalia. That is all." (TI ranking 167/167)

Unpacking aid worker views on corruption

These next thoughtful response captures several themes that merit close attention:

"Where do I begin? One of the problems of BIG AID is the endemic corruption it carries with it. In poor countries, lots of money connected to faceless donors creates a magnetic field around it which distorts markets, expectations and integrity. Battling this is a full time job and demands a canny understanding of the context. This demands battle hardened veterans who stay around and can manage the corruption issues. However, the nature of humanitarian work is one of constant turn over, so this is an issue."
— 56-60yo white male expat aid worker

The idea that large sums of money or resources simply "distort" the equation in many ways and humans being, well, humans, there is a natural tendency to be tempted to pilfer from what may at times appear to be limitless resources. The antidote to this suggested above, "battle hardened veterans" who manage corruption is undercut by the sector wide high turnover rate. Younger, less experienced staff come in and can be easily pulled into illegal or corrupt practices especially when there is a strong need to be culturally sensitive and "fit in." As one respondent put it,

"Indonesia has a lot of corruption. Not just bribes, but more "personal favors" that they don't view as corruption, so it's hard to battle."
      – 36-40yo white female expat aid worker

"Corruption is a way of life here and most of the local authorities see it very differently than in the West. national staff get a lot of family pressure and struggle to explain how things are done differently.
      – 31-35yo white male expat aid worker

The slippery line between corruption and standard cultural practice was made evident in many comments. This is especially true in the case of favoritism, cronyism and nepotism.

"Corruption means different things to different people. Family hiring and 'bak-shish' are just the way of doing business here in the Middle East."
      – 31-35yo white male expat aid worker

Let's first look at family hiring and then *"bak-shish."* As the young female aid worker put it at the beginning of this chapter, *"One man's corruption is another man's wealth redistribution system. I find it hard to judge others on this."* If you have a job and are in a position to hire people or to award contacts in many countries you are bound by cultural expectations to "redistribute the wealth" in order to help out family and friends. This is a textbook example of role conflict where the 'father' role is expected to override the "employee" role.

And what of nepotism? It may be hard to convince some from the Global South that George H. W. Bush didn't hand down his Presidency to his son George H. Bush, and that Bill Clinton is now attempting to pass the Presidency to his wife Hillary Clinton or, in an earlier generation, President John Kennedy appointed Robert Kennedy as Attorney General because he was his brother.

As for "bak-shish" as a way of doing business, yes, tipping someone willingly for good or extra service seems to be fairly ubiquitous not just in the Middle East but elsewhere around the world. But when does *bak-shish* morph into *rashwa* or asking for bribe? In pre-invasion Iraq *rashwa* existed, but asking for a bribe was a punishable – and punished – offense. The current situation in Iraq is that now there is no shame in demanding *rashwa*. The cultural disintegration caused by war has led to this situation. One must ask to what extent has massive and at times sloppy monetary and resource aid – both from the US military and perhaps less so from the humanitarian aid world – contributed to that ugly cultural shift. Aid workers come into contexts like this and face a difficult task not becoming enmeshed.

And with this example a fairly obvious conjecture can be put forward: as cultures face disintegration from disasters – both human-made (e.g., war) or natural is it inevitable that the level of corruption will rise? In the broadest possible terms, social order, which in general can tamp down and control our baser tendencies, can generate corruption-muting norms, and any breakdown in the social order will lead to a breeding ground for the ill-use of power all levels. Just a thought.

This next comment summarizes several points made above and raises a new one regarding "fixers":

> *"Corruption is a tricky term. Internally there are the no-bid contracts and consultancies dished out to friends. None of it violates the letter of the law or policy, but it certainly feels unethical. In country its just the little things, traffic cops, pushing government processes along. Most of this is anecdotal as, with most organizations we use 'fixers' to navigate local bureaucracy. Of course local practices vary widely, in much of Africa I am pleasantly surprised but how little major corruption I am confronted with. Alternatively, in Afghanistan, the utter shamelessness of it was exhausting. This was probably as much a function of the massive sums of money floating around as it was culture."*
> – 31-35yo white male HQ worker

If you use local "fixers" how much can one know about how they are navigating the terrain, especially in situations where language is a major factor?

Yes, I am bringing up Easterly

The following observation has a clear "Easterlyesque" tone (as in William Easterly) and questions the impact of the entire development sector.

> *"When it comes to 'development work,' then they have no excuse for the rampant corruption, which I have witnessed. I really feel that development aid of the big dollar variety has in many places really created corruption, dependency and undercut local efforts at self-development. It's almost as if this industry was in the business of keeping itself busy under the myth of lifting people out of poverty."* – 56-60yo white male expat aid worker

This respondent, a thirty-something female, further critiques the development sector and waxes poetic about the nature of the human condition, imperialism and the fine semantic distinctions that arise when talking about corruption:

"In the organisation, it is bloated with money and many people simply gorge at the trough of development aid. I am thankfully removed from this in my field, I have little reason to interact with others in my organisation. I do see the old boys network everywhere, the British upper middle classes in particular seem to have taken over other organisations, such as parts of the UN for example. Corruption is endemic to the human condition however. Regarding the region (mostly Africa) – there is a fine line between helping ones friends and families and corruption, in some cultural contexts this line is not where we expect. It is imperialism to impose our values on others like this when we have so much 'acceptable' corruption in our own private and public sector. We should get our own house in order (for me, the UK) before we judge others."
— 31-35yo white female expat aid worker

Elsewhere in this book I comment on Easterly's overall critique well summed up by this veteran aid worker. Painting with a brush so broad is always dangerous, though, and may short-circuit more detailed discussions.

Pot calling the kettle black

Here are several comments pointing out that corruption is a fact everywhere and that to narrowly focus on corruption in the developing world is classic Western-centrism.

"Corruption is a problem everywhere. Worst corruption and influence peddaling is in my home country, the US. It bothers me that people complain so much about corruption in the developing world when it is literally magnitudes greater in the US political system." – 26-30yo white male expat aid worker

"Four out of the last seven governors of Illinois have been charged with crimes related to corruption. It is a constant presence in all fields, aid work and otherwise." – 18-25yo white male expat aid worker

"Corruption exists everywhere -and the biggest $ corruption over the years has been in the 'first world' banking/investment sectors. It is perhaps more obvious day-to-day in other places - but exists everywhere."
— 46-50yo white male HQ worker

As a sociologist and as a US citizen I must say that I agree with these assertions. Cockroaches scatter in the light, and to the extent that the spotlight on corruption tends to point outward and not inward, corruption in the West will remain a mostly hidden, metastasizing cancer.

The impact of corruption on organizations, beneficiaries and on the aid workers

That corruption is a negative force seemed to be a common, obvious theme, and some respondents were quite forceful about this point.

> *"Non-internationally recognized government - corruption is everywhere all the time from the shopkeepers and the drivers to the vice president. It is expected."*
> – 18-25yo white female expat aid worker

> *"The government is corrupt, the UN is corrupt, really the whole system is inherently corrupt."* – 26-30yo white female expat aid worker

The human resources and time that are devoted to dealing with corruption can in some – most? – cases drain from efforts to realize the central mission of an aid or development organization. This respondent put it this way:

> *"Although I have not witnessed any corruption in my organisation, the paranoia about corruption affects us all negatively because it is the primary reason for the monumental bureaucracy, box ticking, accountability and reporting requirements, which take up 90% of our time, pulling us away from our real work. It is also the reason why our procurement and recruitment processes are so complex and take forever."*
> – 36-40yo white male expat aid worker

Indeed, if we could all be and act with integrity the world would be a better place. This comment does lead to a good question, though, namely how much overhead – broadly defined – is invested in dealing with or minimizing corruption within the humanitarian aid sector?

This next respondent summarizes one likely common systemic issue and sheds even more light on how aid and development initiatives contribute to corruption.

> *"As I have gained experience in and knowledge of the institutional environments of many different countries, regions and cultures, I have come to understand how deeply corrupting the influence of developed-world institutional actors can become when local authorities and political insiders manipulate the characteristics of engineering-related aid projects to feed the existing hierarchy of endemic corruption within a particular locale, and the aid institutions simply don't have the time or the longer-term awareness to place a higher priority on*

preventing or avoiding that sort of cooption because of their own internal deadlines and personnel advancement objectives."

– 61-65yo white male expat aid worker

A second question, perhaps as important, is what psychological toll does dealing with the complex moral, ethical and personal issues related to corruption (in all forms) day after day take on aid workers? To what extent does this lead to burnout, loss of idealism, and painful soul-searching? How many aid workers have been in situations where making the call to refuse to give a bribe cost necessary succor or even lives in the short run? Every situation is unique, and the "right choice" will always be a judgement call on some level. Living with that burden can be onerous at best, mentally destabilizing at worst.

Concluding thoughts

I began this chapter with some thoughts about how to define corruption. As I read through all 313 narrative responses to our question I learned to appreciate more and more the gift I was being given by all of those who responded to the survey. The aid worker voices concerning corruption were thought provoking, to say the least.

At the end of the day there is much to consider when parsing out the concept of corruption. I am reminded of a comment by Antonio Donini, namely that "Humanitarianism started off as a powerful discourse; now it is a discourse of power, both at the international and at the community level."[4] I think part of the power the West wields is the power to drive the narrative in a self-serving manner and, in the case of corruption, perhaps not looking in the mirror long enough. I also think that this is a conversation worth having often, in depth, with passion and with concrete outcome oriented action as its goal. The topic of corruption raises many issues that for many aid workers are fact of life on a daily basis. The responses to our open ended survey question, a small sample of which you read above, were all over the board, some people responding with confusion, some snarky, but there were many that were well thought out indicating that at least for this question our survey served to generate a cathartic or at least reflective moment where frustrations could be vented.

So, cancer of corruption or the culture of corruption? Yes.

NOTES

1. Karl Marx *The German Ideology: Theses on Feuerbach and Introduction to the Critique of Political Economy* (Amherst, NY: Prometheus Books, 1998, 67.
2. Daniel Maxwell, Peter Walker, Cheyanne Church, Paul Harvey, Kevin Savage, Sarah Bailey, Roslyn Hees, and Marie-Luise Ahlendorf. *Preventing Corruption in Humanitarian Assistance: Final Research Report.* (Berlin: Transparency International, 2008).
3. See this article on primate empathy: Woodruff Health Sciences Center, Emory University. "Evolution of Responses To (Un)fairness." 21 September 2014. http://news.emory.edu/stories/2014/09/de_waal_science_fairness/campus.html
4. Antonio Donini, "Humanitarianism, Perceptions, Power." MSF USA. http://www.doctorswithoutborders.org/humanitarianism-perceptions-power

18 AID WORKER VOICES ON THE FUTURE OF HUMANITARIAN AID

"I really hope it will have more impact on the lives of more and more people. But nowadays it is more and more linked with political and economic agendas of the "powerful" countries so it is losing its credibility. The use of the army also to bring humanitarian relief is it complicating and confusing people about what humanitarian work is."
– 46-50yo white female expat aid worker

"Aid is getting smarter. Vast improvements have been made in just 10 years."
– 26-30yo white female expat aid worker

"The field is becoming increasingly theoretical and ego-driven. Skills that actually save lives are being drowned out by debates on buzzwords."
– 36-40yo white female expat aid worker

Yes, all of the voices above need amplification, clarification and discussion.

We'll get to that.

First, some numbers

Q59 and Q60 ended the survey by asking about the overall direction of humanitarian aid work, offering three response choices then a space for further comment. The modal response at 64% was "Humanitarian aid work is having and will continue to have a moderate positive impact on the lives of more and more people." 26% indicted "a significant positive impact" and 10% reported "minimal impact." Not overly positive, that. And so we end with some aid worker voices on our future, some of which are flip and humorous, some sober. But all are thoughtful in various measure.

Here are the data overall.

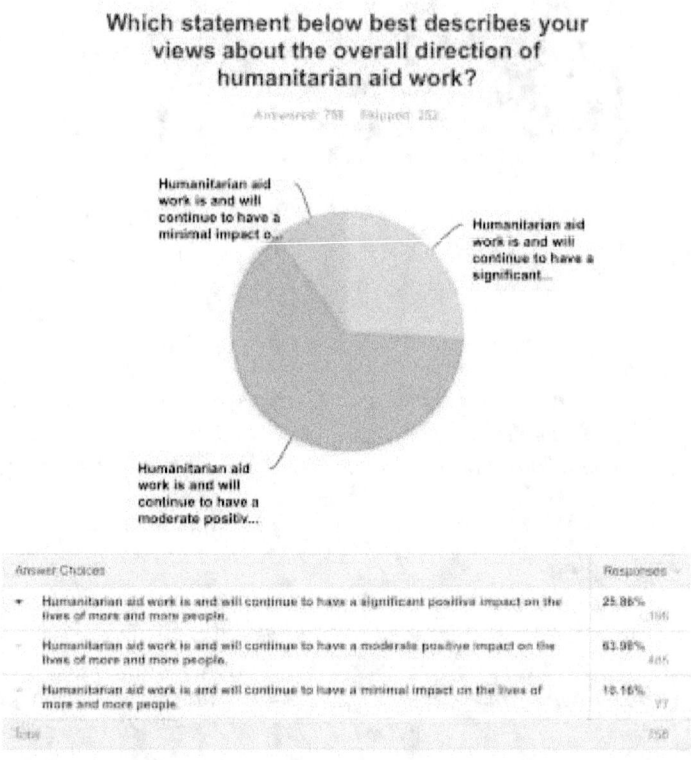

Which statement below best describes your views about the overall direction of humanitarian aid work?

Answered: 758   Skipped: 252

Answer Choices	Responses	
Humanitarian aid work is and will continue to have a significant positive impact on the lives of more and more people.	25.86%	196
Humanitarian aid work is and will continue to have a moderate positive impact on the lives of more and more people.	63.98%	485
Humanitarian aid work is and will continue to have a minimal impact on the lives of more and more people.	10.16%	77
Total		758

Here are the data broken down by gender, with females clustered slightly more toward the "moderate" response and males inflating the numbers on both extremes, "significant" and "minimal." [For data wonks in the crowd, these differences were significant at the p = .05 level.] Looking at just the "significant" numbers it appears that females are much less confident than males. One wonders why this is so, and I have poured through the narrative responses trying to answer that question but have failed to arrive at any firm conclusion.

	Humanitarian aid work is and will continue to have a significant positive impact on the lives of more and more people.	Humanitarian aid work is and will continue to have a moderate positive impact on the lives of more and more people.	Humanitarian aid work is and will continue to have a minimal impact on the lives of more and more people.	Total
Q4: Female	23.26% 120	67.25% 347	9.50% 49	69.73% 516
Q4: Male	31.25% 70	56.70% 127	12.05% 27	30.27% 224
Total Respondents	190	474	76	740

When I compared the results from those who identified as primarily relief workers as opposed to those doing development work the differences were, I think predictable. Relief workers – nearly a third of them – indicated "significant" as compared to only 23% of the development workers, and only 8% – as compared to almost 11% of the development workers indicated "minimal."

	Humanitarian aid work is and will continue to have a significant positive impact on the lives of more and more people.	Humanitarian aid work is and will continue to have a moderate positive impact on the lives of more and more people.	Humanitarian aid work is and will continue to have a minimal impact on the lives of more and more people.	Total
Q19: Relief (disaster response, emergency response, etc.)	31.34% 68	60.83% 132	7.83% 17	34.50% 217
Q19: Development (community development, long-term development, etc.)	23.06% 95	66.02% 272	10.92% 45	65.50% 412
Total Respondents	163	404	62	629

That the overall numbers are so high – 90% of the respondents indicating a moderate or more level of impact – is not reflected in many of the narrative responses discussed below.

Themes

Many themes emerged from the 311 respondents who took the time to address the question about the future of the sector. Below I highlight these themes and provide some representative responses, starting out with examples of those who were both optimistic and those less so.

Those "less so" optimistic about the future

This aid worker first starts by making a legitimate point about our survey question in that our wording forced a choice among "significant" "moderate" or "minimal" impact on peoples' lives and the inference was that the impact would be some degree of positive. Indeed, that is exactly what I had in mind when writing the question. Here's what she said:

> *"Wow. There's an obvious selection missing above. It is not that far-fetched to suggest that a NEGATIVE impact is the net. When taken in sum, aid policies based on 'structural adjustments,' as well as aid dependent on political/military alliances could very well tilt into negative territory, notwithstanding mosquito nets and REMs. Macro aid profoundly affects culture and government. Until aid is withdrawn as a military, political, and cultural weapon, supporting those who swear allegiance to free markets and multinational interests (and then run off with half of the aid money) my bet would be on a grim future for aid as a force for good. Poor nations are crippled by debt while multinationals cart away natural resources and the resulting profits. There will be no net good from aid until it is decoupled. If corruption is endemic to [the country where I now work], the same corruption is endemic to most macro aid."* – 56-60yo white male HQ worker

This writer clearly embraced a big picture view of the sector. The use of the word "weapon" is particularly sharp and helps make her comment a good articulation of the anti-neoliberal/neocolonial perspective held by many in our sample. Please take a look at chapter 17 for more extensive comment about the specific issue of corruption, but in short what is being argued above is that the entire system needs a major – and I think likely impossible – shift in both structure and function of the entire aid industry. In late 2001 when then US Secretary of State Colin Powell called the work of NGOs a 'force multiplier' he laid bare the fact that the core humanitarian principles of neutrality, impartiality and independence have in fact been compromised and that the fourth principle of humanitarianism is, sadly perhaps, additional "collateral damage."[1]

This next section contains many of the same points as the one above and also voices a frequently made distinction between aid and development, with aid for crises having a net positive impact and more long term development efforts being an overall negative.

> *"I think emergency relief work has the best impact – particularly when responding to an acute crisis in a somewhat stable country where specific expertise and materials are needed to bolster the national response. At the other*

end is development work in chronically unstable and corrupt countries where I think humanitarian aid work probably does more harm than good and ultimately helps build and solidify a permanent upper class of wealthy elites who pay lip service to the UN while using vaccine money to build themselves swimming pools and send their children to university in Europe."
> – 31-35yo white female expat aid worker

This third example voices a frustration with the level of intelligence and adaptability the sector shows.

"Compared to the money being invested, we're doing a pretty poor job of getting anywhere. A lot of misguided approaches or self-interested approaches or inappropriate interventions or I could go on and on. Why do we know that poverty is not simple or linear, yet still implement interventions as if it is? We need to get better. We need to be smarter, think more critically."
> – 26-30yo white female expat aid worker

Critiquing more the human resources dimension of the sector, this next aid worker voice echoes a theme I have read over and over throughout this research, namely that with regard to expat workers in general there needs to be a better system that takes into account energy levels, family considerations and the big picture issues of knowledge transfer and continuity of efforts. Her comment is a restatement of the one above in that there is a suggestion that we need to "work smarter, not harder."

"The biggest issue is that they do not get staff into the sector when they are young enough. There should be a push to make vocational way of entering the sector at a younger age to get the "best years" of the staff. i.e. 21-30 when they are more willing to sacrifice their personal lives for their work. Then there needs to be better ways of dealing with staff after 30 when they need a quieter life of their families, but they are often at the peak of their knowledge and what they could contribute to the sector yet seem to begin drifting away from it by then."
> – 26-30yo white male expat aid worker

Finally, we have this pessimistic diagnosis *"The field is becoming increasingly theoretical and ego-driven. Skills that actually save lives are being drowned out by debates on buzzwords."*

And those who were more positive about the future

Positive and optimistic responses were less common among the 311 responses, and generally came with qualifications. Here are a few examples.

"I think humanitarian aid will have a positive impact on more people because disasters will become more frequent. I think humanitarian aid needs to become much more focused and effective to cope with this, and there are serious obstacles to overcome, but I think humanity will continue to support those in need and humanitarian interventions will keep gradually improving. I think the common perception that humanitarian interventions have not improved over the years is wrong, although the pace of change and the retention of institutional knowledge and learning is poor." – 31-35yo white male HQ worker

This first one is referencing disaster relief efforts and says, yes, we're getting better and just in time because there will be more in the future.

This next one is positive in the sense that it points out a fact of humanity, that there will always be those who want to help. Indeed, properly channeling that energy is the issue since we know very clearly that good intentions are absolutely not always directed in a mindful and progressive manner.

"Humanitarian work will always be needed and always be there as long as there will be man-made and natural disasters. Just its "purity" may be different. It certainly is becoming less pure and self-less, but there will always be people in need and always those wanting to help."

– 36-40yo white male expat aid worker

This next example is perhaps the most optimistic of them all, arguing that the "trajectory is changing."

"If you asked me 10 years ago, I'd say, 'cut and run, everyone', but the trajectory is changing. As I've said [numerous] times now, the key is solid evaluation and this is definitely becoming apparent to many organizationss. Also the increasing corporate influence is positive I think – it's a tough change for NGOs but it will force them to act more efficiently and think more about results / gain, versus, 'how do we get more money so we can keep throwing it at things and then produce a glossy pamphlet with this smiling child on it, to get more money.'" – 31-35yo white female expat aid worker

This aid worker argues that the sector is improving at least in terms of evaluation and that this is spurred on by corporate influence.

Finally, this one is a counterpoint to the neoliberal critiques and squarely takes sides in the Sachs vs Easterly squabble. Not to rain on anyone's parade, but what she says below could be seen as innocent.

"I believe the statistics of the impact of aid work can prove that humanity as a whole is improving due to reduced health issues, an increase of education and micro-enterprise enabling people to break out of the cycle of poverty. I think Bill and Melinda Gates really captured this well in their recent annual letter, for instance." – 31-35yo non-white female HQ worker

Is the humanitarian aid sector making positive changes and does the future look bright or bleak? The discussion continues.

Aid is not the same as development

There is a big difference between the relief/disaster response and development work, to be sure, and this difference is highlighted in the responses to the penultimate question on our survey, Q60 "Please use the space below to elaborate on your views about the future of humanitarian aid work." It is clear to me now that if we had separated out relief/disaster response and development work in our questions the responses may have been even more telling. That said, as I have argued elsewhere several times in other chapters, the binary distinction between relief/disaster response and development is, at best, problematic and "pure" examples of either are likely dramatically outnumbered by those that are a mix.

Here are a couple good examples of how a few aid workers felt about this differentiation.

"Distinction between humanitarian and development work should be made. Humanitarian [aid] will continue to serve its purpose, especially for those places where the states are unable to provide relief themselves. Development work - I have no clear idea on the impact it has, and whether it's mostly positive or negative." – 31-35yo white female expat aid worker

"There is really no comparing relief and development..."
– 26-30yo white female expat aid worker

Marx 101

As a sociologist I was somewhat struck by the number of respondents that expressed an understanding of and a concern about the forces of capitalism that seem to be at play vis-a-vis all things international, especially aid work. As I wrote in the earlier chapters, the unfolding algorithm of capitalism is as inexorable as that of biological evolution. But there you go.

"Humanitarian work is going the way of the dinosaur or jersey's free of logos ... soon enough, it will all be green-washing by some corporation to make themselves or others feel good about how the help people. The end-of-history is starting to subsume humanitarian work; eg., capitalism is dollar-for-dollar far larger than any aid agency, even in the poorest areas."

– 36-40yo white male HQ worker

"Probably will go commercialized for profit and things will go much worse. But this isn't humanitarian aid work - that is business. The non-profit category defines the truth of humanitarian work. All the rest is business - which is also really important, but different." – 36-40yo white male expat aid worker

We did ask one question that is somewhat related. As you can see below, there was no agreement on the overall impact on the increasing levels of corporate influence on humanitarian aid efforts, but only 29% of our respondents thought that the overall impact was positive, leaving the remainder, 71% indicating either negligible of even negative overall impact.

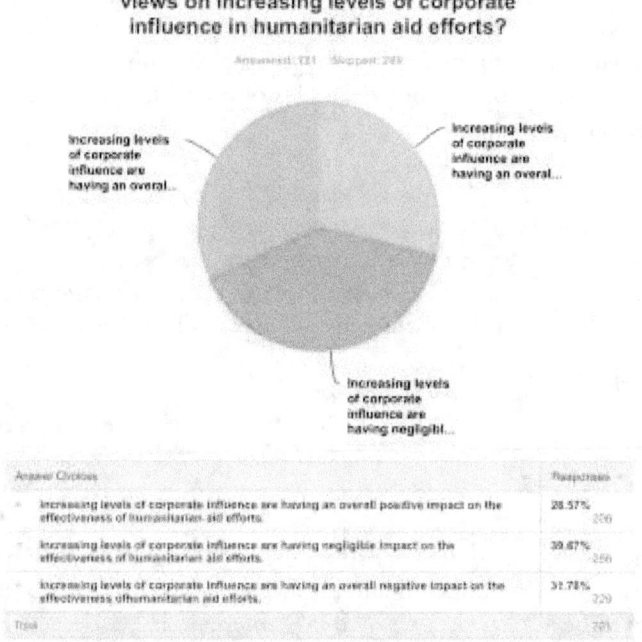

Which statement below best describes your views on increasing levels of corporate influence in humanitarian aid efforts?

Answered: 731   Skipped: 269

Increasing levels of corporate influence are having an overal...

Increasing levels of corporate influence are having an overal...

Increasing levels of corporate influence are having negligibl...

Answer Choices	Responses	
Increasing levels of corporate influence are having an overall positive impact on the effectiveness of humanitarian aid efforts.	28.57%	209
Increasing levels of corporate influence are having negligible impact on the effectiveness of humanitarian aid efforts.	39.67%	256
Increasing levels of corporate influence are having an overall negative impact on the effectiveness of humanitarian aid efforts.	31.78%	229
Total		731

Here is a one voice specifically on this topic.

"There will be more participants from corporate or other non-traditional actors in HAW [humanitarian aid work] *in future, the traditional humanitarian sector needs to prepare for this and develop ways of working to ensure that the standards we hold ourselves to are accepted and utilized by other actors. I believe there will always be a need for humanitarian actors with expertise in particular areas, but that these agencies should be comprised of expert staff from the local area - who understand the capacity of local players, government and find a way to amplify what they are capable of doing."* – 31-35yo white female expat aid worker

What this aid worker had to say about increasing corporate (and other non-traditional) influence is critical, I think, as the sector adapts to a changing global environment. That the sector has worked hard to establish core humanitarian standards is progress but unless there is effective messaging about such standards to these external but growing influences the value of this work will not be maximized. Specifically, there needs to be a commonly accepted set of standards for *all* aid and development work. Getting from where we are to that goal is, indeed, a challenge of significant magnitude.

The future impact of the sector and what we are learning

Some respondents address the hubris embedded in the assumption that we know what we are doing most of the time. Here's what one woman said,

"We are like the frontier doctors – right now we are "bloodletting" and have no clue how to help people, although we may accidentally have a positive effect. But, our efforts will enable future generations to learn from our mistakes – at least we are doing something!" – 31-35yo white female expat aid worker

Our respondents, I think, on the whole agree with this observation; none would shout from the rafters "We have solved the problems related to delivering aid and development assistance!" Most would say the fact that we are learning is important, but that knowledge transfer both within generations of aid workers and from one generation of workers to the next does not happen as effectively as it should.

Another, also somewhat cynical and summary noted,

"I do NOT believe that development work has a longer term positive impact, and I generally do NOT agree with development programmes."
– 31-35yo white female HQ worker

Professionalizing the sector is important but problematic

That there is more need for further professionalization of the sector is a given. How to get there from here is the big question.

> *"I think we need further professionalisation and streamlining, especially for work in increasing numbers of middle income countries. More focus on disaster prevention and mitigation is required."* – 26-30yo white female HQ worker

> *"The professionalization of humanitarian work is/was a good attempt at improving technical competence, but it doesn't seem to have translated much in improved responses. Lessons learned are not learned. Same incompetent people who responded once will respond again."* – 31-35yo white female expat aid worker

> *"It's going to have to get more professional. Unfortunately I think it will continue to be a desirable line of work, which will see lots of people willing to work for free just to get the chance to work for very little money. I think mistakes will be learnt from the major humanitarian crises and how we respond, but there are always new mistakes to make."* – 31-35yo white female expat aid worker

The comments above compliment those described in chapter 15 about MONGOs. Stressing adherence to the Core Humanitarian Standards throughout the aid sector is one positive step in this direction.

Some final thoughts on the future of the sector SEP

The future, if we are sober, is murky at best, and the sense that I got from many respondents is that though there will always be need, and meeting those needs in a meaningful, efficient manner – both in terms of immediate aid and long term development – is not a certainty.

> *"I did not like your choices. A key challenge for humanitarian actors is a very narrow donor base (US+N/W Europe) which is vulnerable to budget cuts. We are also entering a new time where most people live in middle income countries, and their governments have greater capacity. In many cases our business model is no longer so relevant. 'Humanitarian' work has really ballooned in scope and volume during the last 15 years, in part to get around Paris Declaration-type principles and circumvent host country governments. I think this will have to be scaled back. We are also all very confused what 'humanitarian' is – is it defined by the funding source (donor country emergency funding) or is it the type of work (temporary and unplanned)? Much if not*

most work funded by donors through emergency envelopes is really quite routine and planned, but this modality allows less recipient government scrutiny and coordination – for better or worse." – 36-40yo white male expat aid worker

What can be concluded from the above regarding what aid workers thought about the future? Said one,

"For better or worse, aid work needs to continue. Self-assessment in the sector, like this survey and other data sharing and transparency measures, need to continue and expand. This is especially true for funders making decisions on programming that may or may not address the real demands and needs."
– 41-45yo white female HQ worker

Aid workers are a thoughtful bunch who care deeply about what they do and the larger context within which they function, at least those who took the time to respond to our survey certainly seem that way to me. Whether or not one believes there is hope for the future with regard to aid and development work depends upon perspective and level of sobriety, methinks.

Pass the Barbancourt, please.

NOTES

1. Colin Powell, "September 11, 2001: Attack on America." Remarks to the national foreign policy conference for leaders of nongovernmental organizations. 26 October, 2001.

19 ACUTE ON CHRONIC SQUARED: MORE ON THE FUTURE OF HUMANITARIAN AID

"Unfortunately the world is going to see more disasters in the future, particularly natural disasters related to climate change."
– 56-60yo white male expat aid worker

Below I continue presenting and commenting on the 311 comments made by our survey respondents in answer to Q60 about the "future of humanitarian aid."

In *Haiti After the Earthquake* Paul Farmer describes this 2010 event as "acute on chronic."[1] Certainly this description could be used to describe other natural disasters in areas that have a history of marginalization including the 2004 Indian Ocean earthquake and tsunami, numerous Afghanistan-Pakistan earthquakes in the last 20 years, and the 2013 Typhoon Haiyan that hit the Philippines. The list goes on.

A contrasting example of acute not-on-chronic would be the 2011 earthquake and tsunami that hit Japan.

That climate change is impacting the world in significant ways is not in question, and all predictions point to increased weather-related events that are both more frequent and intense. Here is how one of our respondents put it.

"While I think there are positive responses to the world's humanitarian crisis, the bigger choices will negate much of work (i.e. - failure to sign climate treaties; reduce emissions; etc.). There will be positive gains at moderate levels, but unless the inequity of the world and the depletion of its resources is addressed seriously, the problems will only continue to grow." – 41-45yo white female expat aid worker

Another voice here, though I would argue that the line between "humanitarian work" and development is unclear at best.

> *"Humanitarian work, more than development, will always have an important place in the world. Climate change will ensure a lot of difficult times ahead, making large-scale humanitarian deployment a necessity."* – 26-30 white male expat aid worker

The reality of climate change means job security for those who work in humanitarian aid, especially those who respond to disasters like typhoons, floods and blizzards. But what this also means is that there will be increased need for responses to the slow motion natural disasters like chronic, prolonged or unusually extreme drought. Food insecurity will be more common in places where previously it may have never been an issue.

The perfect storm will be when there is acute on chronic squared, that is, when for example an earthquake hits a nation where there is chronic poverty exasperated by food insecurity brought on by increasingly inconsistent or ineffectual rains.

That development work can or should be done to help nations prepare for the likelihood of increased weather-related disasters is an open question according to some aid workers. Here is one comment that touches on this challenge.

> *"I think humanitarian aid will have a positive impact on more people because disasters will become more frequent. I think humanitarian aid needs to become much more focused and effective to cope with this, and there are serious obstacles to overcome, but I think humanity will continue to support those in need and humanitarian interventions will keep gradually improving."*
> – 31-35yo white male HQ worker

Simply put, the aid industry – relief or development focused – cannot and will not "work itself out of a job." From my perspective and based on listening to the aid workers voices, in order to minimize the impact of "acute on chronic squared" events development work will need to be increasingly proactive and thus inevitably contribute even further to the blur between aid and development work.

The "what" in terms of the future may be getting clearer, but the "how" of addressing this future most definitely is not.

NOTES

1. Paul Farmer, *Haiti After the Earthquake* (New York: PublicAffairs, 2011).

20 BIG PICTURE CRITIQUE OF THE AID SECTOR

"We are band-aids born of affluent guilt and survive almost entirely on the donated profits of unjust privilege and power."
– 18-25yo white female expat aid worker

"WTO, WB and IMF policies and corrupt/ignorant/criminal national elites matters million times more any humanitarian program implemented by NGOs."
– 31-35yo white male expat aid worker

Some thoughts as I continue reading, sorting and making sense of aid worker voices on the future of humanitarian aid.

So, I have been reading through – in many cases re-reading and re-reading – the 311 narrative responses to the "future of humanitarian aid work" (Q60) on our aid worker survey and I am struck over and over again with the depth of thought put into some of the responses. Though there were many who responded from a short term or narrow view, many were clearly of the "35,000 foot" and long term perspective.

One theme that I see very clearly is a healthy neo-Marxist/anti neoliberal assessment of the "big picture" relative to not only the aid industry but our entire international community. Many echoed the oft-quoted sentiments of former UNHCR chief Sadako Ogata. "There are no humanitarian solutions to humanitarian problems," said Ogata, explaining that in the many emergencies she oversaw at UNHCR, humanitarian relief in itself was not enough because the problems were caused by political factors.

Here are a few examples.

"The big picture is that developed world is fucking [the] developing world over so that anyone in Europe and America can buy a T shirt and an iPhone. Without more political and economic engagement of developed countries things will remain fucked up in the developing countries (debt, corruption, zero accountability). I hope with growing awareness citizens in developed countries will pressure their authorities more, but I'm a hopeless optimist."
--31-35yo white expat aid worker

And then this one, with just a bit less salt:

"I think humanitarian aid work operates within a system that is built on inequality – we won't see large scale change happen in the lives of people, in terms of long term development, until we start to challenge the structures and systems that result in this inequity in the first place. And the heart of those institutions is within North America and Europe – until we recognize how dependent we are on the oppression and marginalization of others for our own betterment and benefit (i.e. access to cheap disposable goods, foreign foods and fresh imports, temporary foreign workers to fill low-income job vacancies, etc...), humanitarian aid work is just another cog in this bullshit machinery."
--26-30yo white female HQ worker

What I see in all three above meshes well with what I write in the next chapter discussing the long term impact of humanitarian actions, namely that aid does not exist in a vacuum but rather is part of an extremely complex array of non-linear algorithms over which we have little – or no – long term control.

That neoliberal and myopically pro-capitalistic economic policies remain dominant in our world seems to many to be quite self-evident, and arguably these policies impact, well, every aspect of social life on this planet. The respondents above articulate that quite well. They also make the point that there will always be a need for humanitarian aid because the dominant global powers insure inequalities and marginalization.

So, where to go from here? One answer might come from a social thinker from the past whose ideas may be relevant today, "Philosophers have hitherto only interpreted the world in various ways; the point is to change it."[2] This line, in fact, is his epitaph engraved in stone at Highgate cemetery.

More realistically (?) we can all ceaselessly work on shorter term goals of major importance. One positive path is captured by this respondent, arguing for continued professionalization of the sector.

"The sector is professionalizing but still has a way to go. It is a complex sector

to work in and would benefit from a more recognizable professional accreditation system to ensure recruitment of people into the sector is merit and competency based and to dispel the notion that this is an unskilled or vulnerable sector populated by idealistic adventure-seekers."

--31-35yo white male expat aid worker

Echoing a sentiment I have referenced previously, namely that "the problem of the poor is not the problem, the problem is the rich," this next respondent encourages a paradigmatic shift by the affluent nations that can only be brought on by educational work. Though I admire the optimism, I am not holding my breath on this one.

"I think the evidence base continues to show significant impact and improvements in many places. The big challenge is ensuring the complexity of systemic injustice changes the way the wealthy nations live so that aid doesn't become a band aid over deeper problems. For example, if people don't live justly (ethical shopping, investment, simple, enviro friendly, peace building) in the west then we are not really addressing the underlying systemic issues. We need to move from a simple 'give money to this poor child' mentality to a social justice/change the way we all live mentality. Thus increasing importance of educational work rather than just slick marketing and challenges the sector to tell the complex story of change..."

--46-50yo white male HQ worker

This one, more cynical but perhaps at the same time more accurate, sums up a big part of the battle.

"WTO, WB and IMF policies and corrupt/ignorant/criminal national elites matters million times more any humanitarian program implemented by NGOs." --31-35yo white male expat aid worker

To put it in the vernacular, draining the swamp is the only long term solution, and in this case "the swamp" is only getting more entrenched. This respondent makes the same point using what I think is a good analogy.

"Humanitarian aid work is more and more like firefighters. We are not the ones in charge of pursuing those causing the fire to stop them, we just jump from one emergency to the other, and that will not change things for good."

--36-40yo non-white female expat aid worker

That there is meaningful work to be done we can all agree. What that work is and how to best do it is the question that must remain at the forefront all our strategic planning for the future.

NOTES

1. Vivian Tan, "Ogata calls for stronger political will to solve refugee crises." UNHCR, May 27, 2005.
http://www.unhcr.org/en-us/news/latest/2005/5/4297406a2/ogata-calls-stronger-political-solve-refugee-crises.html
2. Karl Marx, "Thesis 11," in *The German Ideology: Including Theses on Feuerbach and Introduction to The Critique of Political Economy* (Amherst, NY: Prometheus Books, 1998).

21 CASTLES IN THE SAND? RESPONDING AS WE MUST, BUT...

"When you are 20, you want to change the world but you accept that it's going to take maybe five years. When you are 25, you decide you just don't want to make the world any worse through your profession, buying choices, politics etc. When you get to 30+, you realise 'Fucking hell, it's way more complicated than anyone can possibly get their head around'." SEP 31-35yo non-white female HQ worker

"I don't think we can change the world - just make it a bit better for a few individuals." SEP 36-40yo white female expat aid worker

Castles in the sand 1.0

This is not an easy chapter to write in large part because I am the director of a program the purpose of which is to work with cohorts of students as they learn how to make sustainable change around the world through meaningful global partnerships, i.e., development work. It is also not easy because I remain unconvinced of my own arguments.

First, two opposing viewpoints, one from a founder of sociology and another from a politician with a flair for rhetoric and, not coincidentally, the founder of the Peace Corps.

> *". . . numerous survivals of the anthropocentric bias still remain and here [in sociology], as elsewhere, they bar the way to science. It dis-pleases man to renounce the unlimited power over the social order he has so long attributed to himself; and on the other hand, it seems to him that, if collective forces really exist, he is necessarily obliged to submit to them without being able to modify*

them. This makes him inclined to deny their existence. In vain have repeated experiences taught him that this omnipotence, the illusion of which he complacently entertains, has always been a cause of weakness in him; that his power over things really began only when he recognized that they have a nature of their own, and resigned himself to learning this nature from them. Rejected by all other sciences, this deplorable prejudice stubbornly maintains itself in sociology. Nothing is more urgent than to liberate our science from it, and this is the principal purpose of our efforts. " — Emile Durkheim (quoted in "Man's Control Over Civilization: An Anthropocentric Illusion", pg. 330, *The Science of Culture*)[1]

"Our problems are manmade — therefore, they can be solved by man. And man can be as big as he wants. No problem of human destiny is beyond human beings. Man's reason and spirit have often solved the seemingly unsolvable--and we believe they can do it again." – John F. Kennedy, *Commencement Address at American University*, June 10, 1963[2]

The Durkheim statement above warns of the anthropocentric illusion of "man's control over civilization" and, in contrast, Kennedy says we are masters of our fate and can mold the social world as we desire if we have the political will and resources.

So who is right?

What of the anthropocentric illusion?

We must continue to build castles in the sand – act on our conviction that we can change the world – because, as anthropologist and self-described "culturologist" Leslie White told us long ago, we must. This is part of what being human means. As one aid worker put it, *"There will always be disasters, there will always be poverty and there will always be some people who feel impelled to try and make a difference."*

To be more direct, we must "fight the fight" of responding to the myriad hot spots of human suffering and injustice around the globe be they in Biafra then or Syria right now. To do less is against not just our better nature, it is against our very human nature. One prototype model for this type of response is Herni Dunant (he of the killing fields at <u>Solerfino</u>), but there were many before him and since that personified this inevitable playing out of our basic human nature. One aid worker put it this way:

"If I didn't believe the above [that aid and development work are making a net positive change overall] *I couldn't continue working doing what we do. Someone I recently spoke with suggested that the world would be*

better if no aid was given anywhere to anyone, and whilst I agree that it is often a hindrance to development and helps certain negative situation perpetuate (war, etc), I found myself passionately defending it, as I truly believe that **we have a moral obligation** *to help others in need of support, whether that is at home or overseas."* (emphasis added) –26-30yo white female expat aid worker

Evolutionary psychologists have reinforced my argument by providing evidence for a fairness module in our brain that, combined with an evolutionary tendency – most would say imperative – for empathy and, more generally stated, morality, we must respond to the suffering of others, especially that which we feel has been unfairly meted out either by natural disaster or human action (or inaction, if that is the case).

What Durkheim in the above quotation offers to us is a view that some may argue is dismal at best and at worst a self-fulfilling prophecy that will doom us to inaction or alternatively raw, selfish hedonism. But those arguments fly in the face of what we know about human nature. We must act as we are: a moral animal.[3]

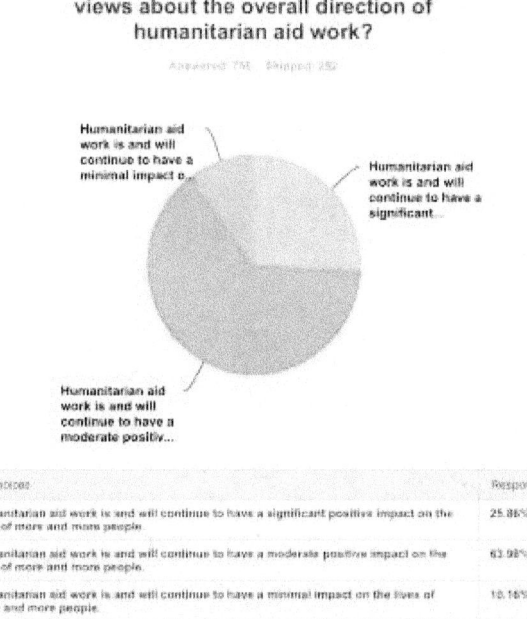

So, what does all this have to do with what our survey respondents said about the future of humanitarian aid? Here they are in the aggregate in

response to Q59, Which statement below best describes your views about the overall direction of humanitarian aid work (above).

Even accounting for the design-challenged wording of the response choices offered, there is a visible, and I would argue both significant and sober, minority of respondents (10.16%) who might agree more with Durkheim than with Kennedy.

Why are they even in this field of work, you might ask, if they feel their efforts will have "minimal impact" on the lives of people? This is a good question, but one answer might be what I have pointed out above: it is who we are as humans. Many human traits appear in populations (for example, height) as a normal curve, most (68% in a true "normal" curve) appearing within one standard deviation from the norm. But there are always those who are two and even three standard deviations from the norm on both ends. Humanitarian aid workers may be one manifestation of the natural distribution of the innate human need to seek fairness, show empathy and act, well, humanely. They exist clustered more on one end of the normal curve and, perhaps, spend their days responding to the actions of those who cluster at the other end of the continuum.

As a short aside I might present the thought that of the nearly 64% who responded "moderate positive impact" there were many who ticked that middle response box as a nod to their self-preservation based need to view their work as meaningful. Were they to dig deeper I offer that it is possible many would have come to the "dark side" and joined the those who were perhaps more realistic. As an aside, I wonder how their sentiment would sound to those that provide money to support their efforts to make "moderate positive impact."

Here are a few responses to the open ended follow up question asking for respondents to elaborate on their views about the future of humanitarian aid work.

> *"This is specific to humanitarian work (emergency response, chronic humanitarian contexts). I do NOT believe that development work has a longer term positive impact, and I generally do NOT agree with development programmes."* –31-35yo white female HQ worker

This first one represents many respondents who made a distinction between emergency response and development work. Indeed, as one respondent put it, *"There is really no comparing relief and development…"* While many felt that the former was necessary and doing positive action, the latter not so much. This next one made me smile and was a good summary of this sentiment.

"Aid work is a band aid. Band aids are good! Transformative structural change is better." –26-30yo white female expat aid worker

This next respondent hits my above points directly, we can't let people die that can be saved (Dunant's ghost appears…).

"As much as I believe that in the long terms humanitarian aid might have a detrimental impact (dependence on aid), I do believe that too many lives would be lost without aid in specific situations. We do need to keep working on linking humanitarian aid to real development."
–31-35yo white female expat aid worker

Elsewhere I discuss the semantic landline that is differentiating between "aid" and "development," but I am haunted by Leslie White and Emile Durkheim. A band aid is, indeed a band aid and the beneficiary of that band aid likely feels grateful having avoided bleeding to death, though I am not convinced that is always the case.

A question arises in my mind. In the case of famine relief can there be any other response than to provide food? Of course not, or so says my Western-centric and hence anthropocentric mind. But is that the most culturally appropriate answer? In part the answer to that question depends upon your point of reference, of course, but that is exactly my point.

Castles in the sand 2.0

What are we accomplishing after all?

So, more aid worker voices to move our journey down this path a bit further.

"I don't think the goal of the development industry should be to eradicate poverty, disease, or save lives – it should be to reduce the barriers that keep people from making informed choices about how to live their lives, be they economic, political, social/cultural, or whatever. Our industry suffers from a persistent messiah complex that, despite its earnest efforts, it can't seem to shake. It is dehumanizing, destructive, and patronizing. Idealism drives burn out, of the "compassion fatigue" variety. Pragmatism makes it easier to let things go when they don't work." – 31-35yo non-white female expat aid worker

"There's a reason all this professional jargon exists. It obfuscates the fact that at the end of the day most aid work doesn't do much of anything." – 36-40yo white male HQ worker

225

"Something an old man told me in West Africa struck me. We were at a big conference on sanitation, and the guy stood up and said '20 years ago I was at a similar conference where we discussed exactly the same issues, with exact same solutions. Now 20 years later we are still discussing the same things.'"– 31-35yo white female HQ worker

Having recently finished Nina Munk's book *The Idealist: Jeffrey Sachs and the Quest to End Poverty*[4] I have a few thoughts on which I'd like to expand.

I'll start by saying that Jeffrey Sachs got it right, finally. "It is what it is," he says in last pages of the book in response to Munk's hard questions about difficulties encountered related to the Millennium Villages Project. The realization that he finally comes to – or reawakens to – is that everything is connected to everything else environmentally, politically and perhaps most importantly, economically both locally and globally. He says exactly that to Munk at the end of the book, "For a long time, I wanted to simplify the problems by putting aside the rich world's issues and so forth and focusing on extreme poverty. But it's all interconnected."[5] I am reminded of the statement from the anthropologist Miles Richardson who said, "...the problem of the poor is not the problem, the problem is the rich."[6] Much truth lies in that statement, and we now have an global 'Occupy' movement that that is shining a bright light onto this reality.

The Sachs team's 147 page *Millennium Villages Handbook*[7] used in the select villages in Africa reported on by Munk and elsewhere was, in a very real sense, the guide to put into place the prescription he expounds in his *The End of Poverty*,[8] his vision – some say promise – to eradicate extreme poverty by the year 2025.

The Millennium Villages Project did the world a great, sobering favor in that it gave perhaps our (i.e., more specifically, the Western, "scientific") world its best shot at trying to solve the problems of the poor and came up -predictably?- short. Not because we didn't try hard enough, but because the assumption is failed.

Certainly if we were listening to history we should have learned this lesson many times over. In his *Doing Bad by Doing Good: Why Humanitarian Action Fails* Christopher Coyne outlines in good detail the failed Kajaki dam project in the Helmand Valley Province in Afghanistan, calling it a "planners problem."[9] His alternative, a rehash of William Easterly's arguing points in *The White Man's Burden: Why the West's Efforts to Aid the Rest have Done So Much Ill and So Little Good* (2006),[10] is the so-called "constrained approach,"[11] not much more than a repackaging of Easterly's "seekers" idea. Both argue this general "bottom-up" approach will have a better chance of success making lasting change.

Coyne argues perhaps the obvious, i.e., that knowledge of the local culture is imperative for development work. He posits, correctly I believe, that "...[we need to appreciate] endogenous rules because existing rules place a constraint on efforts to design and implement what are perceived to be potentially superior formal rules"[12] and further that "...attempting to impose formal rules that are at odds with underlying informal rules is akin too banging a square peg into a round hole – it can be done, but only with significant force and collateral damage."[13] Agreed. But we're still in the weeds here talking about how to engineer sand castles.

Both Easterly and Coyne find support from *Dead Aid: Why Aid Is Not Working and How There Is a Better Way for Africa* by Dambisa Moyo[14] and of course Easterly continues to beat the same drum in his recent offering *The Tyranny of Experts: Economists, Dictators, and the Forgotten Rights of the Poor.*[15]

Easterly, for his part, argues very articulately for the position that by encouraging the rich and simultaneous exploration by many creative people – poor people – for useful and effective solutions to human problems we will all be the better for it. For my money, the Easterly/Coyne/Moyo (*et al.*) arguments sound way too close to the neoliberal rhetoric washing around for the last several decades arguing that the poor just need to be given their rights and respect and they will solve the problem themselves or, rather, the forces of the market will make this happen and the efforts of the rich and newly rich(er) will "trickle down" like so much sweet rain.

The Invisible Hand, in my view, tends to slap the poor and pat the back of the rich. Just sayin'.

The thesis statement for this chapter lies here: our globalized social world comprises one massive complex system – that, if I understand Kurt Godel, Emile Durkheim and Leslie White at all, cannot be meaningfully and permanently changed as a system by purposeful human behavior. Humanity is perhaps the most defining nonlinear system of them all. In short, very subtle, trivial appearing inputs can cause large unpredictable effects in both the short and most definitely in the longer term. Icing on the cake, we are also part of the complex ecosystem of the planet, also most definitely a nonlinear system. This is increasing so as the world gets more interconnected and complex and the rate of social change, especially driven by technology, goes dizzyingly faster and faster. As one aid worker put it,

> *"Compared to the money being invested, we're doing a pretty poor job of getting anywhere. A lot of misguided approaches or self-interested approaches or inappropriate interventions or I could go on and on. Why do we know that* **poverty is not simple or linear**, *yet still implement interventions as if it is? We need to get better. We need to be smarter, think more critically."*
(emphasis added) –26-30yo white female expat aid worker

We are not in charge of how the future will unfold, nor can we ever be. As aid and development work veteran Michael Hobbes put it "Maybe the problem isn't that international development doesn't work. It's that it can't."[16] He chimes in on the above mentioned Millennium Development Goals in a post on his blog, "The Millennium Development Goals were bullshit. And that's OK."[17]

Is there something/someone else at the driver's seat? No, I will not go all Inshallah on you here: the future is not in Allah's hands nor any other God or gods' hands, however much we would like to believe that. If there were a loving God she would not allow the absolute horror that visits upon billions every day, especially the bottom 2 billion that are the focus of much aid and development work. That's my opinion.

It is what it is. Our global community is an unfolding of what may be best described as a set of incomprehensibly numerous and complex algorithms perhaps the two most important of which are biological evolution and capitalism. The future will become what it becomes not *because* of what we – or those like Sachs, Gates, Easterly, Soros and others – want it to become but rather *in spite of* what we what we would like it to become.

To be clear, these fine folks, Easterly, Sachs and the rest are all basing their actions and arguments on one very flawed and hubristic anthropocentric assumption, namely that we are in control of how the global culture unfolds.

There are those who will point to the many human interventions over the centuries that appear to affirm the human capacity to control our civilization. My counter to these examples is that, yes, you can – and as I noted almost *ad nauseam*, we must – build castles in the sand, and some of these castles will be magnificent indeed. But nonetheless these are more testaments to human will than true "directing the unfolding of human history" moments.

In the final pages of Munk's book she talks about the challenging social and economic changes occurring all over Africa that raise a very important question about the efficacy of the MDV's project, namely would much of the change that happened in the target villages occur even despite the massive intervention? The answer, quite likely, is yes. That is, change *in spite of*, not *because*.

I find good support for my position in Steven Pinker's 2011 book *The Better Angels of Our Nature: Why Violence Has Declined*[18] in which he details the very counterintuitive argument that humanity is getting *less* violent over the centuries.

I disagree with what one respondent said when reflecting on the future of humanitarian aid. She said, "*Human beings, we are not good.*"

Humanity is getting more humane in some ways as social institutions slowly evolve to tamp down our more violent tendencies and see ourselves more and more as one humanity. Sociologist G. H. Mead encouraged us to look forward to a time when we would have all humanity as our reference group, our 'generalized other' not just those in our immediate clan.

Can we impact this or that specific life with our actions? Of course. In fact that is what aid and development workers do every day of every year all over the world. Is that impact scalable, the kind that can "end poverty?" That indeed is the question I am attempting to address. I would say "yes" in the short term we can create that appearance, but on a global scale not so much.

The problem of the poor will always be with us, I am afraid.

That's my story and I'm sticking to it.

Ending thoughts on "eradicating extreme poverty by 2025"

Art, as sociologist Georg Simmel pointed out long ago, allows us to make observations about the world in creative, entertaining, and non-linear ways that are sometimes closer to the truth than we dare come with "scientific" thought.[19] Movies, for example, can sometimes allow us to face realities otherwise too stark to otherwise voice. The scenes from the movie *Network* (1976) below nod to Durkheim, I think.

> *"There are no nations. There are no peoples. There are no Russians. There are no Arabs. There are no third worlds. There is no West. There is only one holistic system of systems, one vast and immane, interwoven, interacting, multivariate, multinational dominion of dollars. ... It is the international system of currency which determines the totality of life on this planet. That is the natural order of things today."*

Network executive Arthur Jensen lectures poor TV announcer Howard Beale further...

> *"There is no America. There is no democracy. There is only IBM, and ITT, and AT&T, and DuPont, Dow, Union Carbide, and Exxon. Those are the nations of the world today. What do you think the Russians talk about in their councils of state, Karl Marx? They get out their linear programming charts, statistical decision theories, minimax solutions, and compute the price-cost probabilities of their transactions and investments, just like we do. We no longer live in a world of nations and ideologies, Mr. Beale. The world is a*

college of corporations, inexorably determined by the immutable bylaws of business.'[20]

I am not entirely sure Arthur Jensen/Peter Finch got it wrong back in 1976 in *Network* when describing the nature of global capitalism. No one is in control of how this algorithm plays out, though some learn how to benefit disproportionally.

Jensen uses phrases like "natural order of things" and "immutable bylaws" to describe the world, in effect citing Durkheim. Can we ever reach our goal to "eradicate extreme poverty" at any point in the future? Perhaps not. Though to be clear, I do think that poverty may someday, possibly, be eliminated in our world but that it will not be mindfully engineered by the likes of Gates and Sachs, et al, but rather happen as an organic product of the many dynamic systems at play, that is not because of human agency rather despite it.

NOTES

1. Emile Durkheim, quoted in Leslie White, "Man's Control Over Civilization: An Anthropocentric Illusion," in *The Science of Culture* (New York: Farrar, Straus, and Giroux, 1949). Page 330.
2. John F. Kennedy, "Commencement Address at American University, June 10, 1963. http://www.jfklibrary.org/Asset-Viewer/BWC7I4C9QUmLG9J6I8oy8w.aspx
3. Robert Wright, *The Moral Animal* (New York: Vintage Books).
4. Nina Munk, *The Idealist: Jeffrey Sachs and the Quest to End Poverty* (New York: Doubleday, 2013).
5. Nina Munk, *The Idealist*, 230
6. Miles Richardson, "Culture and the Struggle to be Human." Anthropology and Humanism Quarterly 1 (1976): 2-4.
7. B. Konecky., & C. Palm., eds *The Millennium Villages Handbook: A Practitioners Guide to the Millennium Villages Approach.* New York: Earth Institute at Columbia University, 2008.
8. Jeffrey Sachs, *The End of Poverty*. New York: Penguin Books, 2005.
9. Christopher Coyne, *Doing Bad by Doing Good: Why Humanitarian Action Fails* (Stanford, CA: Stanford University Press, 2013).
10. William Easterly, *The White Man's Burden: Why the West's Efforts to Aid the Rest have Done So Much Ill and So Little Good* (New York: Oxford University Press, 2006).
11. Dambisa Moyo, *Dead Aid: Why Aid Is Not Working and How There Is a Better Way for Africa* (New York: Farrar, Strauss, and Giroux, 2009).
12. William Easterly, *The Tyranny of Experts: Economists, Dictators, and the Forgotten Rights of the Poor* (New York: Basic Books, 2014).
13. Michael Hobbes, "Stop Trying to Save the World." *The New Republic*, November 17, 2014, https://newrepublic.com/article/120178/problem-international-development-and-plan-fix-it
14. Michael Hobbes, "The Millennium Development Goals were bullshit. And that's OK." *Rottin' in Denmark*, Sept 10, 2015. https://rottenindenmark.wordpress.com/2015/09/10/mdgs-bullshit/
15. Steven Pinker, *The Better Angels of Our Nature*. New York: Penguin Books.
16. Georg Simmel, *The conflict in modern culture and other essays* (New York: Techers College Press, 1968).
17. *Network*, 1976. Written by Paddy Chayefsky.

22 THE END: VOICES OF THANKS, SNARK, AND NEXT STEPS

"Am I done yet?"
— 36-40 yo female HQ worker

"I finally feel like I fit somewhere."
— 36-40 yo female expat aid worker

"Did you have an advisor look this [survey] *over before you created it?"*
— 18-25 yo male expat aid worker

Voices of thanks and snark

Yes, we're done. Almost.

The only appropriate end to this exploration of aid worker voices must come from the aid workers themselves. Here are their – and my – parting shots.

Our final question on the survey, Q61, asked "Please use the space below to share your feelings about any of the above questions."

Yes, at the end of a very long survey containing 61 questions and including 23 open-ended "add your comments" questions, nearly 1 in 5 (18%) intrepid souls felt called to put in their last thoughts. To each of these aid workers I say "Thanks!"

Many, in fact, literally shared their feelings with comments like:

"I feel all my cynicism and bitterness coming up :-)"

"It has been good to write these down and share my thoughts – thanks!"

"This is a depressing quiz."

"It has been helpful to reflect and a safe place to write about some of my anger."

Indeed, that the survey provided a "safe place to write about some of [her] anger" speaks to the core purpose of this book that is to provide a place to amplify aid worker voices.

This one from a 31-35yo female HQ worker I think captured the feelings of many when she wrote,

> *"Good questions. Necessary questions. I apologize if I used it as an opportunity to vent. It felt good. And I should probably say that if you'd caught me on a different day, I may have been slightly more optimistic. But I guess the roller-coaster aspect of the job is what we all know."*

That she took responding to the survey as an "opportunity to vent" is one of the main reasons that we kept the survey "live" for so long (14 months). We made the survey public never having a clear plan for how long it would remain available; we had no compelling methodological logic driving this choice, rather the decision was based on the positive cathartic function the survey appeared to be serving for many. Here is another blush from a 31-35yo female expat aid worker:

> *"Very interesting survey and I appreciate the chance to share my views – it is surprising how little time (and few opportunities) one has to actually *think* about things in the busyness of the day-to-day. I wish your survey results could be shared in an open forum (not only virtual) where significant players can be present and honestly reflect for a moment."*

Many of the 181 respondents that took the time to write on this final question commented on how interesting it was to take the survey and many said they'd be very interested to read the final results. Dozens of people wrote just to say "thanks."

Here are a few representative examples:

> *"Interesting and thanks for doing it."*

"Just would like to say that I think it's great that you're doing this work and gathering this info. Wishing you the best of luck with your project."

"This has been a useful exercise in self-reflection. Good luck!"

One young female HQ aid worker went so far as to talk about how she might use some of the questions as a point of departure for workplace discussions.

"I've asked a few of these questions to some of my closer peers – the ones who I feel are on the same page as me, and will partake in a good rant over lunch. But going through this and how important these questions are, for better understanding ourselves and each other, I'm feeling more confident in posing some of these to others. Who knows – maybe even some of those internally-focused, ladder-climbing types just need to be challenged and made to revisit these issues. I may give it a go (albeit in a situation that I can escape quicker than a sit-down lunch)."

Reflections on a career

Some took the opportunity to reflect on their career and aspects of the sector as a whole. One pattern in the responses was clear: many felt that working in the humanitarian aid sector was a meaningful career choice, especially as an alternative to working in the for-profit sector.

I was touched when I read this response below from a young aid worker. His passion and conviction are evident, and I believe his assessment of and motivations for being in the sector are shared by many.

"I think it is easy to see aid workers as a little hedonistic. I think this is true. They can be, and many are. There is definitely a certain something that makes us all tick. But, deep down, something this survey might reveal, they all have very strong motivations for getting into the sector. You see a lot of them talking about work all the time, but not so many talking about their motivations. Many can seem cold to everything, but I think that is a coping mechanism. People get into the sector because they care, and they will always care, they just get a little hardened. It is easy to see this in the way an aid worker will slag off every NGO under the sun to their same-sector colleagues – but in the midst of non-aid workers, they would defend the sector to the death! I do this job because I care. I care because I feel politically driven by the wealth divide the world suffers under. I feel undeserving of the education I have received for free and think everyone should be entitled to the same, and the same opportunities. At the same time, the burning political motivations inside me stop me from being

able to work in a normal sector.

> *I can not physically motivate myself to work for the purpose of making someone else rich. I do not believe in the capitalist system. If I'm not working to directly assist people, I do not work. So, as much as it is a sacrifice to work in this sector, sacrificing money, relationships, stability, friends. It is also a selfish decision. I want to do this work as I get to closely fulfil my ideals, it keeps me motivated, I get to travel, I get to help people, and I don't have to be a 'slave to the system'!"* – 26-30yo male expat aid worker

This next one ends in a quite sober fashion. With very personal words this young woman describes the stages of self-reflection many aid workers go through and uses this moment to vent about the differences between the intense life the "field" and contradiction of working in HQ.

> *"I have been working for the past 5 years in this field, in a variety of locations, such as HQ, refugee camps, field offices, and have experienced different levels of cooperation between humanitarian actors. It seems to me that the bigger the crisis, the brighter the spotlight, and the less inclined people are to work together because they want to shine. Also, my opinion is that humanitarian workers go completely mad, because they see so many things – good and bad – that they have to cope with in their own ways. At one point it becomes much less about the people you are helping because you are very consumed with what is happening with your own self. Also, the fact that you get sniped, stoned, spat on, raped and so on while doing humanitarian work doesn't help keep up idealism. You ask yourself "why am I doing this" more and more often and when you finally get out of it and make it to HQ you feel so removed from the work and start thinking that you work for a multinational for-profit. And then you get bogged down by the salary, benefits and think you deserve it all because you spent time in the field. Just to sum it up, I think I'll be leaving this field soon, because you're of no use to anyone, if you're cynical and burnt out."* – 26-30yo female expat aid worker

Though our respondents were from all age groups there was a definite concentration in the younger ages. The voice below from a legit silverback speaks to the fulfillment sensed by some in the sector.

> *"Overall, my "midlife crisis" going into aid work was a good decision for my wife and me. It was a whole new career of over 20 years that gave me a new perspective on the world. I would not have traded those 20 years for anything. In semi-retirement I continue to do aid work."* – 66-70 yo male expat aid worker

This next voices the frustration of trying to explain the work.

"I think humanitarian work is tough and confusing and those outside of it definitely don't get it and those within it barely get it. It's both good and bad like everything else and though I'm leaving soon, my feelings haven't changed much. Yes, I'm skeptical, but I still believe that working for an NGO is better than working for a corporate entity; my work has more of a chance to do good rather than to help a shareholder. I will probably come back to humanitarian work in some form, but first there are personal projects that I have to do and pursue self-employment options outside of humanitarianism." – 36-40yo male based in HQ

Let the snark begin

Although the tenor of most responses was positive or neutral, there were more than a few (14, to be exact) that felt moved to provide direct, negative feedback, some of which is well taken; the survey questions were not perfectly worded by any means. There were unfortunate question and response wordings, opportunities for easier coding and analysis, perhaps some important topics inadvertently left out, and even an overall tone that could have been more thoughtful or focused. To be clear, I think that much can be learned from those who cared enough to be critical.

A few were just a tad bit patronizing and not very helpful (and yes, I do notice that these all come from males).

"Did you have an advisor look this over before you created it?" – 18-25 yo male expat aid worker

"Poorly worded questions, focus on humanitarian without defining what that is. Subjective responses will be useless in determining and findings when compiled." – 50-55 yo male expat aid worker

"You should work on some of the questions. – 36-40 male expat aid worker

One middle aged (white) male HQ worker commented very thoughtfully *("Seriously, who designed this survey?")* on the wording of many questions and in one case pointed out a flaw common in many surveys, especially those like this one asking about people's perceptions and opinions. With a survey taken at one point in time what you get is more snapshot than moving picture. Listen to how he puts this:

"Every answer here needs to be contextualized in the transition I am

undergoing: I have been working for a donor, and have just transitioned to working for a [African] non-profit. This transition was spurred by positively hating working for a donor (initially I was thrilled). Only time will tell if I end up hating this as much!"

He ended his contribution as a respondent with this:

"Hire a survey designer: 1/4 of these questions were really lousy and would have benefit [sic] from some sharpening up."

I agree with this next one, though he is vague as to what he means by "bias about humanitarian work."

"There seem to be a bias about humanitarian work in general in the questions asked. The rising trend is that corporations, investment and development will solve all the problem. Good if it does but so far injustice and exploitation are growing. There are more hungry people in middle income Countries than in Low Income Countries. Therefore wealth does not solve all problems, injustice remains and more has to be done about it."

A few stressed an issue with the conflation of "humanitarian aid work" versus development activities, none better stated that this:

"I am concerned about your use of language. To me 'humanitarian aid work' is a subset of the aid agenda (which deals with humanitarian crises – droughts, famines, etc.). While I have done 'humanitarian' work before. My country position is almost exclusively 'development' whereby I word with countries to implement systems and change aimed at improving the well being of people over the long term…" – 36-40yo female expat aid worker

Concluding thoughts on the sector

"Related to the questions about explaining the job to people outside the industry, what is nearly impossible to explain is your personal emotional and intellectual response to new situations or the general seriousness of the situations faced: you experience completely new feelings that cause completely unexpected understandings of the world that are very difficult to really completely explain to non-aid workers." – 41-45yo male expat aid worker

Knowing that others hear and, better yet, share or at least can understand feelings and perceptions about the live to which you have devoted yourself is meaningful psychologically. The respondent quoted above – and all of the many hundreds in the preceding chapters – have now had their voices heard and shared. I for one will count that as a net positive toward the goal of creating a more just world for all.

My hope is that in this book I have accomplished the modest goal of effectively presenting and making sense of the aid worker voices that were gifted to me by those who took the time to take our survey. Countless person-hours were spent by 1010 self-identified "aid workers" finding on line and then choosing to complete our survey. Many wrote narrative answers to all of the open-ended questions, sometimes pouring out their hearts and sharing intimate thoughts. My driving logic as I went through the responses was to with fidelity present a summary of all that was said, the good, the bad and the ungrammatical.

My commentary and analysis was just that, analysis of what I heard in all those voices and my modest attempt to use a sociological framework to make sense of it all. That, and a bit of commentary from my perch on the margins of development work, though having been exposed to this kind of work for the last 25 years and directing an academic program engaged in development work and, beginning in 2015, using the Core Humanitarian Standards as part of our syllabi.

Though respondent opinions and observations at times clashed and contradicted, in one sense you can describe this book as an effort to employ crowdsourcing to understand the aid sector. Certainly no one would expect all opinions to be the same since the respondents were diverse in age, gender, racial/ethnic/cultural identity, experiences, and place of employment. But given the depth of thought many put into their responses, taken as a whole I believe that what has been presented captures a great deal of truth about the sector.

And, one more time, a massive THANK YOU to all who participated.

Next steps

"Aid work is part of the wider economic ecosystem. I think we are not really better or worse than anyone else – just a different organ in the body of humanity." – 36-40 yo female HQ worker

I have no doubt that those represented in this book are mostly expat aid workers from the global north. Perhaps a more accurate title might have been "Expat aid worker voices." Fair enough. That said, this book should be best viewed as an exploratory beginning, one that raises some questions and that can light the path for similar work.

Next steps include inviting everyone who reads this book to remain in the conversation and to encourage others to joint. To be heard is to be acknowledged and affirmed, and it is my belief that as the sector gets to know itself better – and the larger social ecosystem of which it is a part – it will be more whole and humane.

ABOUT THE AUTHOR

Tom Arcaro is a sociologist at Elon University and is the founding director of the Periclean Scholars program. His passion for development work began in 1990 with the first of what would be many visits to the Comprehensive Rural Health Project in Jamkhed, India. The seeds for what would eventually become the Periclean Scholars program were planted during that first visit. He lives with his wife and children in Burlington, North Carolina.

www.ingramcontent.com/pod-product-compliance
Lightning Source LLC
Chambersburg PA
CBHW062133280526
45788CB00001B/155